America's Best Pies
2016–2017

America's Best Pies 2016–2017

Nearly 200 Recipes You'll Love

American Pie Council
with Linda Hoskins

Skyhorse Publishing

Copyright © 2016 by the American Pie Council and Linda Hoskins

All rights reserved. No part of this book may be reproduced in any manner without the express written consent of the publisher, except in the case of brief excerpts in critical reviews or articles. All inquiries should be addressed to Skyhorse Publishing, 307 West 36th Street, 11th Floor, New York, NY 10018.

Skyhorse Publishing books may be purchased in bulk at special discounts for sales promotion, corporate gifts, fund-raising, or educational purposes. Special editions can also be created to specifications. For details, contact the Special Sales Department, Skyhorse Publishing, 307 West 36th Street, 11th Floor, New York, NY 10018 or info@skyhorsepublishing.com.

Skyhorse® and Skyhorse Publishing® are registered trademarks of Skyhorse Publishing, Inc.®, a Delaware corporation.

Visit our website at www.skyhorsepublishing.com.

10 9 8 7 6 5 4 3 2 1

Library of Congress Cataloging-in-Publication Data is available on file.

Cover design by Jane Sheppard

Print ISBN: 978-1-5107-1169-3
Ebook ISBN: 978-1-63450-985-5

Printed in China

Table of Contents

APPLE

COMSTOCK CARAMEL APPLE AND DATE PIE

Carolyn Blakemore, Fairmont, WV
2015 APC National Pie Championships
Amateur Division 1st Place Comstock Apple

CRUST
2 cups sifted flour
1 teaspoon salt
1 tablespoon sugar
¾ cup butter-flavored shortening
4 tablespoons water, cold

FILLING
¼ cup caramel sauce
¼ cup dates, chopped
1 tablespoon lemon juice
1 tablespoon orange juice
1 tablespoon orange marmalade
¾ cup sugar
1 (21-oz.) can Comstock apple pie
   filling

⅛ teaspoon salt
3 tablespoons tapioca
3 tablespoons cornstarch
1 teaspoon apple spice
½ teaspoon nutmeg
1 teaspoon cinnamon

CRUMBLE
¼ cup brown sugar
2 tablespoons flour
½ teaspoon cinnamon
2 tablespoons butter

For the Crust: Preheat oven to 400 degrees. Sift flour, salt, and sugar. Cut in shortening with a pastry blender. Sprinkle water on mixture, one tablespoon at a time. Stir with a fork, form a ball. Cover with wax paper. Chill until ready to roll out.

For the Filling: In a bowl, combine caramel sauce, dates, lemon juice, orange juice, and marmalade, and mix together. Add sugar, salt, tapioca, cornstarch, and spices. Mix. Stir in 1 can of Comstock apple pie filling.

For the Crumble: In a cup, stir together crumble ingredients until crumbly. Sprinkle 2 tablespoons of crumble on bottom of crust. Spoon filling into crust, and sprinkle the remaining crumble over the top. Cover with a top crust. Bake 40 minutes, covering the edge with foil.

Comstock Caramel Apple and Date Pie

SLICE OF APPLE SPICE

Marie Salino, Ithaca, NY
2013 APC National Pie Championships
Professional Division Honorable Mention Apple

CRUST
1½ cups flour
½ teaspoon salt
⅔ cup Crisco, chilled
¼ cup ice water
dash of lemon juice

FILLING
7 cups apples (Granny Smith recommended)
¾ cup brown sugar
¾ cup granulated sugar

1 teaspoon cinnamon
1 teaspoon vanilla
2 tablespoons hot pepper jelly
¾ cups cheddar cheese, shredded
¼ cup flour

TOPPING
1 cup flour
dash of cayenne pepper
½ cup brown sugar
½ cup butter, chilled

For the Crust: Preheat oven to 395 degrees. Put flour, salt, and Crisco in bowl. Cut in until it forms crumbs. Mix in ice water and lemon to form a dough ball. Do not over mix. Roll out dough and put in your pie dish. Crimp around all the edges on the crust. Set aside.

For the Filling: Peel and thinly slice all your apples into a large bowl. Mix in your sugars, cinnamon, vanilla, and hot pepper jelly. Let them set for 10 minutes until they form juice. Add ¼ cup of flour and mix. Put shredded cheddar cheese in bottom of pie crust, and add your apple mixture.

For the Topping: Mix flour, cayenne pepper, and brown sugar in a bowl. Cut in butter until the texture becomes crumbly. Sprinkle over apple mixture. Bake in the oven at 395 degrees for 15 minutes. Turn oven down to 350 degrees and bake for another 45 minutes. Let rest before you slice.

APPLE RHUBARB CRUMB PIE

Evette Rahman, Orlando, FL
2013 APC National Pie Championships
Professional Division 1st Place Apple

CRUST
2 cups flour
2 tablespoons sugar
1 teaspoon salt
½ teaspoon baking powder
⅓ cup shortening
⅓ cup unsalted butter
1 tablespoon vinegar
⅓ cup heavy cream

FILLING
6 cups cooking apples, peeled, cored, and sliced
1 cup rhubarb, sliced

2 teaspoons lime juice
1½ tablespoons unsalted butter, cubed
1⅛ cups sugar
3 tablespoons minute tapioca
2 tablespoons cornstarch
½ teaspoon cinnamon
¼ teaspoon nutmeg

TOPPING
1 cup flour
½ cup brown sugar
½ cup unsalted butter, cubed
¼ teaspoon cinnamon

For the Crust: Preheat oven to 375 degrees. Mix dry ingredients together for the crust. Cut in shortening and butter. Add vinegar and cream. Mix together well. Form into two disks and refrigerate for 1 hour. Roll out one disk and place in deep dish pie plate.

For the Filling: Mix filling ingredients together and fill pie plate. Roll out remaining dough and cut into strips. Place several strips across filling, leaving space in between. Bake for 40 minutes.

For the Topping: Mix together topping ingredients thoroughly, until crumbly. Sprinkle over pie and bake an additional 15 minutes. Cool completely before serving.

ALMIGHTY APPLE PIE

John Sunvold, Winter Springs, FL
2014 APC National Pie Championships
King Arthur Flour Apple 1st Place

CRUST
⅓ cup water
1 tablespoon sugar
½ teaspoon salt
8 tablespoons unsalted butter
8 tablespoons lard
2¼ cups King Arthur flour

CARAMEL AND PECAN LAYER
30 Kraft caramels
¼ cup milk
¾ cup pecans

CREAM LAYER
6 oz. cream cheese, softened
⅓ cup powdered sugar
6 oz. Cool Whip

APPLE LAYER
7–8 cups apple (1-inch pieces)
4 tablespoons butter
1 cup brown sugar
3 tablespoons cornstarch
1–2 teaspoons cinnamon
¼ cup frozen apple juice concentrate

For the Crust: Mix water, sugar, and salt. Set aside. Place cold butter, cold lard, and flour in food processor and pulse until butter is the size of peas. Add water mixture and pulse until a dough forms. Place in plastic bag, shape into a disk shape, and chill overnight. Roll out crust and blind bake for around 30 minutes at 350 degrees, or until lightly browned. Cool.

For the Caramel: Melt the caramels with milk. Reserve one-third of this caramel. Add pecan pieces, mix well, and spread into pie crust. Chill.

For the Cream: Mix softened cream cheese and powdered sugar. Fold in Cool Whip. Spread on top of caramel and pecans. Swirl in the reserved caramel into the cream layer. Chill.

For the Apples: Place all ingredients in a covered baking dish at 350 degrees for 30 minutes. Gently stir and check to see if apples are soft. Continue to bake, checking every 5 minutes. Bake until apples are soft. Cool and chill. Spread on the chilled cream later. Chill. Top with favorite whipped topping, caramel sauce, and/or nuts, as desired.

Almighty Apple Pie

HAPPY APPLE-COT GINGER PIE

David Harper, Lone Rock, WI
2014 APC National Pie Championships
Amateur Division 2nd Place King Arthur Flour Apple

CRUST
2 cups King Arthur flour
2 teaspoons salt
1 cup butter-flavored Crisco
10 tablespoons water, cold

CREAM FILLING
½ cup sugar
2 tablespoons cornstarch
2 egg yolks
1¼ cup half-and-half
1 teaspoon vanilla
1 tablespoon butter

APPLE PIE FILLING
4 tablespoons butter
1 heaping tablespoon flour
3 tablespoons white sugar
3 tablespoons brown sugar
dash of cinnamon
dash of nutmeg
2½ pounds cooking apples, peeled,
    cored, and sliced
1 tablespoon lemon juice
¼–½ cup apple cider
¼ cup candied or crystallized ginger,
    chopped into small pieces
1 cup apricot preserves
1 egg, beaten with 1 tablespoon water
sprinkling of white sugar

For the Crust: Preheat oven to 375 degrees. Whisk the flour and the salt together in a large bowl. Add the Crisco and mix with your fingers until combined. Add the water and use a fork to combine. Turn pie dough out onto a floured surface and gather into a circular disk, divide disk into two equal parts. Roll out one disk of dough big enough to fit into a pie plate, trim the edges to about 1 inch overhang. Place in the refrigerator until ready to use. Cover the other disk in plastic wrap and chill until later.

For the Filling: Combine the sugar, cornstarch, egg yolks, and half-and-half together in a heavy saucepan. Cook until filling is thick and bubbly, about 4 to 5 minutes over medium-high heat. Having a heavy saucepan is critical in not scorching your filling. Remove thickened filling and run it through a fine mesh sieve, catching strained filling in another bowl. Add the vanilla and butter and stir until melted and combined. Place plastic wrap directly on top of filling and set aside to cool, about 30 minutes.

For the Apples: In a heavy pan over medium heat, combine the butter, flour, sugars, and spices. Add the apples and lemon juice and sauté until almost tender, about 4 to 6 minutes. If the mixture is too dry/thick, start by adding ¼ cup of cider and add more if necessary to loosen up the filling. Remove from heat and stir in the candied ginger. Cool for about 15 minutes.

Place apricot preserves in a microwave safe bowl and heat until warm and melted. Turn cream filling into the pie shell. Place apple mixture on top of the filling and then spread the apricot preserves on the apple slices. Roll out the other pie crust and cut into strips for a lattice top. Once lattice is on top of the pie, brush the top of the lattice with the beaten egg and sprinkle with sugar. Bake for about 45 minutes or until golden. You may have to cover the crust halfway through the cooking. Serves 8 to 10.

BROWN SUGAR APPLE PIE

Bev Johnson, Crookston, MN
2014 APC National Pie Championships
King Arthur Flour Apple 3rd Place

CRUST
¼ cup + 1 tablespoon ice water
6 tablespoons unsalted butter
2 tablespoons lard
1¼ cups King Arthur flour
½ teaspoon salt

FILLING 1
3 cups apple cider
4 Granny Smith apples
½ cup sugar
⅓ cup King Arthur flour
1 teaspoon cinnamon

FILLING 2
1 cup brown sugar
½ cup unsalted butter, softened
3 tablespoons flour
⅛ teaspoon salt

2 eggs
1 teaspoon vanilla
¼ cup sweetened condensed milk

TOPPING
¾ cup King Arthur flour
¾ cup pecan
½ cup sugar
¼ teaspoon salt
6 tablespoons unsalted butter, cut
    into small pieces

GARNISH
½ cup Kraft caramels
2 teaspoons milk
pecan halves
½ cup chopped pecans

For the Crust: Pour water into a spray bottle and place on crushed ice to chill. Cut butter and lard into small pieces, keep in freezer. Place flour and salt in food processor and pulse to mix. Add chilled butter and pulse 8 to 10 times. Add lard and pulse 5 to 7 times. Spray part of water and pulse 3 times. Continue until water is used up. Form dough into a ball, place in plastic bag and flatten into a disc. Refrigerate for ½ hour. Roll out dough and place in a 9-inch deep dish pie plate. Keep in freezer until ready to use.

For Filling 1: Place apple cider in a sauce-pan and cook over medium heat. Peel and slice apples. Place them in the hot apple cider. Cook until tender. Drain apples, saving apple juice, and return to saucepan. Reduce apple juice. Mix together sugar, flour, and cinnamon. Stir into ½ cup hot apple cider and cook until thickened. Return cooked apple slices to thickened apple cider. Cool. Take pie shell out of freezer. Pour apple mixture into pie shell. Set aside while you make the next layer.

For Filling 2: Preheat oven 400 degrees. Cream brown sugar and butter. Add flour, salt, eggs, vanilla, and milk. Mix thoroughly. Spread over apple mixture. Bake for 30 minutes.

For Topping: Combine flour, pecan, sugar, and salt in food processor. Pulse several times, chopping nuts coarsely. Scatter butter over dry mixture and pulse until resembling fine crumbs. Place in bowl and mix with fingers until crumbly. Refrigerate until ready to use. Remove pie from oven and reduce oven temperature to 375. Place crumbs on top of pie, spreading evenly. Return pie to oven. Bake for 40 minutes. Cover the pie with tented foil for the last 15 minutes to keep from getting too brown. Place on wire rack to cool for 1 hour.

For the Garnish: In a bowl, microwave caramel bits and milk on high for 1 minute, stirring half-way through. Drizzle over entire surface of pie. Press pecan halves into caramel. Sprinkle with the chopped pecans.

Brown Sugar Apple Pie

NUTS ABOUT APPLE PIE

Grace Thatcher, Delta, OH
2015 APC National Pie Championships
Amateur Division Apple 1st Place

CRUST
4 cups flour
1 teaspoon salt
3 tablespoons sugar
1 cup shortening
6–8 tablespoons water, cold
2 cups walnuts

FILLING 1
¼ cup + 2 tablespoons heavy cream
1 teaspoon cinnamon
¼ teaspoon salt
¼ cup water
2 tablespoons light corn syrup
1¼ cups granulated sugar
2 tablespoons butter
1 teaspoon vanilla extract

FILLING 2
4 pounds apples, peeled, cored, and
  thinly sliced

2 tablespoons butter
¾ cups granulated sugar
1½ tablespoons lemon juice
2 tablespoons water
1½ teaspoons cornstarch
1 teaspoon cinnamon
¼ teaspoons vanilla

For the Crust: Preheat the oven to 350 degrees. Into a large mixing bowl, sift the flour, salt, and sugar together. Cut in the shortening with a pastry blender until the mixture develops a course texture. Sprinkle the water over the mixture a spoonful at a time and toss until the dough begins to cohere. Gather the dough into a ball and press together with your hands. Divide the dough into two discs. Cover with plastic wrap and refrigerate for at least one hour before using. Roll and fit one disc of pie crust into a 9-inch deep dish pie pan. Set aside in refrigerator. Put the walnuts on a sheet pan and put into a 325 degree oven for 8 to 10 minutes to toast. Set aside to cool. When the nuts are cooled, rub in a tea towel to remove some of the bitter husks. Put ¾ cup of nuts into the bottom of the pie shell. Set aside the remainder. Roll the other disc of pie crust out and cut lattice strips. Weave lattice top and set aside in the refrigerator to stay cool and make it easier to handle.

For Filling 1: Mix the cream, cinnamon, and salt in a small bowl. Combine the water and corn syrup in a medium saucepan. Pour the sugar in the center of the saucepan, taking care not to let sugar crystals adhere to the sides of the saucepan. Gently stir with a clean spatula to thoroughly moisten the sugar. Cover the pan and bring to a boil over medium-high heat. Cook, covered and without stirring, until the sugar is completely dissolved and the liquid is clear, 3 to 5 minutes. Uncover and continue to cook, without stirring, but gently swirling the saucepan occasionally, until the caramel is a pale golden color, 3 to 5 minutes more. Reduce the heat to medium-low and continue to cook (swirling occasionally) until the caramel is light amber colored and registers about 360 degrees on a candy or instant-read thermometer, about 1 to 3 minutes longer. Remove the saucepan from the heat, add the cream to the center of the saucepan, and stir with a whisk until the bubbling subsides, being sure your hand isn't directly over the pan because the mixture will bubble vigorously. Stir in the butter

Nuts About Apple Pie

and vanilla, and transfer the caramel to a microwave safe bowl. Cool. Pour ¾ cup of the caramel into the bottom of the pie shell.

For Filling 2: Place apples, butter, sugar, salt, and lemon juice in a skillet and cook until apples are softened. Remove the apples to a colander and drain the liquid back into the skillet. Boil until reduced by half. Mix cornstarch thoroughly into the water to make a slurry and add to the skillet with the apple juice and boil until thickened. Remove from the heat and add the cinnamon and the vanilla and whisk until well mixed. Add the apples back in and stir to combine all ingredients. Pour apple filling over the caramel. Arrange the lattice top crust and finish the edge of the pie decoratively. Bake for 30 minutes. After 30 minutes, cover the edge with foil to keep from overbrowning. Bake the pie until the filling bubbles at the edge (approximately 20 minutes). Garnish the pie with a drizzle of remaining caramel and the remaining walnuts, if desired, when the pie has cooled.

BUTTER PECAN CRUMBLE APPLE PIE

Jeanne Ely, Mulberry, FL
2015 APC National Pie Championships
Amateur Division Apple 2nd Place

CRUST

3 cups King Arthur Perfect Pastry
   Blend flour
1 teaspoon salt
1 stick Crisco
1 stick butter
⅓ cup sugar
1 egg
5 tablespoons water, cold
1 tablespoon apple cider vinegar

FILLING

½ cup white sugar
2 tablespoons cornstarch
1 teaspoon cinnamon
¼ cup King Arthur boiled cider
1 cup apple juice
5 large apples
5 tablespoons butter

TOPPING

1 stick butter, softened
2 cups Butter Pecan Cake Mix

For the Crust: Preheat oven to 350 degrees. Cut together flour, salt, Crisco, butter, and sugar until oatmeal-like consistency. Beat egg in a cup, and add water and vinegar. Beat egg mixture and pour into flour mixture. Blend well. Roll out half of the dough and place in 9-inch deep dish pie plate.

For the Filling: Combine sugar, cornstarch, and cinnamon. Stir in boiled cider and apple juice. Cook over medium heat, stirring constantly until thickened. Peel and slice 5 large apples. Melt 5 tablespoons butter in the bottom of a large skillet. Add apple slices and cook until softened slightly, add sauce, and remove from heat. Pour apple mixture into pie shell.

For the Topping: Cut softened butter into cake mix. Place on top of the apples. Bake for approximately 45 minutes or until bubbly and apples are cooked through.

Butter Pecan Crumble Apple Pie

FALL IN LOVE WITH ME APPLE PIE

John Sunvold, Orlando, FL
2015 APC National Pie Championships
Amateur Division Apple 3rd Place

CRUST
1½ cups Windmill cookie crumbs
3 tablespoons sugar
6 tablespoons butter, melted
30 caramels
⅓ cup milk
½ cup almond pieces, toasted

FILLING 1
6 oz. cream cheese, softened
½ teaspoon vanilla extract
⅓ cup powdered sugar
6 oz. Cool Whip

FILLING 2
8–9 cups apple (around ½-inch pieces)
½ cup Honeycrisp apple juice
½ cup Gravenstein apple sauce
3 tablespoons butter
1 cup brown sugar
4 tablespoons cornstarch
1–2 teaspoons cinnamon

GARNISH
1 cup whipped topping
reserved caramel sauce
toasted almonds

For the Crust: Mix all ingredients together and press mixture into a deep pie plate. Bake for 8 to 10 minutes at 350 degrees. Allow to cool to room temperature. Melt caramels with milk. Reserve ⅓ of this caramel. Add toasted almond pieces, mix well, and spread into pie crust. Chill.

For Filling 1: Mix softened cream cheese, vanilla, and powdered sugar. Fold in Cool Whip. Spread on top of caramel and almonds. Swirl in the reserved caramel into the cream layer. Chill.

For Filling 2: Place all ingredients in a covered baking dish at 350 degrees for 30 minutes. Gently stir and check to see if apples are softened. Continue to bake, checking every 5 minutes. Bake until apples are softened. Cool and chill. Spread on the chilled cream (filling 1). Chill.

For the Garnish: Top with favorite whipped topping, caramel sauce (may use some of the reserved caramel layer), and/or nuts, as desired.

Fall in Love with Me Apple Pie

CLASSIC APPLE PIE

Evette Rahman, Orlando, FL
2014 APC National Pie Championships
Professional Division King Arthur Flour Apple, 1st Place

CRUST
2 cups King Arthur flour
1 tablespoon sugar
1 teaspoon salt
⅓ cup vegetable shortening
⅓ cup unsalted butter, cold, diced
¼ cup milk

FILLING
6 Fugi apples, cored, peeled, sliced
  thinly
3 Macon apples, cored, peeled, sliced
  thinly
1 teaspoon lemon juice
1 cup sugar
¼ cup cornstarch
½ teaspoon cinnamon
¼ teaspoon nutmeg
⅛ teaspoon ginger
2 tablespoons unsalted butter, melted
1 egg, beaten with 1 teaspoon water
  (egg wash)
sugar for sprinkling

For the Crust: Mix flour, sugar, and salt together. Cut in shortening and butter. Add milk. Mix together well. Form into two disks and refrigerate for 1 hour. Preheat oven to 375 degrees. Roll out one disk and place in deep dish pie plate.

For the Filling: Mix filling ingredients together and fill pie plate. Roll out remaining dough and cover filling. Cut off excess dough around rim of pie dish. Crimp edges. Brush top crust with egg wash and sprinkle with sugar. Bake for 50 to 60 minutes until golden brown and bubbling. Cover edges with pie crust shield if necessary during baking to avoid overbrowning. Cool completely before serving.

Classic Apple Pie

ALL-AMERICAN APPLE PIE

By Anita VanGundy, DesMoines, IA
2014 Iowa State Fair
1st Place All-American Apple Pie

CRUST
2 cups flour
½ teaspoon salt
⅔ cup shortening
2 tablespoons butter, cold
1 egg
½ water, cold
1 teaspoon vinegar

FILLING
3 Granny Smith apples, peeled and
   sliced
3 Braeburn apples, peeled and sliced

⅓ cup all-purpose flour
1 cup sugar
1 teaspoon cinnamon
1 teaspoon apple pie spice
2 teaspoons lemon juice
2 tablespoons boiled apple cider
½ teaspoon vanilla
2 tablespoons butter, melted

For the Crust: Mix flour and salt. Cut in shortening and butter. Mix egg, water, and vinegar. Add enough liquid to make dough come together, about 7 tablespoons. Shape into 2 discs and refrigerate for 30 minutes. Roll out 1 disc and place in pie pan.

For the Filling: Mix all ingredients in a large bowl. Pour into pie shell. Top with second pie crust. Seal and flute edges. Decorate with cutouts, if desired. Sprinkle with sugar. Bake at 350 degrees for 60 to 70 minutes.

APPLE RUM CARAMEL

Judy Sunvold, Chicago, IL
2014 APC National Pie Championships Amateur Division
1st Place Duncan Hines Comstock/Wilderness Apple

CRUST
1¼ cup graham crackers, crushed
¼ cup sugar
5 tablespoons butter, melted

FILLING 1
6 oz. cream cheese
1¼ teaspoons vanilla extract

FILLING 2
1 can Comstock Apple Pie Filling and
　Topping
¼ cup caramel sauce
½ teaspoon rum extract
½ teaspoon vanilla
½ cup dates, chopped
¾ cup walnuts, chopped

For the Crust: Preheat oven to 350 degrees. In a medium bowl, mix crackers, sugar, and butter. When fully incorporated, press into pan and bake 6 to 8 minutes or until golden in color. Cool. (Note: Depending on depth of pie pan, you may have a little extra.)

For Filling 1: Combine cream cheese and vanilla. When fully incorporated, spread into prepared pie shell. Place plastic wrap on top of surface tightly, and chill for 3 hours or until set.

For Filling 2: Pour apple pie filling into a medium-sized bowl. Pull out apple pieces and cut them into bite-sized pieces and place back into the pie filling can or a small bowl. In the medium-sized bowl, add the caramel sauce, rum extract, and vanilla. Mix until fully incorporated. Add the apples, dates, and walnuts, and mix gently. When fully mixed, pour onto cream cheese layer.

Top with your favorite whipped topping. Garnish and decorate as desired.

THE PERFECT APPLE PIE

Caroline Imig, Oconto, WI
2015 APC National Pie Championships
Professional Division 1st Place Apple

CRUST

²⁄₃ cup + 2 tablespoons shortening
2 cups all-purpose flour
1 teaspoon salt
4–5 tablespoons ice water
1 egg, beaten with 1 teaspoon water
(egg wash)

FILLING

8 cups thinly sliced apples (peeled,
quartered, cored, and sliced cross-
wise)
¾ cup sugar
1 teaspoon lemon juice
1 teaspoon cinnamon
¼ teaspoon apple pie spice
1 tablespoon flour

For the Crust: Preheat oven to 400 degrees. Cut shortening into flour and salt until particles are the size of small peas. Sprinkle in ice water, 1 tablespoon at a time, tossing with a fork until all flour is moistened and a ball of dough can be formed. Add more water, if necessary. Refrigerate dough until ready to roll.

For the Filling: Mix all ingredients with the apple slices. Roll out refrigerated pie crust dough, place in pie pan. Add apple mixture. Top with remaining crust. Cut a few small slashes in top crust for a steam vent. With pastry brush, brush on egg wash (beat one egg with 1 tablespoon of milk). Bake in a 400-degree oven for 10 minutes, then reduce heat to 375 degrees and continue baking for another 20 minutes.

The Perfect Apple Pie

APPLE OBSESSION PIE

Susan Boyle, DeBary, FL
2015 APC National Pie Championships
Professional Division Honorable Mention

CRUST
1 cup shortening, cold
¼ teaspoon salt
2½ cups all-purpose flour
1 egg
1 tablespoon white distilled vinegar
¼ cup ice water

FILLING 1
1 cup sugar
2 tablespoons Clear Jel
2 Jonathan gold apples, peeled, cored, sliced
2 Gala apples, peeled, cored, and sliced
1 Granny Smith apple, peeled, cored, and sliced

2 Pink Lady apples, peeled, cored, and sliced
1 teaspoon apple pie spice
¼ teaspoon ground ginger
2 tablespoons apple jelly

TOPPING
½ cup flour
¼ cup butter
¼ cup sugar
¼ cup pecans, chopped

For the Crust: Mix together shortening, salt, and flour until it resembles coarse crumbs. In another bowl, mix together egg, vinegar, and water. Whisk and then add all at once to shortening/flour mixture. Toss with a fork until mixture forms a ball. Knead and pat into a disk. Refrigerate until ready to use. Roll out pastry and put into a pie dish and crimp.

For the Filling: Mix sugar and Clear Jel together to make a mixture. Toss apples, sugar mixture, apple pie spice, ground ginger, and apple jelly. Toss again to coat evenly. Fill chilled pie crust, pressing down slightly to even the filling.

For the Topping: Mix all ingredients except pecans. Add pecans, then sprinkle on top of pie and add pastry cutouts. Bake at 400 degrees for 15 minutes, then lower temperature to 360 degrees and bake for 45 minutes before slicing.

Apple Obsession Pie

ROCKIN' CHAIR SUNDAY APPLE PIE

Naylet LaRochelle, Miami, FL
2013 APC National Pie Championships
Amateur Division 3rd Place Apple

CRUST

1⅓ cup flour
2 teaspoons sugar
⅛ teaspoon salt
4 tablespoons butter, cold
¼ cup Crisco butter-flavored
  shortening, cold
4–6 tablespoons water
1 teaspoon white wine vinegar

FILLING 1

1 (8-oz.) cream cheese, room
  temperature
⅓ cup sugar
2 eggs
pinch salt
½ teaspoon vanilla bean paste or
  ¾ teaspoon vanilla extract

FILLING 2

3 tablespoons butter
7 medium apples (preferably a
  combination of Granny Smith
  and Golden Delicious, peeled,
  cored, sliced)
⅓ cup light brown sugar
2 tablespoons lemon juice
1 tablespoon cornstarch
1 teaspoon ground cinnamon
⅛ teaspoon ground nutmeg

TOPPING

½ cup flour
⅓ cup light brown sugar
4 tablespoons butter, melted + 1
  tablespoon (cut into small pieces)
⅔ cup walnuts, chopped
⅓ cup toffee bits

For the Crust: Preheat oven to 450 degrees. In a large bowl, combine the flour, sugar, and salt. Using a pastry cutter, cut in the butter and shortening. Drizzle the water and vinegar into the flour mixture and combine with hands until a dough is formed. Shape dough into a disc; cover in plastic wrap. Refrigerate for about 1 hour to chill dough. On a lightly floured surface, roll out dough to fit a 9-inch pie plate. Ease pie dough into pie plate; trim pastry to edge of pie plate. Line crust with foil; add pie weights. Bake 8 to 10 minutes. Remove foil; prick crust. Reduce oven temperature to 375 degrees. Shield edges. Return to oven; bake until the crust is just beginning to turn light brown or partially baked, about 5 to 8 minutes more.

For Filling 1: Preheat oven to 350 degrees. In a medium bowl, beat together cream cheese and sugar until light and fluffy. Add eggs one at a time; beating between each addition. Add salt and vanilla; beat until well combined. Pour filling into pie crust–lined pie plate. Bake 15 to 17 minutes or until cream cheese is set. (Shield pie edge with foil to prevent overbrowning.)

For Filling 2: Meanwhile, in a large, nonstick deep skillet, over medium-high heat, melt butter. Add apples and brown sugar; sprinkle with lemon juice. Cook apples, stirring often, 4 to 5 minutes. Add cornstarch, cinnamon, and nutmeg. Cook, stirring, until apples are just soft and sauce has thickened. Layer apples over cream cheese filling. Dot with 1 tablespoon butter (cut into small pieces).

For Topping: In a medium bowl, combine flour, sugar, and butter until well blended. Stir in walnuts and toffee. Cover apples completely with streusel topping. Bake at 350 degrees 18 to 22 minutes, or until streusel is golden. (Shield edges with foil to avoid overbrowning.) Cool pie thoroughly on a cooling rack, about 2 to 3 hours, before slicing.

APPLE PIE

Andy Hilton, Davenport, FL
2014 APC National Pie Championships
Professional Division Honorable Mention Apple

CRUST
2½ cups all-purpose King Arthur
 flour
1 tablespoon sugar
1 teaspoon baking powder
½ cup butter
½ cup Crisco, cold
8–9 tablespoons water, cold

FILLING
6–7 of your favorite apples
1 teaspoon lemon juice
1 cup sugar + extra for sprinkling

½ teaspoon cinnamon
⅛ teaspoon nutmeg
2½ tablespoons modified cornstarch
2 tablespoons butter

EGG WASH
1 egg
1 tablespoon cold water

For the Crust: Whisk together the dry ingredients in a bowl. Place cold butter and cold Crisco on top of the flour mixture. Cut in with a pastry blender until the butter and Crisco are the size of small peas. Sprinkle with 4 tablespoons of cold water and fluff with a fork. Sprinkle with 4 or 5 more tablespoons of water and fluff until the dough comes together. Form a ball with the dough, wrap in plastic, and place in the refrigerator for 30 minutes. Split dough in half and roll out one half. Use the other half for the top of the pie.

For the Filling: Peel and slice apples, place in a large bowl, and sprinkle with lemon juice.

In another bowl, mix together the dry ingredients. Pour dry ingredients over the apples and blend together.

Place half of the apple filling in the prepared pie crust and dot with butter. Fill the crust with the balance of apple filling and dot with butter. Cover with the top crust and cut in steam vents. Whisk together egg and water. Brush the top of the pie with the egg wash and sprinkle with sugar. Place the pie on a cookie sheet and bake at 400 degrees for 15 minutes. Lower oven temperature to 350 and bake for 45 minutes or until the top is golden brown and the pie juices are bubbling. Remove the pie and cool. Enjoy!

Apple Pie

MAMIE JO'S APPLE PIE

Jill Jones, Palm Bay, FL
2103 APC Crisco National Pie Championships
Amateur Division 2nd Place Apple

CRUST
2 cups flour
½ tablespoons sugar
1 teaspoon salt
1 cup shortening
1 egg
½ tablespoons vinegar
3 tablespoons ice water

FILLING
6–8 Gala apples
2 tablespoons apple juice
½ cup flour
1 teaspoon cornstarch
3 tablespoons brown sugar
½ teaspoon apple pie spice
¾ cup sugar
2 teaspoons cinnamon
½ teaspoon salt
1 tablespoon butter
¼ cup milk
2 tablespoons sugar

For the Crust: Mix flour, sugar, and salt, cut in shortening with a fork or pastry cutter until mix is crumbly. Add egg, vinegar, and water, and mix until it comes together (may be slightly sticky). Scrape out of bowl onto a floured surface, roll into a ball with plastic wrap, and refrigerate for 1 hour. Roll out on floured surface.

For the filling: Peel and slice apples and pour juice over apples, set aside. In bowl, mix flour, cornstarch, brown sugar, apple pie spice, sugar, cinnamon, and salt. Mix well, pour over apples, and toss well. Pour into pie crust. Cube butter into small pieces and place on top of apples. Place top crust on pie and brush with milk and sugar. Vent pie. Bake at 375 for 45 minutes or until crust is nice and golden brown.

SMOKE'N HOT GRILLED APPLE PIE

Rick Johnson, Carpentersville, IL
2013 APC National Pie Championships
Amateur Division 1st Place Apple

CRUST
3 cups all-purpose flour
1¼ cup butter
½ teaspoon salt
⅓ cup lard
½ cup cream cheese
½ teaspoon almond extract

FILLING
6 tablets vitamin C
3 cups water
5 cups Golden Delicious apples
⅓ cup sugar
apple cider
2 tablespoons butter

2 teaspoons cinnamon
½ teaspoon nutmeg
¼ teaspoon ground cloves
¼ teaspoon salt
2 tablespoons Clear Jel

TOPPING
⅔ cup cream cheese
2 cups powdered sugar
2 tablespoons milk
1½ teaspoons vanilla
1 cup walnuts
1 tablespoon butter, melted
pinch salt

For the Crust: Add all ingredients to a food processor and process until it forms a ball. Refrigerate overnight then roll out into 1 large crust and put in heavy ceramic pie plate. Start grill with a small amount of charcoal.

For the Filling: Crush vitamin C tablets and dissolve in water. Slice apples and dip in solution, then add to plastic bag with sugar and refrigerate overnight. Remove apple mixture from plastic bag and drain. Take drained liquid and add enough apple cider to equal 2 cups. In a saucepan, over medium high heat, reduce liquid to 1 cup. Add butter, apples, and remaining ingredients. Pour into crust, and pull crust toward the center and crimp together. Cover tightly with aluminum foil. When the grill is hot, place pie at least 6 inches above charcoal and cover. Pie is done when the filling is bubbling. (Depending on the grill, it may be necessary to use broiler to brown top crust.)

For the Topping: Combine cream cheese and powdered sugar and mix until creamy. Add milk and vanilla, cream well, and pour over pie. Toss walnuts, butter, and salt and roast in 350-degree oven for 15 minutes. Chop walnuts coarsely and top pie.

BLUEBERRY

BLUEBERRY ALMOND FANTASY PIE

Alberta Dunbar, San Diego, CA
2014 APC National Pie Championships
Amateur Division 1st Place Comstock Blueberry

CRUST

1½ cups all-purpose flour
½ teaspoon salt
½ cup Crisco all-vegetable
  shortening
3–4 tablespoons ice water

FILLING

1 (21-oz.) can Comstock blueberry
  filling
2 cups fresh blueberries (or, if frozen, thawed and drained)
¾ teaspoon almond extract
¾ cup toasted almonds, sliced

8 oz. cream cheese, softened
¼ cup fresh lemon juice
2 teaspoons grated lemon peel
8 oz. white chocolate, melted and
  cooled
¾ cup heavy cream, whipped

GARNISH

2 cups heavy cream
¼ cup powdered sugar, sifted
1 teaspoon clear vanilla extract
½ cup toasted almonds, sliced
  (optional)

For the Crust: Preheat oven to 375 degrees. Spoon the flour into measuring cup and level. Mix flour and salt in medium bowl. Cut in shortening using pastry blender or two knives, until flour is blended and forms pea-sized chunks. Sprinkle with 1 tablespoon of water at a time. Toss lightly with a fork until dough forms a ball. Roll on lightly floured board to fit a 9-inch deep dish pie plate with ½-inch overlap. Fold under and flute edges. To blind bake pie, line pie crust with foil overlapping edges. Fill with beans or pie weights. Bake at 375 degrees for 20 minutes. Remove foil and beans. Bake 15 minutes or until golden brown. Cool on rack completely before filling.

For the Filling: In a large bowl, combine Comstock blueberry pie filling with fresh blueberries,

add the almond extract, and sliced almonds. Mix gently and set aside.

In medium bowl, combine cream cheese, lemon juice, and lemon peel. Beat on high until smooth. Beat in white chocolate. Fold in whipped cream.

Place half of blueberry mixture in cooled pie shell. Reserving 2 cups of the cream cheese/white chocolate mixture, pipe over berries. Carefully smooth out piping. Cover with remaining berry filling. Refrigerate 1 hour. Reserve 2 cups topping for around edge of pie. With reserved 2 cups of the cream cheese/white chocolate mixture, create a lattice top.

For the Garnish: Whip cream, powdered sugar, and vanilla together. Pipe whipped cream rosettes around edge of pie. Sprinkle with sliced almonds.

Blueberry Almond Fantasy Pie

BLUEBERRY CRUMBLE PIE

Lori Panchisin, Holly Hill, FL
2014 APC National Pie Championships
Amateur Division 3rd Place Blueberry

CRUST
1 cup all-purpose flour
½ teaspoon salt
⅓ cup + 1 tablespoon Crisco
   shortening
2–3 tablespoons water, cold

FILLING
1 cup granulated sugar
¼ cup + 1 tablespoon all-purpose
   flour
5 cups fresh blueberries, washed

1 tablespoon lemon juice
1 teaspoon pure vanilla extract

CRUMBLE TOPPING
⅔ cup all-purpose flour
¼ cup old-fashioned oats
6 tablespoons brown sugar, packed
¼ cup unsalted butter
¼ teaspoon cinnamon
¼ teaspoon salt

For the Crust: Preheat oven to 350 degrees. Combine flour and salt in a bowl. Cut in shortening until crumbly, using a pastry cutter. Sprinkle with 2 tablespoons cold water. Using a fork, stir until a ball of dough starts to form. If there is still dry flour at the bottom of the bowl, add up to 1 tablespoon water, 1 teaspoon at a time. Do not overmix. Roll into a 12-inch circle on a lightly floured surface with a lightly floured rolling pin. Fit it into a 9½-inch deep dish pie plate, cut off excess dough, leaving ½-inch overlap and tuck under, then flute the edges with your fingers. Set in the refrigerator while you make the filling and crumble topping.

For the Filling: In a large bowl, gently stir sugar, flour, and blueberries together until well mixed. Let stand 10 minutes. Sprinkle lemon juice and vanilla over blueberries and very gently stir to coat. Pour into pie shell.

For the Topping: Mix all topping ingredients together with a pastry cutter until crumbly. Cover pie with crumble topping. Bake on the bottom shelf in a 350-degree oven about 45 minutes until cooked and crumble topping is golden brown. If pie crust starts to get too brown, cover the edges with foil or a pie crust shield.

BLUEBERRY BOUNCE

David Harper, Lone Rock, WI
2014 APC National Pie Championships
Amateur Division 2nd Place Blueberry

CRUST
1 cup flour
1 teaspoon salt
½ cup butter-flavored Crisco
5 tablespoons water, cold

FILLING 1
4 cups fresh blueberries
2 tablespoons lemon juice
2 tablespoons flour
3 tablespoons butter
½ cup white sugar
½ cup dark brown sugar
¼ cup water
pinch cinnamon

FILLING 2
10 oz. mini marshmallows
1 cup of half-and-half
pinch salt
1 cup heavy cream, whipped stiff and
    chilled in refrigerator
1 teaspoon vanilla extract

TOPPING
1 cup whipping cream
¼ cup powdered sugar
1 teaspoon vanilla
lemon zest

For the Crust: Preheat oven to 400 degrees. Whisk the flour and the salt together in a large bowl. Add the Crisco and mix with your fingers until combined. Add the ice water and use a fork to combine. Turn pie dough out onto a floured surface and gather into a circular disk. Roll out the dough big enough to fit into a pie plate. Flute edges for decoration. Prick the bottom and sides of crust with a fork. Place into the refrigerator for 20 minutes. Bake crust until edges are golden brown and bottom is browned also, about 15 to 20 minutes. Cool on wire rack and set aside.

For Filling 1: Combine 3 cups of the blueberries in a large saucepan. Add the lemon juice, flour, butter, sugars, water, and cinnamon. While mixture cooks, use a potato masher to break up the blueberries. Cook over medium heat until mixture is thickened. Remove from heat and stir in the remaining 1 cup blueberries. Set aside to cool while preparing the bounce filling.

For Filling 2: Combine marshmallows, half-and-half, and salt in the top of double boiler. Cook and stir until marshmallows melt. Remove from heat and let cool until very thick, about 30 minutes. Fold in the whipped cream and vanilla until blended.

For the Topping: Turn half Filling 2 into the baked pie crust. Top with half the blueberry mixture. Repeat again with the bounce filling and top with remaining blueberry filling. Chill.

For the Garnish: Whip cream with powdered sugar and vanilla. Top pie with whipped cream and the lemon zest.

Blueberry Bounce

"VIOLET, YOU'RE TURNING VIOLET, VIOLET!" BLUEBERRY PIE

Rick Johnson, Carbondale, IL
2014 APC National Pie Championships
Amateur Division 1st Place Blueberry

CRUST
1½ cup all-purpose flour
½ teaspoon salt
½ cup butter, frozen
3 tablespoons lard
water, chilled

FILLING
8 cups frozen blueberry
1½ cups sugar
1 teaspoon cinnamon
½ teaspoon salt
7 tablespoons Clear Jel

TOPPING
1 cup flour
½ cup sugar
6 tablespoons butter
pinch salt
¾ cup almonds, chopped

GARNISH
1 pint heavy whipping cream
6 tablespoons powdered sugar
4 tablespoons piping gel
1 teaspoon vanilla

For the Crust: Combine flour, salt, and butter in a food processor and process until gravelly. Add lard. Add water a little at a time until dough just starts to hold together. Press into a disk and refrigerate for at least 1 hour then roll into crust.

For the Filling: Combine blueberry and sugar in large zip-top bag and refrigerate overnight. Strain juice and reduce in a large saucepan on medium heat until syrupy. Blend in remaining ingredients and heat until thick, then pour into pie crust.

For the Topping: Combine all ingredients except almonds into food processor and pulse until well combined, then add almonds. Bake at 425 on the bottom rack for 30 minutes, then move pie to top rack and reduce temperature to 350 degrees. Bake for 25 minutes or until topping has browned.

For the Garnish: Combine all ingredients in cold mixing bowl and beat until stiff peaks, then top pie.

"Violet, You're Turning violet, Violet!" Blueberry Pie

CINNAMON CRUNCH BLUEBERRY PIE

Paul Arguin, Atlanta, GA
2015 APC National Pie Championships
Amateur Division 1st Place Blueberry

CRUST
6 oz. flour
$\frac{1}{16}$ teaspoon cinnamon
1½ teaspoon sugar
½ teaspoon salt
$\frac{1}{8}$ teaspoon baking powder
6 tablespoons butter, cold, cut in
   cubes
1 oz. shortening, cold
1 teaspoon cider vinegar
3 tablespoons cold water
1 egg white, lightly beaten

FILLING
30 oz. fresh blueberries
1 Granny Smith apple
zest from 1 lemon
2 teaspoons lemon juice

¾ cup sugar
2 tablespoons minute tapioca,
   finely ground
$\frac{1}{8}$ teaspoon salt

TOPPING
1 cup panko
4 tablespoons butter, melted
¼ cup sugar
½ teaspoon cinnamon
pinch salt

GLAZE
1 cup powdered sugar
1 tablespoon lemon juice
1 tablespoon heavy cream
pinch salt

For the Crust: Mix flour, cinnamon, sugar, salt, and baking powder in a medium bowl. Add butter and cut in by hand with pastry blender until it resembles coarse sand. Add shortening and cut in until pea-sized nuggets of shortening remain. Add water and vinegar and mix with rubber spatula until dough is just holding together. Wrap in plastic and chill in refrigerator 30 minutes. Preheat oven to 425 degrees. Roll out dough into a circle, place in pie plate, and trim any excess. Crimp edge into a decorative pattern and chill another 15 minutes in the freezer. Place a sheet of parchment on the crust and fill with pie weights. Bake crust for 20 minutes on lower oven rack. Remove pie and weights and bake 5 minutes more. Decrease oven temperature to 400 degrees. Brush inside of pie with egg white.

For the Filling: Place blueberries into a vacuum sealable bag. Peel apple and grate finely. Squeeze grated apple through a clean kitchen towel and disperse the grated apple among the blueberries in the bag. Add lemon zest and juice to the bag. Whisk sugar, tapioca, and salt in a bowl and add to bag. Mix well. Seal vacuum bag and cook in immersion circulator at 150 degrees for 1 hour. Pour contents of bag into warm pie shell.

For the Topping: Toss panko with melted butter until well coated. Stir in sugar, cinnamon, and salt. Sprinkle topping on top of blueberries. Cover edge with pie ring and bake on middle rack at 400 degrees for 25 minutes.

For the Glaze: Whisk sugar, lemon juice, cream, and salt, together and drizzle over surface of pie.

Cinnamon Crunch Blueberry Pie

FRESH BLUEBERRY AMARETTO CREAM PIE

Carol Socier, Bay City, MI
2015 APC National Pie Championships
Amateur Division 3rd Place Blueberry

CRUST
¾ cup almonds, sliced and toasted
1 cup all-purpose flour
¼ cup confectioners' sugar
⅛ teaspoon salt
¼ cup unsalted butter, cold and cubed
2 tablespoons shortening, cold
3–4 tablespoons ice water

FILLING
4 oz. cream cheese, softened
¼ cup granulated sugar
1 tablespoon half-and-half
¼ teaspoon amaretto flavoring

1 (1-oz.) square white chocolate, melted
½ cup whipping cream, whipped
4 cups fresh blueberries
1 tablespoon lemon juice
½ cup water
½ cup granulated sugar
¼ cup cornstarch

TOPPING
1 cup heavy whipping cream
2 tablespoons sour cream
1 tablespoon confectioners' sugar
½ teaspoon amaretto flavoring

For the Crust: Place toasted almonds in a food processor. Cover and pulse until almonds are finely ground. Add flour, confectioners' sugar, and salt. Pulse until blended. Remove from blender to mixing bowl. Cut in butter and shortening with pastry blender until pea-sized pieces form. Slowly add cold water until dough ball forms. Shape dough ball into a disk and refrigerate for 20 to 30 minutes. On a lightly floured surface, roll dough to fit 9-inch pie plate. Prick bottom and sides with fork. Bake at 425 degrees for 12 to 14 minutes or until golden brown. Cool before filling.

For the Filling: Beat cream cheese, sugar, half-and-half, and amaretto flavoring in bowl until well blended. Stir in melted chocolate and whipped cream. Pour mixture into cooled crust. Refrigerate while preparing blueberry filling. In a large bowl, mash 1 cup blueberries with lemon juice. Add water. In a large saucepan, combine sugar and cornstarch. Stir in crushed berry mixture. Bring to a boil over medium heat, stirring constantly until mixture thickens. Cool in refrigerator for about 15 to 20 minutes. Fold in remaining blueberries. Spoon over cooled cream cheese layer. Refrigerate for about 3 hours or until set.

For the Topping: In a small bowl, beat whipping cream until soft peaks form. Add sour cream, sugar, and flavoring. Beat until stiff peaks form. Spread or pipe over filling. Garnish with fresh blueberries and toasted almonds, if desired. Serves 8.

Fresh Blueberry Amaretto Cream Pie

BLUEBERRY CHEESEQUAKE CRUMB PIE

David Harper, Lone Rock, WI
2015 APC National Pie Championships
Amateur Division 2nd Place Blueberry

CRUST
1 cup flour
1 teaspoon salt
½ cup butter-flavored Crisco
5 tablespoons water, cold

FILLING 1
1 (8-oz.) package cream cheese
¼ cup powdered sugar
1 teaspoon vanilla
1 teaspoon lemon zest

FILLING 2
4 cups fresh blueberries
2 tablespoons lemon juice
2 tablespoons flour
3 tablespoons butter
½ cup white sugar
½ cup dark brown sugar
¼ cup of water
pinch of cinnamon

TOPPING
⅔ cup flour
⅔ cup old-fashioned oats
½ cup brown sugar
¾ teaspoon salt
1 teaspoon cinnamon
6 tablespoons butter, cold

For the Crust: Preheat oven to 375 degrees. Whisk the flour and the salt together in a large bowl. Add the Crisco and mix with your fingers until combined. Add the water and use a fork to combine. Turn pie dough out onto a floured surface and gather into a circular disk. Roll out the dough big enough to fit into a pie plate. Flute edges for decoration. Place into the refrigerator for 20 minutes. After 20 minutes, use a fork to poke holes in the bottom and sides of the pie crust. Place crust in oven and bake for about 10 to 15 minutes, or until lightly browned and dry. After 10 to 15 minutes of baking, remove the crust from oven and let cool on rack.

For Filling 1: Beat the cream cheese and powdered sugar together in a mixing bowl until smooth. Add the vanilla and lemon zest and whip until incorporated. Spread in the bottom of the cooled pie crust and set aside until later.

For Filling 2: Combine 3 cups of the blueberries in a large saucepan. Add the lemon juice, flour, butter, sugars, water, and cinnamon. While mixture cooks, use a potato masher to break up the blueberries. Cook over medium heat until mixture is thickened. Remove from heat and stir in the remaining 1 cup blueberries. Cool until room temperature.

For the Topping: Combine all the dry ingredients in a bowl, add the chilled butter and, with a fork or fingers, work the butter into the dry ingredients. Don't overwork; you should still see some of the small butter pieces. Place the crumb topping on the blueberry mixture and place in the oven. Bake for 35 to 45 minutes or until topping is browned and crisp. Remove from oven and let cool on wire rack. Since this blueberry pie has cream cheese, I would refrigerate in a covered pie carrier if you have any leftovers.

Blueberry Cheesequake Crumb Pie

BLUEBERRY LEMON CREAM PIE

Devin Davis, Plant City, FL
2015 APC National Pie Championships
Professional Division 1st Place Blueberry

CRUST
10 oz. Pepperidge Farm lemon
　cookies
2 tablespoons flour
4 tablespoons butter, melted
1 tablespoon Crisco, melted

FILLING
2 cups sugar
zest of 1½ lemons
5 egg yolks
⅓ cup lemon juice
1 stick butter, cold and cubed
8 oz. cream cheese, softened
3 cups heavy cream
¾ cup powdered sugar
2 cups frozen blueberries
¾ cup water
1 pint fresh blueberries
¼ cup cornstarch

For the Crust: Preheat oven to 350 degrees. In a food processor, pulse the cookies until they become fine crumbs. Then add the flour, butter, and Crisco, and pulse until the crumbs are moist. Bake for 8 minutes and then let cool completely.

For the Filling: In a food processor, pulse together 1 cup of the sugar and the zest of 1 lemon until the zest is ground fine. Then whisk together the egg yolks and the lemon zest/sugar mixture in a medium-sized bowl until pale yellow, and then whisk in the lemon juice. Cook the egg yolk mixture over a small pot of simmering water for about 10 to 12 minutes or nicely thickened, whisking constantly. Remove from the heat and whisk in the butter one piece at a time, until completely melted and incorporated and then let cool completely; reserve ½ cup of the mixture for later use. In the bowl of an electric mixer, cream the cream cheese and ¼ cup of sugar until smooth and then beat in the lemon custard until smooth. In a separate bowl and using the electric mixer, beat 1 cup of the heavy cream and ¼ cup of the powdered sugar until stiff peaks form and then fold into the cream cheese mixture. Pour half of the lemon filling into the prepared pie crust and then refrigerate. In a sauce pot, combine the frozen blueberries, remaining lemon zest, 1 cup sugar, and the water, and bring to a boil. Cook for 5 minutes and then strain. Return to the pot and bring to a boil, add the fresh blueberries, and cook for 1 minute. In a small bowl, whisk together the cornstarch and ¼ cup of water until smooth then whisk into the boiling blueberry sauce. Cook for 30 more seconds and let cool completely. Spread it over the bottom half of the lemon filling in the pie crust and then refrigerate until the blueberry layer has set and then top with remaining lemon filling. Then whip the heavy cream with the reserved lemon mixture and ½ cup of the powdered sugar until it forms firm peaks. Decorate with the whipped cream mixture and then with more fresh blueberries and lemon zest, if desired.

Blueberry Lemon Cream Pie

BLUEBERRY BLACKBERRY BASIL PIE

Tammi Carlock, Chickamunga, GA
2015 APC National Pie Championships
Professional Division Honorable Mention Blueberry

CRUST
2 cups flour
1 teaspoon salt
⅔ cup Crisco shortening
6–8 tablespoons water, cold

FILLING
6 cups fresh blueberries
1½ cups fresh blackberries
¾ cup sugar
¼ cup cornstarch

1 cup fresh basil leaves
zest of 1 lime
2 teaspoons fresh squeezed lime juice

TOPPING
¾ cup flour
½ cup sugar
¼ teaspoon salt
5 tablespoons butter, cold and cut into small cubes

For the Crust: Mix together flour and salt. Cut in shortening until mixture resembles coarse meal. Add water, 1 tablespoon at a time, mixing with fork until dough holds together. Roll out into circle larger than 9-inch pie plate and press into pie shell and crimp edges. Set aside.

For the Filling: Preheat oven to 375 degrees. In a large saucepan, combine 3 cups blueberries and 1 cup blackberries. Gently mash berries. Stir in sugar and cornstarch. Mix to combine. Add basil leaves and stir gently. Over medium heat, stirring filling often, cook until mixture is thick. Remove from heat and stir in remaining berries, lime zest, and lime juice. Remove basil leaves and set aside filling to cool. Pour filling into the pie shell.

For the Topping: Mix together the dry ingredients in a medium bowl. Cut in butter with a pastry blender until crumbs are coarse. Set aside. Sprinkle the crumb topping on top. Bake for 50 to 60 minutes or until filling is thick and bubbly. Let cool to room temperature.

Blueberry Blackberry Basil Pie

BLUEBERRY LATTICE PIE

Evette Rahman, Orlando, FL
2014 APC National Pie Championships
Professional Division 1st Place

CRUST
2 cups flour
2 tablespoons sugar
1 teaspoon salt
⅓ cup vegetable shortening
⅓ cup unsalted butter, cold, diced
¼ cup milk
1 tablespoon vinegar

FILLING
6 fresh blueberries
2 teaspoons lemon juice
1 cup sugar
3 tablespoons instant tapioca
2 tablespoons cornstarch
½ teaspoon cinnamon
¼ teaspoon nutmeg
2 tablespoons unsalted butter, melted
1 egg, beaten with 1 teaspoon water
    (egg wash)
sugar, for sprinkling

For the Crust: Preheat oven to 375 degrees. Mix flour, sugar, and salt together. Cut in shortening and butter. Add milk and vinegar. Mix together well. Form into two disks and refrigerate for 1 hour. Roll out one disk and place in deep dish pie plate.

For the Filling: Mix filling ingredients together and fill pie plate. Roll out remaining dough and cut into strips. Lay strips across filling or form a lattice design. Cut off excess dough around rim of pie dish. Crimp edges. Brush top crust with egg wash and sprinkle with sugar. Bake for 50 to 60 minutes until golden brown and bubbling. Cover edges with pie crust shield if necessary during baking to avoid overbrowning. Cool completely before serving.

Blueberry Lattice Pie

LEMON BLUEBERRY TARTS

Evette Rahman, Orlando, FL
2014 APC AUI Fine Foods National Pie Championships
Professional Division 1st Place AUI Fine Foods Tart

CRUST
8 AUI Fine Foods Tart shells

FILLING
1 egg yolk
2 tablespoons cream cheese, softened
½ cup whipped topping
½ cup sweetened condensed milk
⅛ cup lemon juice, freshly squeezed
½ tablespoon lemon zest

TOPPING
1 cup fresh blueberries
⅓ cup sugar
1 tablespoon instant tapioca
1 tablespoon cornstarch
2 tablespoons lemon juice

GARNISH
sweetened whipped cream
fresh berries

For the Filling: Beat lemon filling ingredients together until well combined. Divide and spread evenly in tart shells.

For the Topping: In small saucepan over medium heat, cook ½ cup of blueberries and remaining filling ingredients, stirring constantly until very thick. Remove from heat and stir in remaining blueberries. Cool. Divide and spread evenly over lemon layer in tart shells.

For the Garnish: Garnish with sweetened whipped cream and fresh berries.

Lemon Blueberry Tarts

BLUEBERRY CHERRY PIE

Andy Hilton, Davenport, FL
2014 APC National Pie Championships
Professional Division Honorable Mention Blueberry

CRUST
2½ cups all-purpose flour
1 tablespoon sugar
1 teaspoon baking powder
½ cup butter, cold
½ cup Crisco shortening, cold
8–9 tablespoons water, cold

FILLING
5 cups frozen blueberries
2 cups frozen sour cherries
1 cup sugar

3½ tablespoons modified cornstarch
¼ teaspoon nutmeg
2 tablespoons butter

EGG WASH
1 egg
1 tablespoon cold water
2 tablespoons sugar

For the Crust: Whisk together the dry ingredients in a bowl. Place cold butter and cold shortening on top of the flour mixture. Cut in with a pastry blender until the butter and shortening are the size of small peas. Sprinkle with 4 tablespoons of cold water and fluff with a fork. Then sprinkle with 4 or 5 tablespoons of water and fluff until the dough comes together. Form a ball with the dough, wrap in plastic, and place in the refrigerator for 30 min. Split dough in half and roll out one half. Use the other half for the top of the pie.

For the Filling: Combine frozen blueberries, cherries, and almond emulsion. In another bowl, mix together the dry ingredients. Pour dry ingredients over the blueberries and cherries and blend together. Place blueberries and cherry filling in the prepared pie crust and dot with 2 tablespoons of butter. Cover with the top crust and cut in steam vents. Whisk together egg and water. Brush the top of the pie with the egg wash and sprinkle with sugar. Place the pie on a cookie sheet and bake at 400 degrees for 15 minutes. Lower oven temperature to 350 degrees and bake for 45 minutes or until the top is golden brown and the pie juices are bubbling. Remove the pie and cool. Enjoy!

Blueberry Cherry Pie

BLUEBERRY CHEESECAKE PIE

Angela Cacciola, Orlando FL
2015 APC National Pie Championships
Amateur Division
1st Place Duncan Hines Comstock/Wilderness Blueberry

CRUST
1¾ cups graham cracker crumbs
2 tablespoons brown sugar
pinch salt
6 tablespoons butter, melted

FILLING 1
1 (8-oz.) package cream cheese,
    softened
¼ cup sugar
2 cups Cool Whip

FILLING 2
1 (21-oz.) can Comstock blueberry
    pie filling
½ teaspoon cinnamon
¼ teaspoon ground ginger

WHIPPED CREAM TOPPING
2 teaspoons unflavored gelatin
2 tablespoons water, cold
2 cups heavy whipping cream
4 tablespoons white sugar
½ teaspoon vanilla

TOPPING
2 graham crackers, crushed (not
    fine)
¼ cup brown sugar
⅛ teaspoon cinnamon
2 tablespoons melted butter
¼ teaspoon vanilla
2 tablespoons white sugar
pinch salt

For the Crust: Heat oven to 350 degrees. Lightly grease pie pan. Pulse graham crackers in food processor until the consistency of fine crumbs. Add brown sugar, salt, and butter, and mix well. Press into 8-inch pie tin and bake for 12 to 14 minutes until edges are golden brown. Set aside to cool.

For Filling 1: Beat cream cheese and sugar in an electric mixer. Fold in Cool Whip. Pour filling into cooled pie shell. Cool in the refrigerator for 15 minutes.

For Filling 2: Mix ingredients together and spread on top of Filling 1.

For the Topping: Combine gelatin and cold water in a microwave-safe container. Allow to sit for 1 minute, then microwave on high for 15 seconds and allow to cool (not long enough to set). Begin whipping cream in mixer and add gelatin, sugar, and vanilla. Whip until soft peaks form. Pipe on top of pie.

For the Topping: Mix all ingredients together and spread on a cookie sheet sized for a toaster oven. Toast in a toaster oven until fragrant. Sprinkle on whipped topping.

CHERRY

CHEERY CHERRY BOUNCE

David Harper, Lone Rock, WI
2015 APC National Pie Championships
Amateur Division 3rd Place Cherry

CRUST
1 cup flour
1 teaspoon salt
½ cup butter-flavored Crisco
5 tablespoons water, cold

FILLING 1
10 oz. mini marshmallows
1 cup half-and-half
pinch salt
1 cup heavy cream, whipped stiff and
  chilled
1 teaspoon vanilla extract

FILLING 2
2½ cups cherry juice, reserve ½ cup
2 tablespoons butter

½ cup white sugar
½ cup brown sugar
1 tablespoon orange zest
2 tablespoons orange juice
dash cinnamon
3 heaping tablespoons cornstarch
4 cups Wisconsin cherries

TOPPING
1 cup whipping cream
¼ cup powdered sugar
1 teaspoon vanilla
½ cup pistachios or macadamia nuts,
  crushed

For the Crust: Preheat oven to 375 degrees. Whisk the flour and the salt together in a large bowl. Add the Crisco and mix with your fingers until combined. Add the water and use a fork to combine. Turn pie dough out onto a floured surface and gather into a circular disk. Roll out the dough big enough to fit into a pie plate. Flute edges for decoration. Prick the bottom and sides of crust with a fork. Place into the refrigerator for 20 minutes. Bake crust until edges are golden brown and bottom is browned also, about 15 to 20 minutes. Cool on wire rack and set aside.

For Filling 1: Combine marshmallows, half-and-half, and salt in the top of double boiler. Cook and stir until marshmallows melt. Remove from heat and let cool until very thick, about 30 minutes. Fold in the whipped cream and vanilla until blended. Turn half of this filling into the pre-baked crust.

For Filling 2: In a heavy pan over medium heat, combine 2 cups cherry juice, the butter, sugars, orange zest and juice, and cinnamon. Bring this mixture to a boil. Combine cornstarch and reserved ½ cup cherry juice together to make a slurry. Pour this mixture into the boiling cherry juice mixture. Boil for about 2 minutes, stirring occasionally until thickened. Off heat, add the cherries. Cool to room temperature. Cover Filling 1 with half of the Filling 2 mixture. Repeat with Filling 1 and then again Filling 2.

For the Topping: Top with whipped cream and your choice of nuts.

Cheery Cherry Bounce

PART TART VERY CHERRY PIE

Beth Campbell, Belleville, WI
2015 APC National Pie Championships
Amateur Division 1st Place

CRUST
½ cup shortening
1 cup flour
¼ cup cold water
pinch salt

FILLING 1
⅓ cup sugar
⅓ cup cornstarch
1 cup cherry juice
4 cups fresh tart cherries
½ teaspoon ground cinnamon

¼ teaspoon ground nutmeg
¼ teaspoon almond extract

FILLING 2
1 (8-oz.) package cream cheese, softened
1 (14-oz.) can sweetened condensed milk
⅓ cup fresh lemon juice
1 teaspoon almond extract
½ cup whipped cream

For the Crust: Preheat oven to 425 degrees. Cut the shortening into the flour and salt until the particles are the size of small peas. Sprinkle the water into the flour mixture until moistened. Gather the pastry into a ball and refrigerate overnight. Roll pastry out on a floured board. Fold the pastry into quarters, unfold, and ease into pie pan and crimp edges. Fill with pie weights. Bake for 10 minutes or until lightly golden brown. Cool completely.

For Filling 1: In a large saucepan, combine the sugar and cornstarch; gradually stir in the cherry juice until smooth. Bring to a boil; cook and stir until combined for 2 minutes or until thickened. Remove from heat. Add cherries, cinnamon, nutmeg, and almond extract and cook until thickened. Cool completely and pour into cooled pie shell.

For Filling 2: In a large bowl, beat the cream cheese with an electric mixer until light and fluffy. Add the condensed milk, lemon juice, and almond extract. Beat on low until completely combined. Fold into whipped cream until completely blended. Pour on cherry filling layer. Garnish as desired. Chill overnight.

Part Tart Very Cherry Pie

ORCHARD DELICIOUS DOUBLE CHERRY CREAM PIE

Carol Socier, Bay City, MI
2015 APC National Pie Championships
Amateur Division 2nd Place Cherry

CRUST
1½ cups all-purpose flour
2 teaspoon sugar
½ teaspoon salt
½ teaspoon baking powder
½ cup + 1 tablespoon shortening
4–5 tablespoons water, cold

FILLING
1 (15-oz.) can red tart cherries
1 (15-oz.) can sweet Royal Anne
   Cherries in heavy syrup

1 (3-oz.) package cherry Jell-O
1 cup heavy whipping cream
1 (12-oz.) container whipped cream
   cheese spread

TOPPING
1½ cups heavy whipping cream
⅓ cup powdered sugar
½ cup cherry preserves

For the Crust: Whisk together first four ingredients. Cut in shortening with fork or pastry blender until coarse pieces form. Add cold water, 1 tablespoon at a time, tossing with a fork until dough ball forms. Roll out on lightly floured surface to fit 9-inch pie pan. Flute edges and pierce several times with a fork on bottom and sides. Bake in 425-degree oven for 15 to 18 minutes or until golden brown. Cool completely on wire rack before filling.

For the Filling: Drain juice from cherries. Set fruit aside. Dissolve the cherry Jell-O in the drained cherry juice and microwave for 1 minute. Cool to room temperature. Whip cream until peaks form. Add cream cheese and continue beating until smooth. Stir in cooled Jell-O, mixing thoroughly. Fold in drained cherries. Pour into cooled pie shell and refrigerate until set.

For the Topping: Combine whipping cream and powdered sugar. Whip until stiff peaks form. Gently fold in cherry preserves. Spread evenly over top of set pie. Garnish as desired.

Orchard Delicious Double Cherry Cream Pie

AIN'T NO PITS IN THIS CHERRY PIE

Matt Zagorski, Arlington Heights, IL
2015 APC National Pie Championships
Professional Division 1st Place Cherry

CRUST
½ cup whole butter, salted, cold
½ cup butter-flavored Crisco, cold
2 cups all-purpose flour
½ cup cake flour
1 tablespoon powdered sugar
½ teaspoon salt
¼ cup sour cream
½ cup water

FILLING
¾ cup sugar
½ teaspoon salt
9 tablespoon Clear Jel
2 cups cherry juice
1½ tablespoon lemon juice
¼ almond extract
42 oz. tart cherries

TOPPING
1 cup flour
6 tablespoons butter, cold
½ cup brown sugar

EGG WASH
1 egg
1 tablespoon water
2 tablespoons sugar

For the Crust: Cut the butter and Crisco into ¼-inch pieces. Once cut, place in the freezer to harden. Combine the flours, powdered sugar, and salt in a food processor and combine—about 30 seconds. Once the dries are combined, scatter the very cold Crisco and butter pieces over the flour mixture and process thoroughly using 10 (1-second) pulses on the food processor. Make sure the mixture has no fat bits larger than small peas. If so, pulse one or two more times. Remove to a large bowl. Combine the sour cream and water in a glass or bowl and stir to combine. Sprinkle 4 tablespoons of the sour cream mixture over the flour mixture and, with a fork, use a folding motion to incorporate. Add enough additional water that the dough just comes together. It should be slightly damp and cold and should hold together when squeezed. Divide the dough into two piles, shape into balls, and flatten each into a 6- to 8-inch disk. Cover each in plastic wrap and refrigerate at least 2 hours—best if overnight. Before rolling out, let the dough come to just below room temperature. This should take 6 to 7 minutes. The dough should be slightly cool to the touch. Roll to desired thickness and place in pie pan. Place the pan with the rolled out dough in the refrigerator to chill for at least 40 minutes. After 40 minutes in the refrigerator, place the dough and pie pan in the freezer for 20 minutes. While the dough is in the freezer, preheat the oven to 425 degrees and prepare the cherry filling.

For the Filling: Combine the sugar, salt, and Clear Jel together in a bowl and whisk to combine.

Add the cherry juice, lemon juice, and almond extract to the dries and completely mix together. Add the cherries to the wets and pour the whole mixture into the chilled pie shell. Make sure the cherries do not come to the rim of the pie shell. Bake for 35 to 40 minutes more until the cherries bubble—on the sides only is okay; it does not have to be in the middle.

For the Topping: Combine all of the topping ingredients in a food processor and process until the topping looks likes sand. Pour the topping into a bowl and squeeze some of it together to make clumps. Cover the top of the cherry filling with the topping. Use all topping. Whisk together egg and water. Brush egg-wash on the rim of the pie and sprinkle with raw sugar. Place the pie on a sheet pan and place it on the floor of a 425-degree oven for 15 minutes. After 15 minutes, move the pie to the middle of the oven, reduce temperature to 350 degrees.

Ain't No Pits in This Cherry Pie

HAWAIIAN CHERRY PIE

Angela Rumpf, Orlando, FL
2014 APC National Pie Championships
1st Place Comstock Cherry

CRUST
1 (12-oz.) box of Nilla Wafer cookies,
   crushed
½ cup coconut oil, room temp

FILLING
1 (8-oz.) can crushed pineapples,
   undrained
1 box instant vanilla pudding mix
1 (8-oz.) package cream cheese
1 can Comstock Cherry pie filling
½ cup sweetened flaked coconut

For the Crust: Mix together the crushed cookies and warm coconut oil. Press into a 9-inch pie dish. Bake at 350 degrees for 10 minutes. Let cool.

For the Filling: In a large bowl, mix crushed pineapple with its syrup, dry pudding mix, and cream cheese; mix until well. Spoon into pie crust and top with Comstock cherry filling; sprinkle with coconut. Chill at least 2 hours before serving.

RUSTIC CHERRY TART

Andrea Spring, Bradenton, FL
2012 APC Crisco National Pie Championships
Professional Division 2nd Place Cherry

CRUST
½ cup butter-flavored Crisco
1½ cups flour
1 teaspoon salt
½ cup almonds, ground
3 tablespoons sugar
4 tablespoons water, cold

FILLING 1
1 (15-oz.) can cherry pie filling
½ teaspoon almond extract

FILLING 2
4 oz. cream cheese, softened
½ cup sugar
1 egg
½ teaspoon vanilla extract
1 egg yolk, beaten with a few drops
    of water (egg wash)
¼ cup sliced almonds
raw or demerara sugar

For the Crust: Cut Crisco into flour; add salt, almonds, and sugar. Add water and mix. Flatten into large disc and chill for 4 hours.

For Filling 1: Preheat oven to 325 degrees. Cook cherries and almond extract in a saucepan until syrup reduces. Roll out dough and place flat on lightly greased cookie sheet. Divide cherries in half and place half on center of dough, leaving a wide margin around the cherries. Reserve remaining cherries.

For Filling 2: Mix cream cheese, sugar, egg, and vanilla. Spoon on top of cherries. Top with remaining cherries and fold dough in and over filling, leaving open space in center. Brush crust with egg wash. Sprinkle almonds around crust, and then sprinkle with sugar. Bake at 325 degrees for 40 to 50 minutes until crust is golden brown.

UNFORGETTABLE CHERRY PIE

Susan Boyle, Debary, FL
2014 APC National Pie Championships
Professional Division 1st Place Cherry

CRUST
1 cup Crisco shortening, cold
¼ teaspoon salt
2½ cups all-purpose flour
¼ cup almonds, ground
1 egg
1 tablespoon white distilled vinegar
¼ cup water, cold

FILLING
4 cups cherries (red, tart)
1½ cups Bing sweet cherries
½ cup dried tart cherries
1¼ cup sugar
1 teaspoon almond extract
½ teaspoon red food coloring
4 tablespoons cornstarch
1 tablespoon butter

For the Crust: Mix together Crisco, salt, flour, and almonds until it resembles coarse crumbs. In another bowl, place egg, water, and vinegar and whisk. Add egg mixture to flour mixture. Toss with fork until mixture forms a ball, knead and pat into a disk refrigerate until ready to use. Roll out pastry and place in prepared pan. Chill before filling.

For the Filling: In a large bowl, toss together all cherries, sugar, almond extract, food coloring, and cornstarch. Let set for 5 to 10 minutes, re-tossing before adding to prepared crust. Place lattice pastry on top, seal edges, and flute. Bake at 425 degrees for 45 to 55 minutes.

Unforgettable Cherry Pie

SIMPLY CHERRY PIE

Andy Hilton, Davenport, FL
2014 APC National Pie Championships
Professional Division Honorable Mention Cherry

CRUST
2½ cups all-purpose flour
1 tablespoon sugar
½ teaspoon baking powder
½ cup Crisco shortening
½ cup butter
8–9 tablespoons water, cold

FILLING:
5 cups frozen sour cherries
½ cups dried cherries
½ teaspoon almond emulsion
1 cup sugar
3½ tablespoons modified cornstarch
2 tablespoons butter

For the Crust: Preheat oven to 425 degrees. Whisk together the dry ingredients in a bowl. Place cold butter and cold shortening on top of the flour mixture. Cut in with a pastry blender until the butter and shortening are the size of small peas. Sprinkle with 4 tablespoons of cold water and fluff with a fork. Sprinkle with 4 or 5 more tablespoons of water and fluff until the dough comes together. Form a ball with the dough, wrap in plastic, and place in the refrigerator for 30 minutes. Split dough in half and roll out one half. Use the other half for the top of the pie.

For the Filling: Combine cherries and almond emulsion, in a bowl. In another bowl, mix together the dry ingredients. Pour dry ingredients over the cherries and blend together. Place cherry filling in the prepared pie crust and dot with 2 tablespoons of butter. Cover with the top crust and cut in steam vents. Brush the top of the pie with an egg wash and sprinkle with sugar. Place the pie on a cookie sheet and bake at 400 degrees for 15 minutes. Lower oven temp to 350 degrees and bake for 45 minutes or until the top is golden brown and the pie juices are bubbling. Remove the pie and cool. Enjoy!

Simply Cherry Pie

CHERRY MOCHA LATTE PIE

Caroline Imig, Oconto, WI
2014 APC National Pie Championships
Professional Division 1st Place Innovation

CRUST
⅔ cup + 2 tablespoons Crisco short-
    ening
2 cup all-purpose flour
1 teaspoon salt
2 tablespoons cocoa
5–6 tablespoons water, cold

CHOCOLATE BASE
6 tablespoons butter
2 squares (1 oz. each) unsweetened
    chocolate
1 cup sugar
2 eggs, beaten
½ teaspoon vanilla
½ cup all-purpose flour

FILLING 1
4 cups sour cherries
1½ cups sugar
3 tablespoon cornstarch

FILLING 2
¼ cup sugar
1 envelope unflavored gelatin
1 cup water
6 oz. white chocolate baking chips
3 egg yolks
1¼ cup whipping cream
2 tablespoons strong coffee

GARNISH
1 cup cherry filling
whipped cream
chocolate curls (if desired)

For the Crust: Cut shortening into flour, salt, and cocoa until particles are the size of small peas. Sprinkle in water, 1 tablespoon at a time, tossing with a fork until all flour is moistened. Form pastry into a ball, flatten, and roll out. Bake at 375 degrees for 10 minutes.

For the Base: In microwave-safe bowl, melt butter and chocolate. Stir in sugar until well blended. Add egg and vanilla, mix well. Stir in flour until blended. Pour into partially prebaked chocolate crust. Bake at 350 degrees for 12 to 15 minutes. Cool.

For Filling 1: Mix together all ingredients and cook in microwave until boils and thickens. Spread 2 cups cherry filling on chocolate base.

For Filling 2: In a microwave-safe bowl, combine sugar and gelatin. Add water. Cook until mixture boils and gelatin dissolves. Melt white chocolate in microwave, add to water/sugar mixture. In medium bowl, beat egg yolks. Stir three quarters of the hot gelatin mixture into egg yolks, and stir until combined. Return all the mixture to microwave-safe bowl, cook until mixture bubbles. Remove from microwave, cover, and chill about 45 minutes until mixture is the consistency of unbeaten egg whites. Stir occasionally. In a chilled mixing bowl, beat 1¼ cup whipping cream and strong coffee with a mixer until stiff. Fold whipping cream mixture into gelatin mixture. Spoon and spread on top of cherry filling on chocolate base.

For the Garnish: Put additional 1 cup cherry filling center on top of latte filling. Garnish with additional whipped cream and chocolate curls.

Cherry Mocha Latte Pie

COMSTOCK CHERRY CHOCOLATE LOVERS PIE

Carol Socier, Bay City, MI
2015 APC National Pie Championships
Amateur Division Best of Comstock

CRUST
1½ cups chocolate wafer crumbs
¼ cup butter, melted

FILLING
1 (8-oz.) package cream cheese, softened
½ cup granulated sugar
2 tablespoons light cream (half-and-half)
1 teaspoon vanilla extract

1 (1-oz.) square unsweetened chocolate, melted
½ cup whipping cream, whipped
1 can Comstock cherry pie filling

TOPPING
1 cup heavy whipping cream
¼ cup powdered sugar
10–12 maraschino cherries with stems
dark melting chocolate

For the Crust: Preheat oven to 375 degrees. Mix chocolate wafer crumbs and melted butter in bowl. Press onto bottom and up sides of ungreased 8-inch pie pan. Bake 8 minutes in preheated oven. Cool.

For the Filling: Beat cream cheese, sugar, cream, and vanilla in a medium-sized bowl. Divide mixture in half. Stir melted chocolate into half of the cream cheese mixture. Fold whipped cream into remaining cream cheese mixture. Pour chocolate mixture into cooled crust. Top with half of cherry pie filling, then top with whipped cream mixture and remaining pie filling. Chill well.

For the Topping: Combine cream and powdered sugar in cold mixing bowl. Beat until stiff peaks form. Refrigerate until ready to use. Drain stemmed cherries on paper towels. Melt chocolate in melting pot or microwave. Dip cherries into chocolate and set on wax paper. Garnish chilled pie with cream and dipped cherries. Serves 8.

Comstock Cherry Chocolate Lovers Pie

MY CHERRY AMOUR PIE

Evette Rahman, Orlando, FL
2012 Amateur APC Crisco National Pie Championships
Amateur Division 1st Place Cherry

CRUST
1 (10.6-oz.) package Voortman's Almond Crunch Cookies, finely ground
½ cup sweetened flaked coconut, finely ground
½ cup butter-flavored Crisco shortening, melted
6 tablespoons semisweet chocolate morsels
6 tablespoons milk chocolate morsels
½ cup heavy cream

FILLING 1
4 cups dark, sweet, pitted cherries, measured while frozen, then thawed
½ cup tart cherry juice and any drained juice from frozen cherries
⅓ cup sugar

2 tablespoons cornstarch
1 tablespoon salted butter
¼ teaspoon almond extract
2 tablespoons black cherry–flavored gelatin powder

FILLING 2
4 oz. cream cheese, softened
¼ cup sweetened condensed milk
1 tablespoon lemon juice
¼ teaspoon vanilla extract
½ cup powdered sugar
8 oz. container of extra creamy whipped topping

GARNISH
1 cup sweetened whipped cream
toasted sliced almonds
shaved chocolate
mint sprig

For the Crust: Preheat oven to 350 degrees. Mix together cookie crumbs and coconut. Stir in melted Crisco shortening. Press in bottom and up sides of a deep dish pie plate. Bake for 8 minutes. Cool completely. In small saucepan, heat heavy cream until hot. Place both kinds of chocolate morsels in a small bowl. Pour hot cream over chocolate. Let stand 5 minutes. Stir to combine well. Refrigerate until firm, but still spreadable. Spread the chocolate ganache on the bottom and up sides of prepared pie shell and refrigerate.

For Filling 1: In a small saucepan over medium heat, mix cherry juice, sugar, and cornstarch. Cook, stirring frequently, until mixture is very thick. Remove from heat and stir in butter, almond extract, and gelatin powder. Scrape into a medium-sized bowl. Cool 15 minutes. Stir in cherries and refrigerate.

For Filling 2: In large bowl, beat cream cheese until fluffy. Add in condensed milk, lemon juice, vanilla, and powdered sugar. Beat until well combined. Fold in whipped topping. Spread half of cream filling in prepared pie crust. Top with half of cherry filling. Repeat layers with remaining fillings.

For the Garnish: Garnish with whipped cream, toasted sliced almonds, shaved chocolate, and mint sprig, if desired.

My Cherry Amour Pie

LIFE IS A PIE FULL OF CHERRIES

Matt Zagorski, Arlington Heights, IL
2012 APC Crisco National Pie Championships
Professional Division 1st Place Cherry

CRUST
½ cup whole butter, salted, cold
½ cup butter-flavored Crisco, cold
2 cups all-purpose flour
½ cup cake flour
1 tablespoon powdered sugar
½ teaspoon salt
¼ cup sour cream
½ cup water

FILLING 1
1 cup rolled oats
1 cup brown sugar
¼ cup butter

FILLING 2
¼ cup sugar
¼ teaspoon salt
6 tablespoons Clear Jel
2 cans King Orchards Montmorency
   tart cherries (packed in water),
drained and juices set aside
   (about 1⅓ cups)
1 tablespoon lemon juice
¼ teaspoon almond extract
2 tablespoons whole butter, cut into
   ¼-inch pieces
egg wash and sugar for sprinkling
   on crust

For the Crust: Cut the butter and
Crisco into ¼ inch pieces. Once cut,
place in the freezer to harden. Combine
the flours, powdered sugar, and salt in
a food processor and mix for about 30
seconds. Once the dry ingredients are
combined, scatter the very cold Crisco
and butter pieces over the flour mixture
and process thoroughly using 10
(1-second) pulses in the food processor.
Make sure the mixture has no fat bits
larger than small peas. If so, pulse one

or two more times. Transfer to a large bowl. Combine the sour cream and water in a glass or bowl and stir to combine. Sprinkle 4 tablespoons of the sour cream mixture over the flour mixture and, with a fork, use a folding motion to incorporate. Add enough additional water that the dough just comes together. It should be slightly damp and cold and should hold together when squeezed. Divide the dough into two piles, shape into balls, and flatten each into a 6- to 8-inch disk. Cover each in plastic wrap and refrigerate at least 2 hours—best if overnight. Before rolling out, let the dough come to just below room temperature. This should take 6 to 7 minutes. The dough should be slightly cool to the touch. Roll to desired thickness and place in pie pan. Place the pan with the rolled-out dough in the refrigerator to chill for at least 40 minutes. After 40 minutes in the refrigerator, place the dough and pie pan in the freezer for 20 minutes. While the dough is in the freezer, preheat the oven to 425 degrees and prepare the cherry filling.

For Filling 1: Place all of the ingredients in a large bowl and use a fork or your fingers to combine the ingredients. Set aside.

For Filling 2: Combine the sugar, salt, and Clear Jel together in a bowl and whisk to combine. Add the cherry juice, lemon juice, and almond extract to the dry ingredients and completely mix together. Add the cherries to the juice mixture and pour the whole mixture into the chilled pie shell. Make sure the cherries do not come to the rim of the pie shell. Dot the top of the cherries with the whole butter. Cover the cherries with the oatmeal filling. Brush egg wash on the rim of the pie and sprinkle with raw sugar. Place the pie on a sheet pan and place it on the floor of a 425-degree oven for 15 minutes. After 15 minutes, move the pie to the middle of the oven, reduce temperature to 350 degrees, and bake for 45 minutes more until the middle bubbles slightly.

DOUBLE CHERRY PIE

Tammi Carlock, Chickamunga, GA
2012 APC Crisco National Pie Championships
Amateur Division 2nd Place Cherry

CRUST
1⅓ cups flour
½ teaspoon salt
½ cup shortening
3–6 tablespoons water, cold

FILLING
2 cans tart cherries, drained
1 can sweet cherries, drained (reserve 1 tablespoon juice)
¾ cup sugar

2 tablespoons cornstarch
1 tablespoon orange juice

TOPPING
1 cup oats
½ cup flour
1 cup brown sugar
6 tablespoons butter or margarine

For the Crust: Sift flour and salt into a medium-sized mixing bowl. Cut in shortening with a pastry blender. Sprinkle water onto mixture while lightly mixing with fork. Gather into a flat disk and cover with plastic wrap. Refrigerate until chilled. Roll out pastry dough and fit into 10-inch pie plate and crimp edges.

For the Filling: In a saucepan, cook the cherries with the sugar until the sugar dissolves. Mix together the cornstarch and cherry juice, and add to the cherry mixture. Bring to a boil and cook for 2 minutes or until thick. Stir in orange juice, then set aside to let cool.

For the Topping: Mix together oats, flour, and sugar. Cut in butter or margarine with pastry blender. Sprinkle mixture on top of pie. Bake at 350 degrees for about 50 minutes. Cool on wire rack.

Double Cherry Pie

CHOCOLATE

CHOCO-MINT RASPBERRY DREAM PIE

Emily Pearce, Sheboygan Falls, WI
2014 APC National Pie Championships Chocolate

CRUST
1⅓ cup flour
½ teaspoon salt
½ vegetable shortening
3–6 tablespoons water, cold

FILLING 1
1 (8-oz.) package cream cheese, softened
⅓ cup sugar
1 cup sour cream
2 teaspoon vanilla
1 (8-oz.) package Cool Whip

FILLING 2
1½ cups frozen raspberries
½ cup sugar
2 tablespoons water
1 tablespoon + 1 teaspoon arrowroot

FILLING 3
8 oz. dark semisweet chocolate
2 tablespoons + 1¾ cups whipping cream
2 tablespoons butter
1 teaspoon vanilla
½ teaspoon mint extract
3 tablespoons confectioners' sugar
1 (8-oz.) package cream cheese, softened

For the Crust: Preheat oven to 400 degrees. Blend together flour and salt. Cut in chilled shortening with pastry blender, until resembles coarse crumbs. Sprinkle 3 tablespoons water over flour mixture. Mix gently with fork. Add more water by the tablespoon, mixing until dough holds together. Flatten dough into ½-inch-thick round disk and cover in plastic wrap. Refrigerate at least 30 minutes. Place dough on lightly floured surface. With floured rolling pin, roll dough outward from center into circle 2 inches wider then pie plate. Ease crust into pie plate and trim evenly around plate. Place a sheet of aluminum foil over crust and form up the sides. Put in pie weights or unbaked beans. Bake for 10 to 15 minute or until light golden brown. Set on rack to cool.

For Filling 1: Beat cream cheese until smooth; gradually beat in sugar. Blend in sour cream and vanilla. Fold in Cool Whip, blending well. Spoon into crust. Chill until set.

For Filling 2: Combine raspberries, sugar, and 1 tablespoon water. Cook in microwave for 5 minutes. Mix arrowroot with remaining 1 tablespoon water and add to raspberry mixture. Stir until thick, then cool. Once cool, pour over cream cheese layer and refrigerate.

For Filling 3: In a medium saucepan over low heat, cook the chocolate with the 2 tablespoons of whipping cream, stirring constantly for 2 to 3 minutes, until the chocolate in melted and the mixture is thick. Add the butter, vanilla, and mint extract, and stir to combine, cooking for another minute. Remove from the heat.

In a large bowl with an electric mixer, beat the confectioners' sugar and cream cheese together at medium speed until fluffy, 2 to 3 minutes. Add the melted chocolate mixture, and stir to combine. Set aside. In a medium bowl with an electric mixer, whip the remaining 1¾ cups whipping cream until light and fluffy. Fold the whipped cream gently but thoroughly into the chocolate mixture. Spread gently over the raspberry sauce. Refrigerate.

For the Garnish: Decorate with whipping cream and fresh raspberries. If desired, add chopped Andes chocolates.

Choco-Mint Raspberry Dream Pie

CHOCOLATE TURTLE PIE

Rick Johnson, Carbondale, IL
2014 APC National Pie Championships
Amateur Division 2nd Place Chocolate

CRUST
2 cups flour
2 tablespoons sugar
½ cup butter
½ teaspoons salt
1 cup roasted pecans, chopped
cold water

FILLING 1
1½ cup butter
2¼ cup sugar
6 oz. unsweetened chocolate, melted
1½ teaspoon vanilla bean paste
6 pasteurized eggs

TOPPING
1½ pints heavy whipping cream
6 tablespoons piping gel
3 tablespoons powdered sugar
1 tablespoon vanilla extract
½ cup caramel sauce
1 teaspoon salt

GARNISH
¾ cup roasted pecans, chopped
caramel drizzle

For the Crust: Preheat oven to 375 degrees. Combine flour, sugar, butter, and salt in a food processor and process until gravelly. Add pecans and water a little at a time until dough just starts coming together. Press into a disk and refrigerate for at least 1 hour, then roll into crust. Blind bake crust at 375 degrees for 20 minutes or until browned. Cool in refrigerator

For the Filling: Combine butter and eggs and beat until fluffy. Add melted chocolate, vanilla, and 2 eggs, and beat on high for 10 minutes. Add 2 more eggs and beat for additional 10 minutes. Finally add remaining eggs and beat until creamy.

For the Topping: Add ingredients to a cold mixing bowl and beat to stiff peaks then top pie.

For the Garnish: Sprinkle roasted pecans and follow with caramel drizzle.

Chocolate Turtle Pie

RUTH'S PARK AVENUE CHOCOLATIER PIE

John Sunvold, Winter Springs, FL
2014 APC National Pie Championships
Amateur Division 1st Place Chocolate & Best of Show

CRUST
14 graham cracker sheets (crumbs)
    (about 1.5 cups)
3 tablespoons sugar
6 tablespoons butter, melted
30 caramels
¼ cup milk
¾ cup pecan pieces

FILLING 1
6 oz. cream cheese, softened
⅓ cup powdered sugar
6 oz. Cool Whip

FILLING 2
3 oz. bittersweet or unsweetened
    chocolate
1⅛ cup fine sugar
¾ cup butter
1 teaspoon vanilla
3 pasteurized eggs

GARNISH
whipped topping
caramel drizzle
nuts

For the Crust: Preheat oven to 350 degrees. Mix graham cracker crumbs and sugar. Mix in melted butter. Press into a pie plate and bake for 8 to 10 minutes in a 350-degree oven. Allow to cool. Melt caramels with ¼ cup milk, then add pecan pieces. Spread mixture over the bottom of the cooled pie crust.

For Filling 1: Mix cream cheese with powdered sugar. Fold in Cool Whip and spread on top of the caramel pecans.

For Filling 2: Melt chocolate and set aside to cool. Place sugar in food processor and make the sugar powdery. In a mixer, cream the butter and sugar. Add the cooled chocolate and vanilla, and beat with a mixer for 2 minutes. Add and egg and beat for 5 minutes. Scrape the bowl. Add another egg and beat for 5 minutes. Scrape the bowl. Add the last egg and beat for 5 minutes. Scrape the bowl and beat for 1 more minute. Spread over Filling 1, cover, and place in the refrigerator for 2 hours.

For the Garnish: Top with favorite whipped topping. Garnish with caramel topping, chocolate, or nuts, as desired.

Ruth's Park Avenue Chocolatier Pie

CHOCOLATE RASPBERRY PASSION PIE

Evette Rahman, Orlando, FL
2014 APC National Pie Championships
Professional Division 1st Place Chocolate

CRUST
1½ cups chocolate cookie crumbs, finely ground
6 tablespoons unsalted butter, melted
¾ cup semisweet chocolate morsels
½ cup heavy cream

FILLING 1
2 tablespoons cream cheese, softened
¼ cup strained puréed raspberries
¼ cup powdered sugar
1 cup whipped topping

FILLING 2
¼ cup unsalted butter, softened
2 tablespoons powdered sugar
⅛ teaspoon salt
¼ cup pasteurized egg product
2 oz. semisweet chocolate, melted
¼ cup plain whipped cream

GARNISH
sweetened whipped cream
raspberries

For the Crust: Preheat oven to 350 degrees. Mix together cookie crumbs and melted butter. Press and shape crust in a 9-inch pie dish. Bake for 8 minutes. Cool completely. Heat morsels and heavy cream in glass bowl in microwave until very hot. Stir until thoroughly mixed together. Chill in refrigerator until thickened enough to be spreadable. Spread on crust.

For Filling 1: Mix all ingredients together and chill until firm. Spread on pie crust.

For Filling 2: With electric mixer, beat, until smooth, all ingredients, except whipped cream, to make chocolate mousse. Fold in whipped cream. Spread on top of raspberry filling in pie crust. Chill at least 4 hours or until set.

For the Garnish: Garnish with sweetened whipped cream and raspberries.

Chocolate Raspberry Passion Pie

SCANDINAVIAN CHOCOLATE PIE

Jeanne Ely, Mulberry, FL
2015 APC National Pie Championships
Amateur Division 1st Place Chocolate

CRUST
1 package Oreo cookies
1 stick butter

FILLING
½ cup margarine
¾ cup sugar
4 squares 70% dark chocolate + ½
   cup milk chocolate chips, melted
   and cooled slightly
3 eggs
1 cup heavy whipping cream

TOPPING
1 cup lingonberry preserves
1 (14.5-oz) jar wild lingonberries
½ cup lingonberry juice
1 tablespoon cornstarch

GARNISH
¾ cup heavy whipping cream
¼ cup confectioners' sugar
¼ teaspoon vanilla bean paste

For the Crust: Crush Oreo cookies and melt the butter in the microwave. Add the melted butter slowly to crushed cookies. Press into 9-inch deep pie dish. Freeze for approximately 10 minutes. Move to refrigerator.

For the Filling: Cream together margarine and sugar. Stir in cooled chocolate. Add 1 egg at a time, beating 5 minutes between each egg. Whip the heavy whipping cream until stiff. Fold the chocolate mixture into the whipped cream. Spoon into the pie dish, smoothing out the top. Chill until firm.

For the Topping: Combine cornstarch and lingonberry juice in small dish. Place lingonberry preserves and lingonberries in small saucepan, add cornstarch mixture to lingonberries. Cook over medium-high heat until thickened. Cool completely and place on top of set chocolate.

For the Garnish: Whip all ingredients together until stiff. Spoon into star-tipped pastry bag. Swirl into rosettes around the edge just inside the crust. Keep cold in the refrigerator until ready to serve.

Scandanavian Chocolate Pie

CHOCOLATE BANANUTELLA PIE

Christopher Taylor, Atlanta, GA
2015 APC National Pie Championships
Amateur Division 2nd Place Chocolate

CRUST
1½ cup all-purpose flour
1¼ teaspoons sugar
½ teaspoon salt
⅛ teaspoon baking powder
8 tablespoons unsalted butter, cold,
    in 8 pieces
4 tablespoons vegetable shortening, cold
1 teaspoon cider vinegar
¼ cup water, cold

FILLING 1
3 fl. oz. heavy cream
½ teaspoon corn syrup
3 oz. 60% chocolate, chopped
2–3 large bananas

FILLING 2
2½ cups half-and-half
⅓ cup sugar
6 egg yolks

2 tablespoons cornstarch
¼ cup Nutella hazelnut spread
5 tablespoons butter
7 oz. very dark chocolate
    (70% cacao), chopped
1 teaspoon hazelnut extract

GLAZE
3 oz. dark chocolate
3 tablespoons Nutella hazelnut spread
⅓ cup heavy cream
¼ teaspoon hazelnut extract

TOPPING
1 cup heavy cream
2 tablespoons powdered sugar
2 tablespoons piping gel
¼ teaspoon banana extract

GARNISH
⅓ cup chopped hazelnuts, toasted

For the Crust: Mix flour, sugar, salt, and baking powder in the bowl of a food processor. Pulse in the butter until the pieces are the size of large beans. Pulse in the shortening until mixture resembles coarse, wet sand and no pieces are larger than peas. Add the vinegar to the water. Pulse in the water mixture until incorporated but before a dough ball forms. Remove the dough from the processor and pat into a 4-inch disc on a sheet of plastic wrap. Wrap tightly and refrigerate for at least 3 hours. Roll the pie dough out to a circle large enough to fill a 9½-inch-deep dish pie pan. Line the pan with the rolled crust and crimp the edges as desired. Freeze for 30 minutes. Meanwhile, preheat oven to 425 degrees. Line the dough with parchment paper and pie weights. Bake for 18 minutes. After 18 minutes of baking, remove the weights and parchment. Continue baking until the crust is golden brown, 5 to 10 minutes more. Allow the crust to cool completely.

For Filling 1: Bring the heavy cream and corn syrup to a simmer. Pour over the chopped chocolate. Whisk to combine. Spread a thin layer of the chocolate mixture on the bottom of the prepared crust. Slice the bananas into thin slices and layer on top of the chocolate. Spread the remaining chocolate over the banana slices. Refrigerate while preparing the second filling.

For Filling 2: Bring half-and-half and sugar to simmer in saucepan, stirring frequently. Whisk the yolks and cornstarch together in a bowl. Slowly add the hot dairy mixture to the egg yolk mixture, whisking constantly. Return mixture to the sauce-

Chocolate Bananutella Pie

pan. Whisking constantly, heat the mixture until the mixture boils. Boil for 1 minute. Mixture will thicken. Remove from heat. Whisk in the Nutella, butter, chocolate, and hazelnut extract until fully incorporated. Allow to cool to room temperature before pouring over chocolate banana layer. Allow to set completely, at least 2 hours, before topping with Chocolate Hazelnut Glaze.

For the Glaze: Add the chocolate and Nutella to a medium bowl. Heat the cream to a simmer. Pour the hot cream over the chocolate and Nutella. Whisk to combine. Whisk in the hazelnut extract. Allow to cool until just warm. Pour over the top of the pie and spread evenly.

For the Topping: Whip the cream and sugar until soft peaks form. Whip in the piping gel and extract until stiff peaks form. Decorate the top of the pie, as desired.

For the Garnish: Sprinkle on top of glaze.

TIM'S TUXEDO JUNCTION PIE

John Sunvold, Orlando, FL
2015 APC National Pie Championships
Amateur Division 3rd Place Chocolate

CRUST
26 Oreos
5 tablespoons butter
6 oz. cream cheese
⅓ cup powdered sugar
6 oz. Cool Whip

FILLING
3 oz. bittersweet or unsweetened
  chocolate
1⅛ cup fine sugar

¾ cup butter
1 teaspoon vanilla extract
3 pasteurized eggs

GARNISH
whipped topping
caramel topping
Oreo cookie crumbs

For the Crust: Preheat oven to 375 degrees. Place whole cookies in food processor and pulse until cookies resemble wet sand. Melt butter, pour over cookie crumbs, and mix until butter is evenly distributed. Press crumbs evenly into pie pan. Bake crust at 375 degrees for 10 minutes. Let cool. Mix cream cheese with powdered sugar. Fold in Cool Whip and spread over cooled crust.

For the Filling: Melt chocolate and set aside to cool. Place sugar in food processor and make the sugar powdery. In a mixer, cream the butter and sugar. Add the cooled chocolate and vanilla, and beat with a mixer for 2 minutes. Add and egg and beat for 5 minutes. Scrape the bowl. Add another egg and beat for 5 minutes. Scrape the bowl. Add the last egg and beat for 5 minutes. Scrape the bowl and beat for 1 more minute. Spread on the pie, cover, and place in the refrigerator for 2 hours.

For the Garnish: Garnish as desired.

Tim's Tuxedo Junction Pie

CHOCOLATE HEAVEN PIE

Andy Hilton, Davenport, FL
2015 APC National Pie Championships
Professional Division 1st Place Chocolate

CRUST
2 cups chocolate sandwich cookies
5 tablespoons butter

FILLING 1
6 tablespoons butter
1¾ cups heavy cream
10 oz. milk chocolate chips
6 oz. semisweet chocolate chips

FILLING 2
1½ cups heavy whipping cream
7 oz. white chocolate chips (Nestles
  works very well)
12 oz. cream cheese
½ cup sugar

FILLING 3
1¼ cup sugar
¼ cup + 2 tablespoons cornstarch
8 tablespoons cocoa powder
4 large egg yolks
2½ cup whole milk
½ cup heavy cream
1½ cups unsweetened whipped
  cream

GARNISH
whipped cream
white and milk chocolate curls

For the Crust: Preheat oven to 350. Combine cookies in a food processor and grind them to a crumb. Pour them into a bowl. Melt butter and mix it into the crumb. Press 1½ cups of crumb into a 9-inch pie pan, using the back of a spoon to form the crumb into a crust. Take an empty pie pan and press it into the pie pan with the crumb and press firmly. Remove empty pan and bake crust for 4 minutes in a 350-degree oven. Remove and let cool.

For Filling 1: Using a 2-quart saucepan, melt and warm butter and cream on low to medium heat. Add both chocolates and honey, and stir gently on low to medium heat until smooth. Do not be concerned about having small bits of chocolate; you may strain ganache to remove them. Fill pie crust one-third of the way with warm ganache, cover with plastic, and refrigerate 2 hours.

For Filling 2: Using a heavy saucepan, bring ½ cup heavy cream to a simmer, remove from heat. Add the white chocolate and gently stir until smooth and creamy. Beat cream cheese and sugar with a stand mixer until smooth. Scrape the walls and beater, beat again for another minute. Mix in chocolate mixture, mix for 1 minute. Whip 1 cup heavy cream to stiff peaks, fold in cream cheese mixture to the whipped cream. Fill another third of the pie, cover with plastic, and refrigerate overnight.

For Filling 3: Mix sugar, salt, cornstarch, and cocoa powder together in large bowl. Whisk in

Chocolate Heaven Pie

egg yolks and ¼ cup of the milk to form a paste. Combine 2¼ cups of milk and ½ cup heavy cream in a heavy 3-quart saucepan. Heat slowly until the mixture just starts to boil. Remove from the heat and whisk a small amount of the heated cream, ¼ cup, into the egg yolk paste to temper the eggs. Add the rest of the heated cream to the egg paste and whisk together. Pour mixture through a strainer and return to a clean saucepan. Heat on medium-high and stir continually until everything thickens. Pour into a bowl and cover with plastic so the plastic is touching the cream; this will keep a skin from forming on the cream. Place in the refrigerator to cool for 3 to 4 hours. Blend in enough whipped cream to the base to make pastry cream but thick enough to hold a pie slice. Fill the last one-third of the pie.

For the Garnish: Use whipped cream and chocolate curls as desired.

DECADENT CHOCOLATE TURTLE

Tammi Carlock, Chickamunga, GA
2015 APC National Pie Championships
Professional Division Honorable Mention

CRUST
2 cups flour
1 teaspoon salt
⅔ cup Crisco shortening
6–8 tablespoons water, cold

FILLING
1 cup half-and-half
4 tablespoons butter
8 oz. 60% cacao bittersweet chocolate
¾ cup unsweetened cocoa
1¼ cup sugar
4 tablespoons flour
dash salt

3 egg yolks
2 whole eggs
2 teaspoons vanilla
1 cup pecans, chopped

TOPPING
2½ cups large pecan halves, toasted
¾ cup sugar
¼ cup water
¼ cup butter
½ teaspoon salt
⅓ cup heavy cream

For the Crust: Mix together flour and salt. Cut in shortening until mixture resembles coarse meal. Add water, 1 tablespoon at a time, mixing with fork until dough holds together. Roll out into circle larger than 9-inch pie plate, press into pie shell, and crimp edges. Set aside.

For the Filling: Preheat oven to 350 degrees. In a small saucepan, combine half-and-half, butter, and chocolate over medium heat, stirring frequently until chocolate is melted and smooth. Set aside. In a medium bowl, combine dry ingredients. Add to chocolate mixture and combine. Add egg yolks and eggs and combine well. Stir in pecans. Pour mixture into pie shell. Bake for 45 to 50 minutes until pie is set in the middle. Remove from oven and cool on wire rack.

For the Topping: In a small saucepan, combine sugar and water. Let cook over medium heat, stirring occasionally, until mixture begins to turn a caramel color. Remove from heat and add butter and salt, stirring to melt the butter. Add cream and continue stirring. If mixture begins to harden, heat again over low heat and stir. Place pecans on top of pie in a circular pattern going all around and filling in all the way to the center. Pour caramel mixture over top.

Decadent Chocolate Turtle

GERMAN CHOCOLATE PIE

Evette Rahman, Orlando, FL
2015 APC National Pie Championships
Professional Division 1st Place Innovation

CRUST
1½ cups chocolate cookie crumbs,
   finely ground
6 tablespoons unsalted butter, melted
¾ cup semisweet chocolate morsels
½ heavy cream

FILLING 1
½ cup evaporated milk
¼ cup brown sugar
1 egg yolk
½ teaspoon vanilla
⅛ teaspoon salt
¾ cup sweetened coconut flakes
⅓ cup pecans, chopped

FILLING 2
¼ cup unsalted butter, softened
2 tablespoons powdered sugar
¼ cup pasteurized egg product
2 oz. semisweet chocolate, melted
¼ cup plain whipped cream

GARNISHES
sweetened whipped cream
toasted coconut
pecans

For the Crust: Preheat oven to 350 degrees. Mix together cookie crumbs and melted butter. Press and shape crust in a deep pie dish. Bake for 8 minutes. Cool completely. Heat morsels and heavy cream in glass bowl in microwave until very hot. Stir until thoroughly mixed together. Chill in refrigerator until thickened enough to be spreadable. Spread on crust.

For Filling 1: In a small saucepan, whisk together first five ingredients. Cook over medium heat until thickened, stirring constantly. Remove from heat and stir in coconut and pecans. Cool completely. Spread on top of chocolate layer in crust.

For Filling 2: With electric mixer, beat, until smooth, all ingredients, except whipped cream. Fold in whipped cream. Pour into pie shell. Chill at least 4 hours or until set.

For the Garnish: Garnish with sweetened whipped cream, toasted coconut, and pecans.

German Chocolate Pie

WACKY WISCONSIN SNOWBALL PIE

David Harper, Lone Rock, WI
2015 APC National Pie Championships
Amateur Division 2nd Place Innovation

CRUST
1 cup flour
1 teaspoon salt
½ cup butter-flavored Crisco
5 tablespoons water, cold

CHOCOLATE CAKE*
3 cups flour
2 cups sugar
⅓ cup cocoa
2 teaspoons baking soda
1 teaspoon salt
2 tablespoons vinegar
2 teaspoons vanilla
¾ cup vegetable oil
2 cups water, cold

FILLING
1 cup heavy cream
1 tub marshmallow fluff
1 teaspoon vanilla extract

TOPPING
1½ cup shredded coconut
few drops red food coloring
1 cup whipping cream
¼ cup powdered sugar
1½ teaspoon vanilla

*This recipe makes two 9-inch cakes. You will only need one for this recipe.

For the Crust: Preheat oven to 375 degrees. Whisk the flour and the salt together in a large bowl. Add the Crisco and mix with your fingers until combined. Add the ice water and use a fork to combine. Turn pie dough out onto a floured surface and gather into a circular disk. Roll out the dough big enough to fit into a pie plate. Flute edges for decoration. Prick the bottom and sides of crust with a fork. Place into the refrigerator for 20 minutes. Bake crust until edges are golden brown and bottom is browned also, about 15 to 20 minutes. Cool on wire rack and set aside. Reduce oven temperature to 350 degrees.

For the Chocolate Cake: Line two 9-inch round cake pans with parchment paper. Mix all ingredients in order listed in a large bowl until no lumps remain. Divide batter between both pans. Bake for 20 to 25 minutes or until tooth-pick inserted in center comes out clean. Cool on wire racks.

For the Filling: Whip heavy cream until stiff. Remove from mixer bowl and set aside. Put marshmallow fluff in mixer bowl and whip until smooth. Add back to mixer the whipped cream and add vanilla. Whip until incorporated and thick. Place about ½ cup of the filling on bottom of pie crust. Take a cake and cut it in half horizontally, creating two thinner layers. Place one of the cake layers on the marshmallow filling. Spread the rest of the marshmallow filling on the cake layer. Top with remaining cake.

For the Topping: In a mixer, place coconut and a few drops of red food coloring. Turn mixer on low and mix until coconut turns pink. You may have to add more drops of food coloring to make the color pink you like. Whip cream with sugar. Garnish pie with whipped cream and pink coconut.

CHOCOLATE BUZZ PIE

Patricia Lapiezo, LaMesa, CA
2015 APC National Pie Championships
Amateur Division Best of Show

CRUST

10 Pepperidge Farm Milano dark
  chocolate cookies, finely ground
6 Oreo cookies, finely ground
2 tablespoons butter, melted

FILLING

7 oz. semisweet chocolate, finely
  chopped
¾ cup coffee ice cream (Trader
  Joe's Coffee Blast)
3 cups miniature marshmallows
1½ cups heavy whipping cream
¼ cup powdered sugar

TOPPING

1 (8-oz.) package cream cheese,
  softened
½ cup powdered sugar
½ cup white chocolate chips
⅓ cup coffee ice cream, melted
⅛ teaspoon instant espresso
1–2 teaspoons coffee flavoring
1 cup heavy cream
¼ cup powdered sugar
chocolate espresso beans, if desired

For the Crust: Preheat oven to 350 degrees. Combine the crust and butter and press into 9½-inch pie pan. Bake at 350 degrees for 8 minutes. Remove from oven and cool.

For the Filling: In a microwave-safe bowl, combine the chocolate, ice cream, and marshmallows and heat 1 minute. Stir and continue heating at 30-second intervals until chocolate is melted and marshmallows begin to melt. Whisk ingredients together until smooth. Cool. Remove approximately ⅓ cup of filling and spread over bottom of crust. Refrigerate. In a large mixing bowl, beat the whipping cream with the powdered sugar until soft peaks form. Fold 1 cup into the chocolate mixture. Continue beating the remaining cream until stiff.

Fold into chocolate mixture. Spread in pie pan and smooth top.

For the Topping: In a large bowl, beat the cream cheese and ½ cup powdered sugar until well blended. In a microwave-safe bowl, place the ice cream, chips, and espresso powder. Microwave on high at 30-second intervals until melted, stirring occasionally. If espresso doesn't completely dissolve, strain mixture. Cool and then beat into cream cheese mixture until well blended. Add coffee flavoring to taste. Beat the 1 cup heavy cream with ¼ cup powdered sugar until stiff and fold into cream cheese mixture. Decoratively pipe over top of pie, and if desired, decorate with chocolate espresso beans.

Chocolate Buzz Pie

TRIPLE CHOCOLATE DELIGHT PIE

Andy Hilton, Davenport, FL
2014 APC National Pie Championships
Professional Division Honorable Mention Chocolate

CRUST
2 cups chocolate sandwich cookie
   with cream filling
5 tablespoons butter

CHOCOLATE GANACHE
4 tablespoons butter
1½ cups heavy cream
10 oz. milk chocolate chips
6 oz. semisweet chocolate chips

FILLING
1½ cups heavy whipping cream
5 oz. white chocolate chips (Nestles
   works very well)
12 oz. cream cheese
½ cup sugar

CHOCOLATE PASTRY CREAM
1¼ cups sugar
Pinch of salt
¼ cup + 2 tablespoons cornstarch
8 tablespoons cocoa powder
4 large egg yolks
2½ cups whole milk
½ cup heavy cream
1½ cups unsweetened whipped
   cream

For the Crust: Combine cookies in a food processor and grind them to a crumb. Pour them into a bowl. Melt butter and mix it into the crumb. Press 1½ cups of crumb into 9-inch pie pan, using the back of a spoon to form the crumb into a crust. Take an empty pie pan and press it into the pie pan with the crumb and press firmly. Remove empty pan and bake crust for 4 minutes in a 350-degree oven. Remove and let cool.

For the Ganache: Using a 2-quart saucepan, warm butter and cream on low to medium heat. Add both chocolates and honey, stir gently on low to medium heat until smooth. Do not be concerned about having small bits of chocolate; you may strain ganache to remove them. Fill pie crust one-third full with warm ganache, cover with plastic, and refrigerate 2 hours.

For the Filling: Using a heavy saucepan, bring half of heavy cream to a simmer, remove from heat. Add the white chocolate and gently stir until smooth and creamy. Beat cream cheese and sugar with a stand mixer until smooth. Scrape the walls and beater, beat again for another minute. Mix in chocolate mixture, mix for 1 minute. Whip 1 cup heavy cream to stiff peaks, fold cream cheese mixture into the whipped cream. Fill another one-third of the pie, cover with plastic, and refrigerate overnight.

For the Chocolate Pastry Cream: Mix sugar, salt, cornstarch, and cocoa powder together in large bowl. Whisk in egg yolks and ¼ cup of the milk to form a paste. Combine 2¼ cups of

Triple Chocolate Delight Pie

milk and ½ cup heavy cream in a heavy 3-quart saucepan. Heat slowly until the mixture just starts to boil. Remove from the heat and whisk a small amount of the heated cream, ¼ cup, into the egg yolk paste to temper the eggs. Add the rest of the heated cream to the egg paste and whisk together. Pour mixture through a strainer and return to a clean saucepan. Heat on medium to high and stir continually until everything thickens. Pour into a bowl and cover with plastic so the plastic is touching the cream; this will keep a skin from forming on the cream. Place in the refrigerator to cool for 3 to 4 hours. Blend in enough whipped cream to the base to make pastry cream but thick enough to hold a pie slice. Fill the remaining one-third of the pie. Garnish with whipped cream and white and milk chocolate curls.

LOVER'S PIE

Jeanne Ely, Mulberry, FL
2012 Amateur Crisco Classic Amateur Division
Chocolate 1st Place

CRUST
1 package Oreo cookies
⅔ cup butter-flavored Crisco

FILLING
½ cup margarine
¾ cup sugar
4 squares unsweetened chocolate,
   melted and cooled
2 eggs
1 cup heavy whipping cream

TOPPING
1 cup sugar
2 tablespoons cornstarch
1 (8-oz) can 7-Up
1 teaspoon lemon juice
3 oz. box strawberry Jell-O
1 pint strawberries

GARNISH
¾ cup heavy whipping cream
¼ cup confectioners' sugar
¼ teaspoon vanilla bean paste

For the Crust: Crush Oreo cookies and melt the Crisco in the microwave. Add the melted Crisco slowly to crushed cookies. Press into 9-inch heart-shaped pie dish. Freeze.

For the Filling: Cream together margarine and sugar. Stir in cooled chocolate. Add 1 egg at a time, beating 5 minutes between each egg. Whip the heavy whipping cream until stiff. Fold the chocolate mixture into the whipped cream. Spoon into the pie dish, smoothing out the top. Chill until firm.

For the Topping: Combine sugar, cornstarch, and 7-Up in a small saucepan. Heat, stirring constantly until mixture becomes clear and thickens. Stir in lemon juice and strawberry Jell-O. Cool. Clean strawberries and slice in half. Dip in the strawberry Jell-O mixture and place on top of the set chocolate filling until the filling is covered. Cool.

For the Garnish: Whip all ingredients together until stiff. Spoon into star-tipped pastry bag. Swirl into rosettes around the edge just inside the crust. Keep cold in the refrigerator until ready to serve.

Lover's Pie

CHOCOAHOLIC LOVERS PIE

Alberta Dunbar, San Diego, CA
2012 APC Crisco National Pie Championships
Amateur Division 3rd Place Classic Chocolate

CRUST
1¼ cups all-purpose flour
½ teaspoon salt
½ cup Crisco vegetable shortening
4–5 tablespoons water, cold

FILLING 1
6 oz. cream cheese, softened
¼ cup half-and-half
1 teaspoon Kona coffee extract
6 oz. semisweet chocolate, melted
   and cooled
¾ cup heavy cream, whipped

FILLING 2
6 oz. cream cheese, softened
¼ cup half-and-half
1 teaspoon pecan extract
6 oz. white chocolate, melted and
   cooled
¾ cup heavy cream, whipped

¾ cup toasted pecans, ground
¾ cup toffee baking bits

FILLING 3
6 oz. cream cheese, softened
¼ cup half-and-half
1 teaspoon pecan extract
6 oz. milk chocolate, melted and
   cooled
¾ cup heavy cream, whipped

TOPPING
2½ cups heavy cream
¼ cup powdered sugar, sifted
1 teaspoon pecan extract

GARNISH (OPTIONAL)
¼ cup pecans, ground
¼ cup toffee bits

For the Crust: Preheat oven to 450 degrees. Spoon the flour into measuring cup and level. Mix flour and salt in a medium bowl. Cut in shortening using pastry blender or two knives until flour is blended and forms pea-sized chunks. Sprinkle with 1 tablespoon of water at a time. Toss lightly with a fork until dough forms a ball. Roll out on lightly floured board to fit a 9-inch deep dish pie plate with ½ inch overlap. Fold under and flute edges. Prick bottom and sides with a fork. Bake at 450 degrees for 12 minutes or until golden brown. Cool on rack completely before filling.

For Filling 1: Place cream cheese, half-and-half, and coffee extract in a medium bowl. Beat on high until well-blended and smooth. Beat in cooled chocolate. Beat well with wooden spoon, and then fold in whipped cream. Carefully spread in pie shell. Smooth top and place in freezer.

For Filling 2: Repeat instructions for filling 1 with filling 2. Carefully fold in pecans and toffee bits when folding in whipped cream. Spread over Layer 1 and smooth top. Chill until set.

For Filling 3: Repeat instructions for filling 1. Spread over filling 2 and smooth top. Chill until set.

For the Topping: Place topping ingredients in a medium bowl and beat on high until stiff peaks form. Fill pastry bag with medium tip and pipe topping all over pie.

For the Garnish: Sprinkle pecans and toffee bits on top of pie before serving.

Chocoaholic Lovers Pie

IRRESISTIBLY NUTTY FRANGELICO CHOCOLATE TARTS

Susan Boyle, Debary, FL
2014 APC AUI Fine Foods National Pie Championships
Professional Division Honorable Mention AUI Fine Foods Tarts

CRUST
8 AUI Fine Foods Tarts

FILLING
8 oz. chocolate cream cheese
3 tablespoons Frangelico
2 tablespoons powdered sugar
1 tablespoon sour cream
½ cup toasted hazelnuts, finely
　　ground (reserve 4 teaspoons of
　　hazelnuts for tart shells)
chocolate straws, for garnish

HAZELNUT GANACHE RECIPE
1 pound semisweet chocolate chips
½ teaspoon butter
1 pint regular whipping cream
1 teaspoon white corn syrup
3 tablespoons Frangelico

For the Filling: Whip chocolate cream cheese and Frangelico until creamy. Slowly add sugar and sour cream, continue to whip, add ground hazelnuts to mixture, and mix for a couple minutes until smooth. Fill a 14-inch piping bag with a number-32 tip with filling. In each of the tart shells, sprinkle a teaspoon of finely ground hazelnuts. On top of the nuts, pipe a generous amount of filling in shell, then drizzle with hazelnut ganache. Pipe a swirl of whipped topping, add more hazelnut ganache, drizzle, and add some decorative chocolate straws to enjoy!

For the Ganache: Cook over medium heat until chocolate reaches 78 degrees. Strain. Let cool for drizzle.

CITRUS

LEMON CURD SUPREME PIE

George Yates
2014 APC National Pie Championships
Amateur Division 3rd Place Citrus

CRUST
1½ cups graham cracker crumbs, crushed
½ cup vanilla wafers, crushed
¼ cup toasted almonds, ground
3 tablespoons sugar
5 tablespoons unsalted butter, melted
1½ teaspoon lemon juice

LEMON CURD
3 eggs
4 egg yolks
1 cup sugar
1 tablespoon lemon zest
⅔ cup fresh lemon juice
4 tablespoons unsalted butter, softened
⅛ teaspoon salt

FILLING
1 tablespoon unflavored gelatin
⅔ cup water
1 cup sugar
¾ cup fresh lemon juice
5 eggs, separated, reserving egg whites
1½ tablespoons lemon zest, freshly grated

GARNISH
2 cups heavy whipping cream
4 tablespoons powdered sugar
1 teaspoon clear vanilla extract

For the Crust: Preheat oven to 350 degrees. In a medium bowl, combine graham cracker and wafer crumbs, ground almonds, and sugar. Stir lemon juice in melted butter until combined. Press crumb mixture into 9-inch or 10-inch deep dish pie pan. Bake for 10 minutes. Cool completely before filling.

For the Lemon Curd: Whisk eggs, yolks, and sugar in a saucepan until thick. Whisk in zest, juice, butter, salt, and cook over medium-low heat, stirring constantly until very smooth and thick. Remove from heat. Cool to room temperature. Cover and refrigerate.

For the Filling: In a heavy-bottomed saucepan, sprinkle the gelatin over the water and let stand for a few minutes to soften. Add ½ cup sugar and the lemon juice; mix well. Then add the egg yolks and whisk until blended. Place over moderate heat and cook, stirring constantly, until the mixture thickens slightly and barely reaches a simmer, 5 to 10 minutes; do not allow it to boil. Stir in the lemon zest. Pour the gelatin mixture into a bowl and refrigerate, stirring occasionally, until completely chilled. In a medium bowl, beat the egg whites until soft peaks form, then add the remaining ½ cup sugar and beat until stiff peaks form. Gently fold the lemon filling into the whites and pour the filling into pie crust. Chill until firm. Spread curd over filling; chill again until firm.

For the Garnish: Beat together the whipped cream, powdered sugar, and vanilla; garnish with whipped cream, pipe around border edge of pie. Decorate with fresh raspberries, sliced lemon and sliced almonds, and raspberry jam. Refrigerate until ready to serve.

Lemon Curd Supreme Pie

PINING FOR PINEAPPLE ORANGE PIE

Beth Campbell, Belleville, WI
2014 APC National Pie Championships
Amateur Division 1st Place Citrus

CRUST
1¼ cup graham cracker crumbs
3 tablespoons sugar
⅓ cup butter, melted

FILLING
1 (3-oz.) package orange Jell-O
1 (3-oz.) package pineapple Jell-O
1 (20-oz.) can of crushed pineapple
1 (11-oz.) can of mandarin oranges

1 cup heavy whipping cream
1 package (4 serving) vanilla instant
 pudding

GARNISH
whipped cream
mandarin oranges
pineapple rings

For the Crust: Preheat oven to 350 degrees. Combine the crumbs and sugar in medium-sized bowl. Stir in the melted butter until thoroughly blended. Pack mixture firmly into a 9-inch pie pan and press firmly to bottom and sides, bringing crumbs evenly up to the rim. Bake in 350 degrees oven for 8 minutes.

For the Filling: Put the Jell-O, crushed pineapple with juice, and mandarin oranges with the juice into a saucepan. Heat until the Jell-O is dissolved. Take off the heat and put into the refrigerator until it starts to set. Whip the heavy whipping cream until stiff peaks form. Add the instant vanilla pudding and stir until completely mixed into the whipped cream. Gently fold into the filling mixture.

Once combined, spoon the filling mixture into the baked and cooled graham cracker crust.

For the Garnish: Garnish with additional sweetened whipped cream, mandarin oranges, and pineapple rings, if desired.

Pining for Pineapple Orange Pie

LEMON ROSEMARY CREAM PIE

Patricia Lapiezo, LaMesa, CA
2014 APC National Pie Championships
Amateur Division 2nd Place Citrus

CRUST
1 cup unsalted butter, softened
¾ cup granulated sugar
1 large egg
1 teaspoon vanilla
2½ cups all-purpose flour, sifted
1 tablespoon fresh rosemary, chopped
¾ teaspoon coarse salt
melted butter

FILLING
1 (8-oz.) package cream cheese, softened
4 oz. white chocolate, melted
1 (14-oz.) can sweetened condensed milk
½ cup frozen lemonade concentrate, thawed
1 (3.5-oz.) package instant lemon pudding
1 cup heavy whipping cream, stiffly beaten

LEMON CURD
2 egg yolks
½ cup granulated sugar
½ cup unsalted butter
2 whole eggs
1 tablespoon rosemary, chopped
3 oz. fresh lemon (or lime) juice
pinch salt
1 teaspoon grated lemon peel
⅛ teaspoon fresh rosemary, finely chopped

GARNISH
whipped cream

For the Crust: Beat butter and granulated sugar in large bowl until light and fluffy, about 2 minutes. Mix in whole egg and vanilla. Add flour, rosemary, and salt, and mix until combined. Halve the dough and form into a log. Chill until firm. Cut into ¼-inch slices and bake cookies in a 375-degree oven until golden brown. Cool. Grind enough cookies to make approximately 2 cups. Add approximately ⅓ cup melted butter or enough to have the consistency of wet sand. Press into bottom and up sides of a 9-inch pie dish. Bake at 350 degrees for 10 minutes. Cool.

For the Filling: In a large mixing bowl, beat cream cheese until smooth. Add melted chocolate and beat until blended. Beat in sweetened condensed milk until blended. On low speed, blend in lemonade until thickened. Beat in the pudding mix until smooth. Fold in whipped cream. Refrigerate while preparing topping.

For the Lemon Curd: In a large saucepan, beat the yolks and sugar together until well blended. Stir in the remaining ingredients. Cook over medium-low heat, stirring constantly, until thickened and resembling a thin hollandaise sauce. Do not bring to a boil. When thickened, pour at once into a strainer. Discard residue. Pour over top of pie to within 1 inch of sides. Sprinkle with ⅛ teaspoon rosemary.

For the Garnish: Decorate edge of pie with sweetened whipped cream.

Lemon Rosemary Cream Pie

HAPPY-GO-LUCKY LEMON RASPBERRY PIE

David Harper, Lone Rock, WI
2015 APC National Pie Championships
Amateur Division 1st Place Citrus

CRUST
1 cup flour
1 teaspoon salt
½ cup butter-flavored Crisco
5 tablespoons water, cold

FILLING 1
1 cup raspberry purée (2 cups of fresh raspberries yields about 1 cup purée)
2 tablespoons fresh lemon juice
1 envelope plain gelatin
1½ cups heavy cream

FILLING 2
1 envelope plain gelatin
¾ cup lemon juice, reserve ¼ cup
4 eggs, separated, save the whites
1 cup sugar
¼ teaspoon salt
1 tablespoon lemon zest
½ cup heavy cream, whipped stiff

GARNISH
1 cup whipping cream
¼ cup powdered sugar
1½ teaspoons vanilla
4 cups raspberries
lemon zest

For the Crust: Preheat oven to 375 degrees. Whisk the flour and the salt together in a large bowl. Add the Crisco and mix with your fingers until combined. Add the water and use a fork to combine. Turn pie dough out onto a floured surface and gather into a circular disk. Roll out the dough big enough to fit into a pie plate. Flute edges for decoration. Prick the bottom and sides of crust with a fork. Place in the refrigerator for 20 minutes. Bake crust until edges are golden brown and bottom is browned also, about 15 to 20 minutes. Cool on wire rack and set aside.

For Filling 1: Put raspberry purée in a small saucepan. Combine gelatin and lemon juice together to soften in a small bowl, about 2 minutes. Heat raspberry purée until very hot but not boiling. Add the gelatin mixture to hot purée and stir until gelatin has dissolved. Remove from heat. Cool until room temperature, about 20 to 25 minutes. While mixture is cooling, whip the 1½ cups of heavy cream until stiff peaks. When raspberry mixture is room temperature, fold in the whipped cream until no white streaks remain. Place half the mixture in the baked pie shell and cover the top with fresh raspberries. Top with other half of raspberry mixture, covering the berries. Top with fresh berries again. Set in refrigerator and make the lemon filling.

For Filling 2: Whip the ½ cup whipped cream until stiff and set in refrigerator until later use. Sprinkle the gelatin over the ¼ cup lemon juice

Happy-Go-Lucky Lemon Raspberry Pie

and let soften for a few minutes. In a double boiler, combine egg yolks, ½ cup lemon juice, ½ cup of the sugar, and salt. Cook over boiling water (water not touching the bottom of the pan) until mixture is thickened, about 5 minutes. Add the gelatin and lemon zest. Stir to combine. Remove from double boiler and cool in a pan of ice water. Cool for about 10 minutes, stirring occasionally. Beat the egg whites until soft peaks form and beat in the other ½ cup sugar. Beat until stiff peaks form. Fold the lemon mixture into the egg whites until no streaks remain. Fold in the whipped cream until no white streaks remain. Place on top of the raspberry mixture and mound it high. Let set in the refrigerator overnight.

For the Garnish: When ready to eat, top with whipped cream (whip whipping cream, vanilla, and sugar), raspberries, and lemon zest.

ALMOST A MIMOSA BREEZY ORANGE PIE

Naylet LaRochelle, Miami, FL
2015 APC National Pie Championships
Amateur Division 2nd Place Citrus

CRUST
1¾ cup honey graham crackers,
  finely crushed
¼ cup sugar
6 tablespoons butter, melted

FILLING 1
½ cup pineapple juice
1 teaspoon unflavored gelatin
8 oz. cream cheese, softened
⅔ cup grated coconut in heavy
  syrup, mostly drained

FILLING 2
⅔ cup orange juice
2¼ teaspoons unflavored gelatin
¾ cup heavy whipping cream

1 cup powdered sugar
½ teaspoon orange zest, grated
½ teaspoon orange extract
½ teaspoon vanilla extract
2 (15-oz.) cans mandarin oranges,
  well drained, chopped, squeezed
  lightly to drain liquid

TOPPING
sweetened whipped cream
1 cup mandarin oranges, very well
  drained, do not chop
toasted coconut flakes

For the Crust: Preheat oven to 375 degrees. In a large bowl, mix cracker crumbs, sugar, and butter until well combined. Press mixture onto bottom and up the sides of pie plate. Bake 8 to 10 minutes. Let cool.

For Filling 1: In a small bowl, add pineapple juice. Sprinkle gelatin over juice; let sit 5 minutes. Microwave gelatin mixture about 15 seconds, or until dissolved completely. In a large bowl, beat cream cheese until fluffy. Very slowly add pineapple-gelatin mixture. Stir in coconut. Pour filling into pie crust. Refrigerate 2 to 3 hours or until set.

For Filling 2: In a small bowl, add orange juice. Sprinkle gelatin over juice; let sit 5 minutes. Microwave gelatin mixture about 30 seconds, or until completely dissolved. Set aside to cool. In a large bowl, add whipping cream; beat until stiff peaks form. Fold in powdered sugar. In a large bowl, combine orange-gelatin mixture, orange zest, orange and vanilla extract, and mandarin oranges. Fold orange mixture into whipped cream. Spread orange filling over coconut-pineapple layer. Refrigerate 2 to 3 hours or until set.

For the Topping: Pipe whipped cream around edge of set pie. Arrange mandarin oranges in center. Sprinkle coconut over whipped cream. This pie will need to firm up for at least 6 hours or overnight.

Almost a Mimosa Breezy Orange Pie

DOUBLE THE CITRUS SMOOTHIE PIE

Carol Socier, Bay City, MI
2015 APC National Pie Championships
Amateur Division 3rd Place Citrus

CRUST
1 package lemon-filled Oreo sandwich cookies (30–32 cookies)
1 tablespoon powdered lemonade mix
4 tablespoons unsalted butter, melted

FILLING 1
8 oz. cream cheese, softened
1 package orange smoothie mix
½ cup orange juice (Tropicana, with
  lots of pulp)
1 cup heavy whipping cream

FILLING 2
1 cup sugar
5 tablespoons cornstarch
½ teaspoon salt
1¾ cups orange juice (Tropicana,
  with lots of pulp)
4 egg yolks
½ cup fresh squeezed lemon juice
2 tablespoons butter
1 teaspoon grated lemon peel
1 teaspoon grated orange peel

For the Crust: Preheat oven to 350 degrees. Place cookies and lemonade mix in food processor. Pulse until finely ground. Transfer to bowl. Mix in melted butter, tossing until evenly mixed and crumbly. Spread evenly across bottom and sides of 9-inch pie pan. Bake 5 minutes in 350-degree oven. Cool before filling.

For Filling 1: Beat the cream cheese and smoothie mix in a large bowl until smooth. Add orange juice, mixing well. Whip cream until peaks form. Fold into cream cheese mixture. Spread half of mixture over bottom of cooled pie crust. Use other half of mixture for garnish.

For Filling 2: In a large saucepan, mix sugar, cornstarch, and salt. Whisk in orange juice. Cook and stir over medium-high heat until thickened. Cook and stir 2 minutes longer. In small bowl, whisk a small amount into beaten egg yolks. Return all to pan. Bring mixture back to a gentle boil and cook and stir for 2 more minutes. Remove from heat. Gently stir in lemon juice, butter, and lemon and orange peel. Spoon over cream cheese layer and refrigerate until cool. Pipe or spread remaining cream cheese mixture over top. Garnish as desired.

Double the Citrus Smoothie Pie

JUST PEACHY KEY LIME HABANERO PIE

Jaynie Buckingham, Austin, TX
2015 APC National Pie Championships
Professional Division 1st Place Citrus

CRUST
1½ cups Vanilla Wafers crumbs
3 tablespoons sugar
6 tablespoons butter

FILLING
1 can condensed milk
4 egg yolks
1 cup peach habanero jelly, reduced
½ cup key lime juice
lime zest

For the Crust: Mix sugar and crumbs together. Melt butter and add to crumb mixture. Press into greased pie pan and set in freezer for about 5 to 7 minutes.

For the Filling: In a medium bowl, gently whisk together condensed milk, egg yolks, $1/3$ jelly, key lime juice, and zest. Pour into the prepared, cooled crust. Chill completely 3 hours then top with remaining jelly. Garnish with whipped cream.

Just Peachy Key Lime Habanero Pie

CLASSIC KEY LIME PIE

Evette Rahman, Orlando, FL
2015 APC National Pie Championships
Professional Division Honorable Mention Citrus

CRUST
1½ cups graham cracker crumbs
¼ cup sugar
5 tablespoons unsalted butter, melted

FILLING
¾ cup key lime juice
2 whole eggs
3 egg whites

2 (14-oz.) cans sweetened condensed milk
⅛ teaspoon kosher salt
½ tablespoon lime zest

GARNISH
sweetened whipped cream
lime zest
berries

For the Crust: Preheat oven to 350 degrees. Mix crust ingredients together. Press into deep dish pie plate. Bake for 8 minutes. Cool.

For the Filling: Mix filling ingredients together and pour into pie shell. Bake 25 minutes. Cool completely in refrigerator.

For the Garnish: Garnish with whipped cream, zest, and berries.

Classic Key Lime Pie

BASIL KEY LIME PIE WITH BERRY COULIS

Patricia Lapiezo, LaMesa, CA
2015 APC National Pie Championships
Amateur Division 1st Place Key Lime

CRUST
9 whole graham crackers, finely ground
3 tablespoons granulated sugar
5 tablespoons butter, melted

FILLING
6 egg yolks
1 (14-oz.) can sweetened condensed milk
½ cup heavy cream
½ cup key lime juice
1 tablespoon fresh basil, finely chopped

KEY LIME CURD
2 whole eggs + 2 egg yolks
½ cup unsalted butter, cut into small pieces
½ cup granulated sugar
3 oz. key lime juice
pinch salt
1 teaspoon grated lime peel
chopped basil

BERRY COULIS
4 oz. fresh strawberries
4 oz. blueberries
4 oz. fresh raspberries
3 tablespoons granulated sugar
4 oz. fresh blueberries
2 teaspoons lemon juice

For the Crust: Preheat oven to 350 degrees. Combine the graham cracker crumbs, sugar, and butter, and press into a 9-inch pie pan. Bake for 10 minutes. Remove from oven and cool completely.

For the Filling: Beat the egg yolks in a bowl with condensed milk and cream. Gradually whisk in the lime juice to thicken the custard. Fold in basil. Pour into prepared crust and bake 15 minutes. Cool to room temperature and prepare lime curd.

For the Key Lime Curd: In a large saucepan, beat the yolks and sugar together until well blended. Stir in the remaining ingredients. Cook over medium-low heat, stirring constantly, until thickened and resembling a thin hollandaise sauce. Do not bring to a boil. When thickened, pour at once into a strainer. Discard residue. Poor over prepared pie filling and sprinkle with chopped fresh basil. Refrigerate overnight to set.

For the Berry Coulis: In a medium saucepan, combine the ingredients until berries become soft. Place in blender and purée until smooth. Decorate edge of pie with sweetened whipped cream, if desired, and serve with berry coulis.

Basil Key Lime Pie with Berry Coulis

UNDER THE CABANA KEY LIME COCONUT PIE

Naylet LaRochelle, Miami, FL
2015 APC National Pie Championships
Amateur Division 2nd Place Key Lime

CRUST
1¾ cups honey graham crackers,
   finely crushed
¼ cup sugar
7 tablespoons butter, melted
½ cup roasted macadamia nuts,
   chopped

FILLING
1 (8-oz.) package cream cheese
2 tablespoons sugar
1 (14-oz.) can sweetened condensed
   milk
3 egg yolks

1 whole egg
½ teaspoon vanilla bean paste
2 teaspoons lime zest
⅔ cup key lime juice*
1 (17-oz.) can grated coconut in
   heavy syrup, drained, divided

GARNISH
1¼ cup heavy whipping cream
¼ cup powdered sugar
roasted macadamia nuts, chopped
lime slices

*Exact amount of lime juice may vary slightly depending on tartness of the
   lime. Taste to adjust.

For the Crust: Preheat oven to 375 degrees. Lightly spray a 9-inch pie plate with cooking spray. In a large bowl, combine ground cookie crumbs, sugar, and butter until well combined. Stir in nuts. Press mixture onto bottom and up the sides of pie plate. Bake 8 to 10 minutes. Let cool.

For the Filling: In a large bowl, beat cream cheese and sugar until light and fluffy. Slowly add condensed milk; beat until combined. Add egg yolks, egg, vanilla, lime zest, and lime juice; beat until just combined. Stir in 1/3 cup of grated coconut (drained) and 3 tablespoons of heavy syrup. (Reserve remaining grated coconut for later use.) Pour into cooled crust. Bake at 350 degrees for 30 to 35 minutes or until pie is set. Refrigerate pie 4 to 5 hours or until well set. Before topping pie with whipped cream, sprinkle remaining grated coconut (well drained) over top of pie to about 1 inch from the edge.

For the Garnish: In a large bowl, beat heavy whipping cream until soft peaks form. Add powdered sugar; continue to beat until stiff peaks form. Pipe whipped topping over pie. Top with nuts; garnish with lime slices.

Under the Cabana Key Lime Coconut Pie

ANNIE'S KEY LIME PIE

Grace Thatcher, Delta, OH
2014 APC National Pie Championships
Amateur Division 1st Place Key Lime

CRUST
1 cup (4-oz.) graham crackers
3 tablespoons sugar
1 tablespoon lime zest
½ cup pistachios
4 tablespoons butter, melted

FILLING
¼ cup water
1¼ teaspoons gelatin
¼ cup sugar
1 tablespoon lime zest
1 (8-oz.) block cream cheese
1 (14-oz) can sweetened condensed
   milk
⅓ cup instant vanilla pudding mix
¾ cup key lime juice
1 teaspoon vanilla extract

For the Crust: Process all ingredients except butter in food processor until grahams are ground fine, then stream in the melted butter until all is incorporated. Press crust into a 9-inch pie pan and bake at 350 degrees for 10 to 15 minutes until slightly browned.

For the Filling: Put gelatin in water to soften. Process sugar and lime zest for one minute. Add cream cheese and process well. Scrape down sides of work bowl. Add sweetened condensed milk and pudding mix and blend until well mixed. Put gelatin mixture into microwave and cook on high for 15 seconds. Stir to dissolve and add along with juice and vanilla to processor and mix well. Pour into cooled pie shell, smooth top, and refrigerate for at least 5 hours. Garnish with whipped cream, lime slices, and chopped pistachios, if desired.

Annie's Key Lime Pie

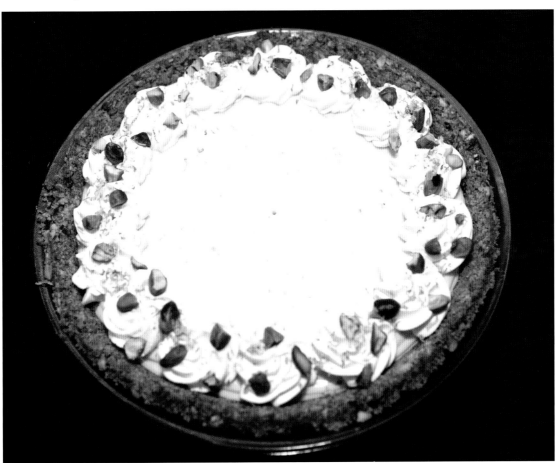

CRAZY GOOD PINEAPPLE PIE

Grace Thatcher, Delta, OH
2014 APC National Pie Championships
Amateur Division 1st Place Open

CRUST
2 cups flour
½ teaspoon salt
10 tablespoons Crisco shortening
3–4 tablespoons water, cold

BRAISED PINEAPPLE
1 pineapple
1 cup brown sugar
2 teaspoon lime juice
1 teaspoon vanilla bean paste
Pinch each cinnamon, nutmeg,
  ginger

FILLING
6 oz. mascarpone
3 tablespoons sugar
4 tablespoons heavy cream
Pinch of salt

PINEAPPLE MOUSSE
1½ tablespoons pineapple juice concentrate
1⅛ teaspoon gelatin
½ cup pineapple juice concentrate
  (thawed)
½ cup sugar
1 tablespoon lime juice
Pinch of salt
¼ teaspoon pineapple extract
1 cup heavy cream, whipped
¼ teaspoon vanilla extract

For the Crust: Into a large mixing bowl, sift together the flour and salt, and then add all of the Crisco shortening. Cut the shortening into the flour with a pastry blender until the mixture develops a course texture. Sprinkle the water over the mixture a spoonful at a time, and toss until the dough begins to cohere. Gather the dough into a ball and press together with your hands, cover with plastic wrap, and refrigerate for at least 1 hour before using. Roll and fit into a 9-inch pie plate. Bake at 400 degrees until golden brown.

For the Braised Pineapple: Core and cut pineapple into long wedges or rings and set aside. Put brown sugar, lime juice, vanilla bean paste, and spices into a large stainless steel skillet. Turn to low heat to melt the sugar and mix the ingredients and then add the pineapple. Turn heat to medium-low and cook covered for 10 minutes on the first side and 7 additional minutes for the remaining side. Reserve syrup. Set aside to cool.

When cool, cut pineapple into thin slices to make 1½ cups. There will be some left over. Measure ¾ cups of syrup and 1 tablespoon of clear gel. Whisk until smooth and bring to a boil over medium-high heat. Set aside to cool.

For the Filling: Place mascarpone in a medium-sized mixing bowl and set aside. Mix together sugar and cream to dissolve the sugar. Add cream mixture to the mascarpone and stir to combine. When combined, whisk until the mixture takes on a thicker consistency. Do not over beat. Spread this mixture on to the bottom and half way up the sides of the prepared pie shell. Add the sliced pineapple over the

Crazy Good Pineapple Pie

mascarpone layer. Spread with about ½ cup of the thickened syrup. Put into the refrigerator to stay cool while preparing the pineapple mousse.

For the Pineapple Mousse: Add the gelatin to the 1½ tablespoons of pineapple juice concentrate to bloom gelatin, about 5 minutes. Prepare an ice water bath. In a small saucepan add the pineapple juice, sugar, lime juice, and salt. Cook and stir until the mixture comes to a boil. Add the gelatin mixture and stir to dissolve completely. Add the pineapple extract. Put in the ice water bath to cool to 60 degrees. In the meantime, whip the cream with the vanilla to soft peaks. When the pineapple mixture is cooled, stir in ⅓ of the whipped cream to lighten. Fold in the remaining whipped cream until mixture is uniformly colored. Scrape onto the top of the pie to mound in the center. Refrigerate the pie for at least 4 hours to set completely. Decorate with reserved pineapple chunks and reserved syrup piped decoratively over the pie.

CHOCOLATE KEY LIME PIE

Deb Knicos, Bangor, PA
2014 APC National Pie Championships
Amateur Division 2ⁿᵈ Place Key Lime

CRUST
30 chocolate wafers
3 tablespoons sugar
5 tablespoons unsalted butter

FILLING
4 eggs yolks
1 (14-oz.) can sweetened condensed
  milk
½ cup fresh key lime juice (approximately 17 key limes)
2 teaspoons lime zest, grated

TOPPING
1 cup heavy cream
⅓ cup powdered sugar
½ key lime zest, grated

GARNISH
2 key limes
1 square of a semisweet chocolate
  bar

For the Crust: Preheat oven to 350 degrees. In food processor, pulse chocolate wafers and sugar. Melt butter. In large mixing bowl, add cookie crumbs and butter, press them into 9-inch pie plate, bake for 5 minutes. Place on wire rack, set aside.

For the Filling: Use electric mixer, beat egg yolks until thick and light yellow, don't over mix. Turn mixer off, add sweetened condensed milk. Turn speed to low and mix in half of the lime juice. Once the juice is incorporated, add other half of juice and zest and continue to mix until blended (just a few seconds). Pour mixture into pie crust, and bake for 12 minutes to set the yolks and kill any salmonella in the eggs. Let cool 15 minutes before refrigerating. Let chill 4 hours.

For the Topping: In electric mixer with wire whisk attachment, add cold heavy whipping cream with powdered sugar, and whip until stiff peaks of cream form. In plastic piping bag, spoon in whipping cream and pipe cream around top of pie. Lightly zest with key lime over entire pie.

For the Garnish: Cut 2 key limes into 8 slices, slit half of each slice, twist, and place slice in 8 spots around pie. With grater, lightly grate chocolate all over pie.

Chocolate Key Lime Pie

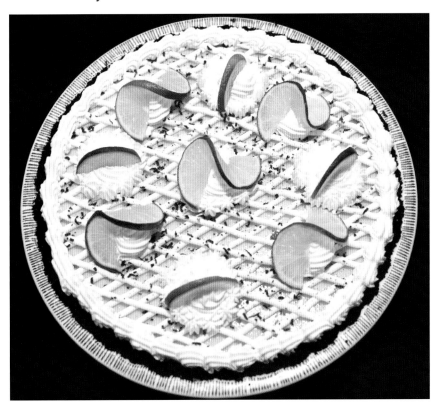

THE KEY (LIME) TO HAPPINESS

John Sunvold, Orlando, FL
2015 APC National Pie Championships
Amateur Division 3rd Place Key Lime

CRUST
1½ cup graham cracker crumbs
5 tablespoons melted butter
3 tablespoons sugar

FILLING:
¾ cup key lime juice
2 cans sweetened condensed milk
2 large eggs
2 egg yolks
⅓ cup boysenberry preserves

For the Crust: Mix graham cracker crumbs and sugar, add the melted butter, and press into a 9- to 10-inch pie plate. You may not use all of it if you use a shallow pan. Bake at 350 degrees for 8 to 12 minutes. Cool.

For the Filling: Mix juice, condensed milk, whole eggs and egg yolks, and pour into cooled crust (use a much of the key lime mix as your pan will hold). Drop spoonfuls of preserves on top of key lime mix and create marble effect by moving a knife around this mix. Do not over mix or it will lose the marble effect. Bake for 15 to 20 minutes in 375-degree oven. Chill pie. Spread the boysenberry preserves on top of pie. Chill.

For the Garnish: Top with favorite whipped cream topping, plus lime zest, graham cracker crumbs, berries, preserves, white chocolate, and/or nuts if desired. Decorate pie as desired. Chill and serve.

The Key (Lime) to Happiness

CLOUD 9 LEMON MERINGUE PIE

Evette Rahman, Orlando, FL
2014 APC National Pie Championships
Professional Division 1st Place Citrus

CRUST
1¼ cup flour
1 tablespoon sugar
½ teaspoon salt
3 tablespoons vegetable shortening
3 tablespoons unsalted butter, cold, diced
2 tablespoons milk
½ tablespoon vinegar

FILLING
4 egg yolks
2 (14-ounce) cans sweetened condensed milk
½ cup freshly squeezed lemon juice
1 tablespoon lemon zest

TOPPING
4 egg whites
¼ teaspoon cream of tartar
½ cup sugar
¼ teaspoon vanilla extract

For the Crust & Filling: Preheat oven to 350 degrees. Mix flour, sugar, and salt together. Cut in shortening and butter. Add milk and vinegar. Mix together well. Form into a disk and refrigerate for 1 hour. Roll out disk and place in deep dish pie plate and crimp edges. Place in freezer for 15 minutes. Blind bake crust for 15 minutes. Mix filling ingredients together. Pour into pie shell and bake 20 minutes.

For the Topping: Heat oven to 400 degrees. Beat egg whites until foamy. While beating, add cream of tartar. Slowly add sugar and vanilla extract. Beat until firm and glossy, but not dry. Spread over hot pie, completely covering, sealing up to the crust edges. Return to oven and bake for 5 minutes or until meringue is a light golden brown. Cool at room temperature for 2 hours. Chill in refrigerator for 4 to 6 hours until set.

TROPICAL ISLAND DELIGHT PIE

Patricia Smith, Deltona, FL
2014 APC National Pie Championships
Amateur Division 3rd Place Innovation

CRUST
2½ cups flour
1 cup Crisco, cold
¼ teaspoon salt
1 egg
1 tablespoon white vinegar
¼ cup water, cold

FILLING
4 eggs
1 small can crushed pineapple,
   drained

1 can flaked coconut
2 cups sugar
1½ sticks unsalted butter
1 tablespoon cornmeal
½ teaspoon vanilla bean paste

GARNISH
1 cup whipped cream
toasted coconut
pineapple bits

For the Crust: Mix flour, Crisco, and salt until it resembles coarse crumbs. Mix together eggs, water, and vinegar. Whisk and add to flour mixture. Toss with fork until mixture forms a ball and pulls from side of bowl. Knead and pat into a disk. Refrigerate until ready to use. Roll out pastry, place in pan, flute edges, and chill before baking.

For the Filling: Combine and mix all ingredients well. Pour into chilled prepared pie crust.

Bake at 350 degrees for 50 minutes. If a toothpick inserted into the center does not come out clean, bake another 10 minutes. Cool before garnishing

For the Garnish: Whip topping and spread on top of chilled pie. Sprinkle with toasted coconut and pineapple bits.

LIME COCONUT CHESS PIE

Tammi Carlock, Chickamunga, GA
2014 APC National Pie Championships
Professional Division Honorable Mention Citrus

CRUST
1 cup flour
1 teaspoon salt
⅔ cup Crisco shortening
6–8 tablespoons water, cold

FILLING
3 whole eggs
3 egg yolks
1¼ cups sugar
½ teaspoon salt
¾ cup heavy cream

½ cup fresh squeezed lime juice
2 tablespoons butter, melted
zest of 1 lime
¾ teaspoon vanilla
1 cup coconut flakes

TOPPING
1 cup heavy whipping cream
¼ cup powdered sugar
1 teaspoon vanilla
1 teaspoon lime zest (optional)
¼ cup coconut flakes (optional)

For the Crust: Preheat oven to 350 degrees. Mix together flour and salt. Cut in shortening until mixture resembles coarse meal. Add water, 1 tablespoon at a time, mixing with fork until dough holds together. Roll out into circle larger than 9-inch pie plate and press into pie shell and crimp edges. Set aside.

For the Filling: Mix together the eggs, egg yolks, sugar, and salt in a bowl. Stir in the cream, lemon juice, butter, lime zest, and vanilla. Add the coconut. Whisk together well. Pour into pie shell and bake for 45 minutes or until set. Let cool completely on a wire rack.

For the Garnish: Mix the cream on high speed using an electric mixer until soft peaks form. Add the sugar and vanilla and continue beating until stiff peaks form. Pipe on pie, add some lime zest and additional coconut, if desired.

CREAM

FLUTTERBY BUTTERSCOTCH PIE

Jennifer Nystrom, Morrow, OH
2015 APC National Pie Championships
Amateur Division 2nd Place Cream

CRUST

⅓ cup + 1 tablespoon water, cold
1 tablespoon cider vinegar
1 teaspoon salt
1 teaspoon sugar
3 cups all-purpose flour
¾ cups vegetable shortening, cold
½ cup butter, cold, cut into cubes

FILLING

4 tablespoons butter
1 cup dark brown sugar, firmly
    packed
4 tablespoons cornstarch

2 cups whole milk
3 large egg yolks
1 teaspoon Butter Vanilla (available
    from King Arthur or in the cake
    decorating section)
⅛ teaspoon salt

GARNISH

1 cup heavy whipping cream
2 tablespoons dark brown sugar,
    firmly packed
½ teaspoon Butter Vanilla
toffee bits

For the Crust: Preheat oven to 375 degrees. In a small bowl, mix together water, cider vinegar, salt, and sugar. Stir to dissolve sugar and salt. Put bowl in the freezer to get very cold while you continue with the rest of the dough. In the bowl of a food processor, put your flour and vegetable shortening that has been cut up in small chunks. Pulse about 5 times or until well incorporated. Add butter that has been cut up in small cubes to the flour mixture. Pulse again about 6 times or until it looks like small peas. You should still see some butter chunks. While pulsing, pour the now very cold water/vinegar mixture into the food processor until the dough just begins to come together. Turn dough out onto a lightly floured counter and shape into two discs. Cover each disc tightly in plastic wrap. Refrigerate for at least an hour or overnight.

Take out one disc (reserving the other disc for another use) and roll out to fit into a 9-inch pie plate. Cover pie dough with parchment paper and fill with pie weights. Bake in preheated oven for 20 minutes. Take out the parchment paper and pie weights and continue to bake for another 5 to 10 minutes or until just beginning to turn golden brown. Take crust out and cool completely while making the filling.

For the Filling: Put the butter and the brown sugar into a large saucepan and, over medium-low heat, melt the butter and mix the brown sugar, stirring constantly. Cook another 2 minutes. Take off the heat. In a small bowl, beat

Flutterby Butterscotch Pie

the egg yolks. In a separate large bowl, mix the cornstarch with 1 cup of the milk until completely combined. Add the beaten egg and salt and whisk well. Whisk in the remaining milk. Add the milk mixture very slowly to the pan with the brown sugar/butter mixture, whisking constantly. Cook over medium-low heat, whisking constantly, until thickened, about 25 to 30 minutes. Take off the heat and whisk in the Butter Vanilla until well blended. Pour butterscotch filling into completely cooled pie crust. Place plastic wrap directly on the butterscotch mixture and refrigerate for at least 3 hours.

For the Garnish: When ready to serve, put whipping cream, brown sugar, and Butter Vanilla in a large mixing bowl. Whip on high until thick. Spread on pie and top with toffee bits, if desired.

STRAWBERRY BANANA CREAM DREAM PIE

David Harper, Lone Rock, WI
2015 APC National Pie Championships
Amateur Division 3rd Place Cream

CRUST
2 cups graham cracker crumbs
¼ cup powdered sugar
1 stick of butter, soft

FILLING
1 cup sugar
¼ cup cornstarch
4 egg yolks
2½ cups half-and-half
2 teaspoons vanilla
dash almond flavoring
2 tablespoons butter

GARNISH
1 cup whipping cream
¼ cup powdered sugar
1½ teaspoon vanilla
bananas
fresh strawberries
toasted pecans (optional)

For the Crust: Mix together the graham cracker crumbs, powdered sugar, and the butter until combined. Press into a 9-inch pie plate until even layer is achieved. Place in refrigerator until later use.

For the Filling: Combine the sugar, cornstarch, egg yolks, and half-and-half together in a heavy saucepan. Cook until filling is thick and bubbly, about 4 to 5 minutes over medium-high heat. Having a heavy saucepan is critical in not scorching your filling. Remove thickened filling and run it through a fine mesh sieve, catching strained filling in another bowl. Add the butter and vanilla and stir until melted and combined. Place plastic wrap directly on top of filling and set aside to cool completely in refrigerator, about 30 minutes. Place one-third of filling on bottom of chilled pie crust. Cover filling with banana slices and strawberry slices. Cover fruit with another one-third of filling. Cover filling with banana and strawberry slices. Top with remaining filling. Place plastic wrap on top and chill for at least 3 to 4 hours or overnight.

For the Garnish: Top with whipped cream, extra strawberry slices, and toasted pecans if you wish.

Strawberry Banana Cream Dream Pie

COOL BANANAS PIE

John Sunvold, Orlando, FL
2015 APC National Pie Championships
Amateur Division 1st Place Cream

CRUST
1/3 cup water
1 tablespoon sugar
1/2 teaspoon salt
8 tablespoons unsalted butter
8 tablespoons lard
2 1/4 cups flour
30 caramels
1/2 cup milk
1/2 cup pecan pieces

FILLING 1
4 oz. cream cheese, softened
1/2 cup powdered sugar
4 oz. Cool Whip

FILLING 2
5/8 cup sugar
1/4 teaspoon salt
1/4 cup cornstarch
1 1/2 cup cream
1 cup milk
5 egg yolks
1 tablespoon vanilla extract
2 tablespoons butter
2–4 bananas

GARNISH
whipped topping
nuts
caramel

For the Crust: Mix water, sugar, and salt. Chill in refrigerator. Place cold butter, cold lard, and flour in food processor and pulse until butter is the size of peas. Add water mixture and pulse until a dough forms. Place in plastic bag, shape into a disk, and chill overnight. Roll out crust and blind bake for around 30 minutes at 350 degrees or until lightly browned. Cool. Melt caramels with milk and pecans and spread over the crust. (Sugar or egg wash on pie crust is optional.)

For Filling 1: Combine all ingredients and spread over caramel/pecan mixture. Slice bananas and arrange over cream cheese mixture.

For Filling 2: Mix sugar, salt, and cornstarch in a pot. In a bowl, whisk cream, milk, and egg yolks slightly. To the pot, slowly add the egg yolk/cream/milk mixture. Heat over medium heat, whisking frequently, until thick and bubbling (but not rapidly boiling). Once the cream is bubbling, continue to cook and whisk for 30 more seconds. Finally, add the vanilla and butter and mix until the cream is smooth. Set aside. Cover bananas with filling 2. Place a plastic sheet over the cream to prevent a skin from forming on the cream filling. Place in refrigerator until completely chilled.

For the Garnish: Top with your favorite whipped topping. Garnish with nuts, caramel, or decorate as desired. Chill 4 hours before serving.

Cool Bananas Pie

PEARL BAILEY'S CREAM PIE

Matt Zagorski, Arlington Heights, IL
2015 APC National Pie Championships
Professional Division
1st Place Cream

CRUST
¼ cup butter-flavored Crisco, cold
¼ cup whole butter, salted, cold
1 cup all-purpose flour
¼ cup cake flour
½ tablespoon powdered sugar
¼ teaspoon salt
⅛ cup sour cream
¼ cup water

FILLING
1½ cup whipping cream, whipped
¾ cup sugar

½ tablespoons instant Clear Jel
2½ oz. Bailey's Irish Cream
12 oz. cream cheese
⅓ cup unsweetened cocoa powder
1 banana, cut into slices
12 ladyfingers, store bought

TOPPING
½ large chocolate bar
1 cup whipping cream
2½ tablespoons sugar

Pearl Bailey's Cream Pie

For the Crust: Preheat oven to 400 degrees. Cut the fats into ¼-inch pieces, then place in the freezer to harden. Combine the flours, powdered sugar, and salt in a food processor and combine, about 30 seconds. Once the dries are combined, scatter the very cold Crisco and butter pieces over the flour mixture and process thoroughly using 10 (1-second) pulses on the food processor. Make sure the mixture has no fat bits larger than small peas. Remove to a large bowl. Combine the sour cream and water and stir to combine. Sprinkle 2 tablespoons of the sour cream mixture over the flour mixture and use a folding motion to incorporate. Add additional water so the dough just comes together. It should be slightly damp and cold and should hold together when squeezed. Shape the dough into a ball and flatten into a 6- to 8-inch disk. Cover in plastic wrap and refrigerate at least 2 hours, or overnight. Before rolling out, let the dough come to just below room temperature, roughly 6 to 7 minutes. The dough should be slightly cool to the touch.

Roll to desired thickness and place in pie pan. Chill rolled-out dough in pan for at least 40 minutes.

After 40 minutes in the refrigerator, place the dough and pie pan in the freezer for 20 minutes. Take the dough and pie pan out of the freezer, line the bottom of the pie shell with a parchment circle, and then add about 1 to 1½ pounds of ceramic pie weights.

Place the pie shell on a cookie sheet and bake on the floor of the oven for 20 minutes, and then remove the weights and parchment paper.

Dock or prick the dough with a fork to let air escape and return the shell to the middle rack of the oven to cook for another 6 to 8 minutes or until the bottom of the crust is golden brown. If the crust bubbles, prick it again with a fork.

When the pie crust is golden brown, remove it from the oven and let cool completely before filling.

For the Filling: Whip the whipping cream to soft peaks. Set aside.

Combine the sugar and instant Clear Jel together. In a stand mixer, combine the Bailey's Irish Cream with the cream cheese and beat together with an electric mixer for 1 to 2 minutes until smooth.

Gently fold the cheese mixture into the whipped cream. Adjust the cream cheese mixture to taste (this usually means to add more Bailey's).

Place about one-third of the flavored cream cheese mixture on the bottom of your cooled pie crust. Top the cream cheese with the cocoa powder, the sliced bananas, and a row of ladyfingers. Top the ladyfingers with another one-third of the Bailey's cream cheese.

Add the sugar to the remaining 2 cups of whipping cream and whip into stiff peaks.

For the Garnish: Garnish the top of the pie with the whipping cream and chocolate curls. Refrigerate for at least 4 hours before serving so the flavors can come together.

Chef's Notes:
Use a vegetable peeler on the chocolate bar to make the chocolate shavings. This works best if the chocolate is cold. Work fast, as the heat of your hand will cause the chocolate to melt and become very messy.

GERMAN CHOCOLATE CREAM PIE

Amy Freeze, Avon Park, FL
2015 APC National Pie Championships
Professional Division Honorable Mention Cream

CRUST

2½ cups graham cracker crumbs
½ cup pecans, finely chopped
2 tablespoons sugar
6 tablespoons butter, melted

FILLING 1

⅔ cup sugar
¼ cup cornstarch
5 egg yolks
2 cups whole milk
½ teaspoon salt
1 tablespoon butter
1 cup heavy cream
4 oz. German chocolate, chopped
2 oz. semisweet chocolate, chopped

FILLING 2

1 (12-oz.) can evaporated milk
4 egg yolks
1½ cups sugar
1½ teaspoons vanilla extract
¾ cup butter, softened
1 cup sweetened coconut flakes
1 cup pecans, chopped

GARNISH

½ cup semisweet chocolate chips
2 tablespoons heavy cream

For the Crust: In a large bowl, combine cookie crumbs, pecans, sugar, and melted butter. Press into a 9-inch deep dish pie plate. Bake at 350 degrees for 10 minutes. Cool completely before filling.

For Filling 1: In a saucepan, combine sugar, cornstarch, egg yolks, milk, salt, butter, and heavy cream. Whisk over medium heat until thick and bubbly. Remove from heat and whisk in chopped chocolates until melted. Pour into prepared crust. Refrigerate until set.

For Filling 2: In a saucepan, combine evaporated milk, egg yolks, sugar, vanilla, and butter. Cook over medium heat until thick, bubbly, and lightly brown. Remove from heat. Stir in coconut and pecans. Spread over chocolate cream. Refrigerate until set.

German Chocolate Cream Pie

For the Garnish: In a small bowl, combine chocolate chips and cream. Microwave in 30 second intervals. Pour melted ganache into a piping or zipper bag. Drizzle over coconut-pecan layer.

BANANA BLISS PIE

John Sunvold, Orlando, FL
2014 APC National Pie Championships
Amateur Division 1st Place Cream

CRUST
1½ cup graham cracker crumbs
6 tablespoons butter, melted
3 tablespoons sugar

FILLING 1
2 tablespoons butter
2 tablespoons corn syrup
2 tablespoons cream
⅓ cup semisweet chocolate chips
1 cup powdered sugar

FILLING 2
⅝ cup sugar
¼ teaspoon salt
¼ cup cornstarch
1½ cups cream
1 cup milk
5 egg yolks
1 tablespoon vanilla extract
2 tablespoons butter
2–4 bananas, sliced

GARNISH
whipped cream
nuts
chocolate

For the Crust: Mix graham cracker crumbs and sugar, add the melted butter, and press into a 9- to 10-inch pie plate. You may not use all of it if you use a shallow pan. Bake at 350 degrees for 8 to 12 minutes. Cool.

For Filling 1: Mix butter, corn syrup, and cream, and heat over medium until boiling. Stir constantly. Add chocolate chips and stir until melted. Once fully combined, slowly add powdered sugar. Mix completely, then carefully spread the chocolate onto the bottom of the crust (may include a thin layer around the sides of the crust to hold the crust together).

It cools quickly, so you must spread immediately. Top with a single layer of mini chocolate chips (around ⅛ cup). Chill.

For Filling 2: Mix sugar, salt, and starch in a pot. In a bowl, whisk cream, milk, and egg yolks slightly. To the pot, slowly add the egg yolk/cream/milk mixture. Heat over medium heat, whisking frequently, until thick and bubbling (but not rapidly boiling). Once the cream is bubbling, continue to cook and whisk for 30 more seconds. Finally, add the butter and vanilla and mix until the cream is smooth. Set aside. Cut 2 to 4 bananas, and cover the chocolate layer with bananas and the warm vanilla cream. Place a plastic sheet over the cream to prevent a skin from forming on the cream filling. Place in refrigerator until completely chilled.

For the Garnish: Top with your favorite whipped topping. Garnish with chocolate and nuts, as/if desired. May also cover with chocolate-covered banana pieces. Chill 4 hours before serving.

NUTTY BUTTERSCOTCH PIE

Alberta Dunbar, San Diego, CA
2014 APC National Pie Championships
Amateur Division 2nd Place Cream

CRUST
1½ cups all-purpose flour
½ teaspoon salt
½ cup Crisco all-vegetable
    shortening
3–4 tablespoons water, cold

FILLING:
8 oz. cream cheese softened
1½ cups cold milk
1 (4 servings) package French vanilla
    instant pudding mix

1 (11-oz.) package butterscotch chips,
    melted and cooled
1 teaspoon vanilla extract
1 cup heavy cream whipped
1½ cups unsalted macadamia nuts,
    ground

FOR THE TOPPING:
2½ cups heavy cream
¼ cup sifted powdered sugar
1 tablespoon clear vanilla extract
½ cup macadamia nuts, ground

For the Crust: Preheat oven to 450 degrees. Spoon the flour into measuring cup and level. Mix flour and salt in medium bowl. Cut in shortening using pastry blender or two knives until flour is blended and forms pea-sized chunks. Sprinkle with 1 tablespoon of water at a time. Toss lightly with a fork until dough forms a ball. Roll on lightly floured board to fit a 9-inch deep dish pie plate with ½ inch overlap. Fold under and flute edges and prick bottom with fork. Bake at 450 degrees for 10 to 12 minutes or until golden brown. Cool on rack completely before filling.

For the Filling: In large bowl, combine cream cheese and milk. Beat on high until smooth. Add pudding mix. Mix 2 minutes until well blended and smooth. Add vanilla, beat well.

Fold in cooled chips. With wooden spoon, fold in whipped cream and macadamia nuts. Turn into cooled crust, spread evenly, and smooth top. Chill 30 minutes.

For the Topping: Combine all ingredients in medium bowl. Beat on high until stiff peaks form. Reserve 2 cups for piping around edge of pie. Frost pie smooth. Pipe large rosettes around edge of pie. Garnish with the ground macadamia nuts as desired. Another optional garnish is butterscotch leaves, which are macadamia nuts dipped in butterscotch.

Nutty Butterscotch Pie

COASTAL COCONUT CREAM PIE

Amy Freeze, Avon Park, FL
2014 APC National Pie Championships
Amateur Division 3rd Place Cream

CRUST
2 cups coconut shortbread cookies, crushed
⅛ cup sugar
5 tablespoons butter, melted

FILLING 1
8 oz. cream cheese, softened
2 whole eggs
2 egg yolks

1 can cream of coconut
1 cup milk
1 teaspoon coconut extract
1 cup sweetened coconut flakes

FILLING 2
2 cups heavy whipping cream
1½ cups powdered sugar
½ cup fresh coconut shavings

GARNISH
½ cup shortbread cookie crumbs
chocolate sea shells

For the Crust: In a bowl, combine cookie crumbs, sugar, and butter. Press into a 9-inch deep dish pie plate. Bake at 350 degrees for 10 minutes. Allow to cool to the touch before filling.

For Filling 1: In a medium bowl, beat cream cheese until smooth. Add eggs and egg yolks, one at a time, beating well after each addition. Add cream of coconut, milk, and coconut extract. Pour into a large sauce pot. Cook over medium heat until filling thickens and begins to bubble.

Pour into cooled crust. Top with coconut and refrigerate.

For Filling 2: In a cold bowl, beat whipping cream and powdered sugar until stiff. Mound filling over cream and coconut filling. Top with coconut shavings.

For the Garnish: Sprinkle middle of pie with cookie crumbs. Garnish with chocolate sea shells

Coastal Coconut Cream Pie

MAX'S COO COO FOR COCONUT PIE

Matt Zagorski, Arlington Heights, IL
2010 APC Crisco National Pie Championships
Professional Division Honorable Mention Cream

CRUST

2 cups all-purpose flour
½ cup cake flour
1 tablespoon powdered sugar
½ teaspoon salt
½ cup butter-flavored Crisco
½ cup plus 2 tablespoons whole butter, salted
½ cup ice cold water
¼ cup sour cream

FILLING

2 tablespoons corn starch
⅔ cup granulated sugar
¼ teaspoon fine salt
6 large egg yolks
2 cups coconut milk
4 teaspoons, divided vanilla bean paste (or vanilla extract)
5 teaspoons, divided coconut extract
2 tablespoons cold unsalted butter, cut into pieces
3 ounces white chocolate, finely chopped (about ½ cup)
2 cups whipping cream
5 tablespoons sugar
1 cup coconut, shredded and toasted

For the Crust: Cut the fats into ¼" pieces and place in a metal bowl. Once cut, place the cut fats in the freezer to harden. Once the fat is very, very cold (almost frozen—do not rush it), place the flours, powdered sugar, and salt in the bowl of a food processor and process for 5–10 seconds to distribute the dries evenly. Scatter the fats over the flour mixture and process thoroughly. Make sure the mixture has no fat bits larger than small peas. Remove the dough to a large bowl. Combine the sour cream and water and stir to combine. Sprinkle about two thirds of the ice water mixture over the flour mixture and use a folding motion to incorporate. Add enough additional water that the dough just comes together. It should be slightly damp, cold, and hold together when squeezed (this is very important!).

Divide the dough in two, shape into balls, and flatten each into a 2-inch disk. Wrap each in plastic wrap and refrigerate at least 4 hours (or overnight if possible). Before rolling out, let the dough come to just below room temp. It should be slightly cool to the touch, 10 minutes.

If it is too cold, the dough will crack when rolled out. Roll to a $\frac{1}{8}$" thickness and place in pie pan. Place back in the refrigerator to chill, about 40 minutes. Once chilled, place in the freezer for 20 minutes. To blind bake the pie shell, pre-heat the oven to 400 degree for at least 20 minutes. Line the bottom of the pie shell with parchment paper and then add about 1.5 lbs of pie weights.

Place the pie shell on a cookie sheet and bake on the floor of the hot oven for 20 minutes.

After 20 minutes, remove the weights and parchment. Prick the dough with a fork to let air escape and return the shell to the middle rack of the oven to cook for another 5–8 minutes more or until the bottom of the crust is golden brown. If the crust starts to bubble, prick it again with a fork. When the pie crust is golden brown, remove it from the oven and let cool completely before filling.

For the Filling: Toast coconut: Preheat oven to 350 degrees. Spread shredded coconut on a rimmed baking sheet and bake, stirring once or twice, until golden, about 5 to 10 minutes. Be careful not to let it burn. Set aside to cool. This can be done a day ahead.

Whisk together the corn starch, sugar, and salt in a medium mixing bowl. Add the egg yolks and whisk to combine. Heat the coconut milk in a medium sauce pan over medium-high heat; bring to a boil. Pour about a third of the hot coconut milk into the egg mixture and whisk to combine. Pour the tempered egg mixture back into the sauce pan with the rest of the coconut milk and then place the whole mixture over medium-high heat. Whisking constantly and vigorously until thickened, bring the mixture to the boil. When

Max's Coo Coo for Coconut Cream Pie

the mixture is fully thickened, it should pull away from the sides of the pan slightly. Do not let it bubble long. Remove from the heat.

Whisk 3 teaspoons of the coconut and 2 teaspoons of vanilla extract, the butter, and white chocolate into the custard until completely smooth. Strain through a fine sieve into a clean bowl (if necessary);

Press a sheet of plastic wrap directly onto the surface of the pastry cream, then place in the refrigerator to cool down until ready to use. Fill the cooled pie shell with the cooled filling. If you have time, cover the filling with plastic wrap and place the pie back in the refrigerator for 2–3 hours to set. Do not panic if you do not have time to do this.

Whip the 2 cups of whipping cream with 4–5 tablespoons of sugar and the remaining 2 teaspoons of the coconut and vanilla extracts until you achieve soft peaks. Taste; adjust to your personal preference. Remove the chilled and filled pie from the refrigerator, remove the plastic wrap (if necessary) and place the whipped cream on top of the coconut cream filling.

Sprinkle the toasted coconut on top of the whipping cream for a finishing garnish.

HAWAIIAN TROPICAL PIE

Andy Hilton, Davenport, FL
2014 APC National Pie Championships
Professional Division Honorable Mention Cream

CRUST
8 oz. short bread cookies
1 cup macadamia nuts, chopped
8 tablespoons butter

FILLING 1
1 cup crushed pineapple, drained
½ oz. unflavored gelatin
1½ cup heavy whipping cream
5 oz. white chocolate chips
12 oz. cream cheese
½ cup sugar
1 cup heavy whipping cream
¼ cup sugar

FILLING 2
1 cup whole milk
1 cup coconut milk
1 cup sugar
3 tablespoons cornstarch
5 large egg yolks
pastry cream

GARNISH
1 tablespoon coconut flavoring
1 cup coconut flakes
½ cup toasted coconut flakes
1 quart whipping cream

For the Crust: Combine cookies in a food processor and grind them to a crumb. Pour them into a bowl and add the macadamia nuts. Melt butter and mix it into the crumb. Press 1½ cups of crumb into 9-inch pie pan, using the back of a spoon to form the crumb into a crust. Take an empty pie pan and press it into the pie pan with the crumb and press firmly. Remove empty pan and bake crust for 4 minutes in a 350-degree oven. Remove and let cool.

For Filling 1: Place crushed pineapple in a bowl, sprinkle and mix the gelatin, and set to the side to firm. Using a heavy saucepan bring half of heavy cream to a simmer, remove from heat. Add the white chocolate and gently stir until smooth and creamy. Beat cream cheese and sugar with a stand mixer until smooth. Scrape the walls and beater, beat again for another minute. Mix in chocolate mixture, mix for 1 minute, add pineapple mixture, and mix for a minute. Whip 1 cup heavy cream to stiff peaks, fold cream cheese mixture into the whipped cream. Fill the pie crust halfway with pineapple mousse, cover with plastic, and refrigerate overnight.

For Filling 2: In a medium saucepan, slowly heat the milk, coconut milk, sugar, and cornstarch, using medium-high heat. Stir constantly to keep the milk from burning, and heat until the mixture begins to simmer. Add and stir in 2 to 3 tablespoons of the milk mixture to the eggs yolks; this will temper the eggs. Stir in another 3 tablespoon and blend together. Pour the egg

Hawaiian Tropical Pie

mixture back into the milk mixture and mix well. Pour milk and egg mixture through a strainer and quickly put the mixture back on medium to high heat and stir constantly until the mixture thickens. This will take a few minutes because the cornstarch needs to boil just a bit to thicken. Once the mixture thickens, pour it into a bowl and place plastic right on the cream to prevent a skin from forming and place cream into the refrigerator to cool.

For the Garnish: Whip cream and sugar to firm peaks. With a whip attachment, blend coconut flakes and coconut flavoring into Filling 2 base. Fill the balance of the pie with coconut cream, garnish with whipped cream, toasted coconut and candied pineapple.

CLASSIC COCONUT CREAM PIE

Beth Campbell, Belleville, WI
2014 APC National Pie Championships
Amateur Division 3rd Place Open

CRUST
½ cup shortening
1 cups flour
½ cup shredded coconut
pinch salt
¼ cup water, cold
1 cup coconut spread (can be found at most Chinese stores or in Chinese aisle of grocery store)

FILLING
1 cup whole milk
1¾ cup unsweetened coconut milk (13.5 fl. oz. can)
½ cup sugar

4 tablespoons flour
2 large eggs (slightly whisked)
4 tablespoons butter
1½ cups shredded coconut
1 teaspoon coconut extract
1 teaspoon vanilla extract

TOPPING
1 (9.5-oz.) jar coconut curd

GARNISH
¾ cup whipping cream
½ cup powdered sugar

For the Crust: Cut the shortening into the flour and coconut until the particles are the size of small peas. Dissolve the salt into the cold water. Sprinkle in the water until the flour mixture is moist. Gather the pastry into a ball and refrigerate overnight. Roll pastry out on floured board. Fold the pastry into quarters, unfold, and ease into the pie pan. Bake at 375 degrees for 7 to 8 minutes or until golden brown but not burned. You may have to put a pie shield or aluminum foil on the outer edge if you notice it is getting too brown. Cool completely. Gently spread ½ cup of the coconut spread over the baked crust. (The rest can be either used on the top of the curd layer later on or used to garnish the pie if you like).

For the Filling: In a large pot, combine the whole milk, coconut milk, and sugar. Slowly whisk in the flour a little at a time and cook until thickened over medium heat. Remove from heat and take part of the hot mixture and combine half of it with the eggs and then return all of it to the pan, whisking constantly. Let simmer for another 3 minutes or until it reaches a nice, thick consistency. Remove from heat and stir in butter, coconut, and the extracts. Pour into the prebaked piecrust coated with the coconut spread. Cool completely in the refrigerator with a piece of plastic wrap to stop a skin from forming.

For the Topping: Warm the coconut curd (if you need to) until it is a good consistency for smearing on the top of the coconut-filling layer.

For the Garnish: In a large bowl, beat the whipping cream until soft peaks form. Add the ½ cup of powdered sugar and whip until peaks are stiff, but don't overbeat. Top the coconut spread layer with the whipped cream. You can also garnish with toasted coconut, the rest of the coconut spread, or white chocolate curls, if desired.

COO COO FOR COCONUT CREAM PIE

Dionna Hurt, Longwood, FL
2014 APC National Pie Championships
Professional Division 1st Place Cream

CRUST
3 cups Nilla cookies
½ cup butter, melted
2–3 tablespoons sugar

FILLING
3 tablespoons cornstarch
1 cup heavy cream
1 can coconut milk
1 (14-ounce) can sweetened condensed milk

3 egg yolks, beaten
1 tablespoons butter
1 tablespoon vanilla extract
1 cup shredded sweetened coconut

GARNISH
Sweetened whipped cream

For the Crust: Pre-heat oven to 350 degrees F. In food processor, grind cookies into crumbs. Transfer crumbs to mixing bowl. Add sugar and melted butter, toss with fork. Pour into pie dish and press into bottom and up the sides. Bake for 15 minutes, let cool.

For the Filling: In a heavy saucepan, dissolve the cornstarch in the cream; stir in sweetened condensed, cream, coconut milk and egg yolks. Cook and stir until thick and bubbly. Remove from heat add butter and vanilla extract & shredded coconut. Pour into pie crust and chill for 2 or more hours.

For the Garnish: Garnish with sweetened whipped cream around the edge.

Coo Coo for Coconut Cream Pie

STUFFED CRUST CHERRY SUNDAE PIE

Phyllis Szymanek, Toledo, OH
2012 APC Crisco National Pie Championships
Amateur Division 1st Place Cream

CRUST
2 cups Pillsbury all-purpose flour
1 tablespoon sugar
1 teaspoon salt
½ cup butter-flavored Crisco, chilled
4 tablespoons butter
1 teaspoon vinegar
5 tablespoons water, cold

FILLING 1
⅓ cup sugar
1½ tablespoon cornstarch
¼ teaspoon lemon zest
1 (16-oz.) jar Wienke's pitted sour
    cherries, drain and save 1 cup juice
⅛ teaspoon almond extract
1 tablespoon butter
1 beaten egg + 1 teaspoon water

FILLING 2
1 (8-oz.) package cream cheese,
    softened
1 cup water
⅔ cup sweetened condensed milk
1 (3.4-oz) package instant vanilla
    pudding
¼ teaspoon almond extract
1 (12-oz.) container Cool Whip
1 cup pecans, chopped and divided
1 (10-oz.) jar maraschino cherries
    with stems, drained (set aside 8
    cherries, cut up remaining)

GARNISH
¼ cup Smucker's Hot Fudge Topping
    (warmed)

For the Crust: In a mixing bowl, combine flour, sugar, and salt; add Crisco and butter. With pastry cutter, cut into pea-sized pieces. Mix together vinegar and water. Add 1 tablespoon of vinegar/water mixture at a time until dough forms into a ball. Shape dough into a log and cut ¾ of log and flatten for bottom of crust and ¼ for the top. Chill for 2 hours.

For Filling 1: In a small saucepan, combine sugar, cornstarch, and lemon zest. Add cherry juice and cook over medium heat until thick, about 5 minutes. Remove from heat and add cherries, extract, and butter. Roll out bottom crust on floured surface and place into 9-inch deep pie dish; flute edges. Pour filling into pie dish. Roll out the remaining ¼ dough for a top crust. Using an 8-inch pie dish, turn upside down and cut an 8-inch circle in rolled out dough. Place over cherries. Seal crust to sides. Brush with egg wash. Prick sides of crust and top with a fork. Cover inside and edges of crust with foil. Bake at 375 degrees for 20 minutes. Remove foil and bake 15 to 20 minutes longer or until crust is golden brown. Cool on wire rack.

For Filling 2: In a large mixing bowl, beat cream cheese until light. Gradually beat in water and condensed milk. Add pudding mix and extract. Fold in 2 cups of Cool Whip; add ½ cup nuts and chopped cherries. Pour over the pie crust and chill for 4 to 6 hours. Garnish with remaining Cool Whip, cherries, and ½ cup pecans.

For the Garnish: Drizzle with fudge topping.

Stuffed Crust Cherry Sundae Pie

I CANNOT TELL A LIE . . . WASHINGTON CREAM PIE!

David Harper, Lone Rock, WI
2014 APC National Pie Championships
Amateur Division 2nd Place Innovation

CRUST
2 cups flour
2 teaspoons salt
1 cup butter-flavored Crisco
10 tablespoons water, cold

VANILLA FILLING
1 cup sugar
¼ cup cornstarch
4 egg yolks
2½ cups half-and-half
2 teaspoons vanilla
2 tablespoons butter

HOT MILK SPONGE CAKE
1½ cup all-purpose flour
1½ teaspoons baking powder
¾ teaspoon salt
¾ cup whole milk
6 tablespoons butter

2 teaspoons vanilla
1½ cup sugar
1½ cups seedless jelly, your choice
   (I use either raspberry or cherry)

CHOCOLATE SAUCE
8 ounces semisweet chocolate
¾ cup heavy cream
2 tablespoons light corn syrup
1 teaspoon vanilla

GARNISH
1 cup heavy cream
¼ cup powdered sugar
1 teaspoon vanilla
grated chocolate

For the Crust: Preheat oven to 400 degrees. Whisk the flour and the salt together in a large bowl. Add the Crisco and mix with your fingers until combined. Add the water and use a fork to combine. Turn pie dough out onto a floured surface and gather into a circular disk. Roll out the dough big enough to fit into a pie plate. Flute edges for decoration. Bake crust until edges are golden brown and bottom is browned also, about 15 to 20 minutes. Cool on a wire rack and set aside.

For the Filling: Combine the sugar, cornstarch, egg yolks, and half-and-half together in a heavy saucepan. Cook until filling is thick and bubbly, about 4 to 5 minutes over medium-high heat. Having a heavy saucepan is critical in not scorching your filling. Remove thickened filling and run it through a fine mesh sieve, catching strained filling in another bowl. Add the vanilla and butter and stir until melted and combined. Place plastic wrap directly on top of filling and set aside to cool, about 15 minutes. Place about

I Cannot Tell A Lie . . . Washington Cream Pie!

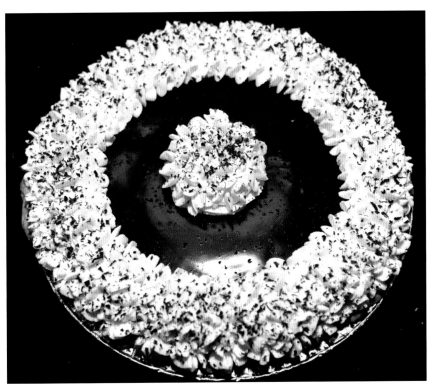

¾ cup of the cream filling over the bottom of the pie crust.

For the Cake: Heat oven to 325 degrees. Grease two 9-inch cake pans and line with parchment paper. Grease the parchment. Combine the flour, baking powder, and salt in a bowl. Heat the milk and butter in a pan until butter is melted. Remove from heat and add the vanilla. Cover to keep warm. With a mixer, whip the eggs and sugar on high speed for about 5 minutes. Once mixed, add the hot milk mixture and whisk by hand until incorporated. Add the dry ingredients and mix until incorporated. Divide the batter between the two prepared pans and bake for about 25 minutes or until a toothpick comes out clean. Cool cakes in pan. When cool, run a small knife around the edge of pan and turn out onto a wire rack. Remove parchment and turn cakes right-side up. (You will only need one cake for this recipe, so enjoy the other cake for something else.) Take one of the cooled cakes and trim it so it can fit in the pie crust. You may have to trim around the edge so it will fit nicely in the crust. Once you have the correct fit, carefully cut the cake in half horizontally so that you have 2 even cake layers. Place one of the cake layers on the cream filling, cut-side up. Spread ¾ cup of jelly on the cake layer.

Cover the jelly with the rest of the cream filling. Carefully spread the rest of the jelly on the cut side of the other cake layer and place the cake layer on the cream filling, jelly-side down. Place cake in refrigerator for about 10 minutes.

For the Chocolate Sauce: Meanwhile, combine all the ingredients for the chocolate sauce in a microwaveable bowl and cook for about 1 minute. Remove from microwave and stir until combined. Let cool for about 10 minutes. Once the cake is cool, carefully poor chocolate over the top of the cake until cake is covered. Place back in refrigerator for about 1 hour to let filling and chocolate set up.

For the Garnish: Whip cream with vanilla and powdered sugar. Garnish the top of cake with whipped cream in a decorative pattern and grate chocolate on top.

CREAM CHEESE

STRAWBERRY BLACKBERRY CREAM CHEESE PIE

Devin Davis, Plant City, FL
2014 APC National Pie Championships
Amateur Division 1ˢᵗ Place Cream Cheese

CRUST
20 shortcake cookies
2 tablespoons sugar
2 tablespoons flour
2 tablespoons butter, melted
1 tablespoon Crisco, melted

FILLING 1
8 oz. cream cheese, softened
1 (7-oz.) container marshmallow fluff
1 (8-oz.) container Cool Whip

FILLING 2
12 oz. frozen blackberries
½ cup sugar
½ teaspoon lemon zest
¼ cup + 2 tablespoons water, divided
2 tablespoons cornstarch

FILLING 3
1 quart strawberries, chopped, divided
½ cup sugar
¼ cup + 2 tablespoons water, divided
¼ teaspoon lemon zest
2 tablespoons cornstarch

GARNISH
2 cups whipped cream
strawberries
blackberries

For the Crust: Preheat oven to 350 degrees. In a food processor, pulse cookies until they turn into fine crumbs. Transfer to a small bowl and stir in sugar and flour. Then mix in the butter and Crisco until all the crumbs are moistened. Press into the bottom and sides of a 9-inch pie plate and bake for 8 minutes. Set aside and let cool completely.

For Filling 1: Using an electric mixer, beat together the cream cheese and marshmallow fluff until combined. Then fold in Cool Whip and refrigerate until ready to use. Spread half the cream cheese mixture into the bottom of the cooled crust.

For Filling 2: In a small pot, combine first three ingredients and ¼ cup of water and bring to a boil and cook for 5 minutes or until blackberries are soft and begin to break down. Using a spoon or fork, mash the blackberries and then strain out the seeds from the sauce. Return sauce to the pot and bring to a boil. Whisk together the cornstarch and remaining water in a small bowl and then whisk into the boiling blackberry sauce. Cook for 30 more seconds or until thick and let cool completely. Spread filling over the cream cheese layer and put in the refrigerator until the blackberry filling is set. Spread the remaining cream cheese filling over blueberry filling.

For Filling 3: In a small pot, combine half the strawberries, the sugar, ¼ cup of water, and lemon zest and bring to a boil. Cook for 5 minutes. In a small bowl, whisk together the cornstarch and remaining water and then whisk into the boiling strawberry mixture. Cook for 30 more seconds or until thick and let cool. Once cool, stir in the remaining chopped strawberries. Top pie with the strawberry filling. Refrigerate for 4 hours or overnight.

For the Garnish: Garnish with whipped cream and fresh strawberries and blackberries, if desired.

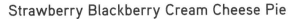

Strawberry Blackberry Cream Cheese Pie

LEMON CREAM CHEESE PIE

George Yates
2014 APC National Pie Championships
Amateur Division 2nd Place Cream Cheese

CRUST

1½ cups graham cracker crumbs, crushed
½ cup vanilla wafers, crushed
¼ cup toasted almonds, ground
3 tablespoons sugar
1½ teaspoons lemon juice
5 tablespoons unsalted butter, melted

FILLING 1

8 oz. cream cheese, softened
¼ cup granulated sugar
½ teaspoon vanilla
1 egg

FILLING 2

½ cup granulated sugar
2 tablespoons cornstarch
dash salt
1 cup water
2 egg yolks
2 tablespoons fresh lemon juice
1 tablespoon butter

GARNISH

2 cups whipping cream
4 tablespoons powdered sugar
1 teaspoon clear vanilla extract
raspberries, if desired
lemon, if desired

For the Crust: Preheat oven to 350 degrees. In a medium bowl, combine crumbs, ground almonds, and sugar. Stir lemon juice in melted butter until combined. Press crumb mixture into bottom of a 9-inch deep dish pie pan and 1-inch up sides.

For Filling 1: Prepare the cream cheese filling by mixing cream cheese with sugar, vanilla, and egg, using an electric mixer. Mix well until smooth. Pour cream cheese filling into crust and bake for 30 minutes or until center is cooked. A knife stuck in the middle of the filling should come out mostly clean. Remove from oven and let cool.

For Filling 2: Make the lemon filling by combining sugar with cornstarch, salt, and water in a small saucepan. Set mixture over low heat and bring to a simmer, stirring often. Whisk in egg yolks, then add lemon juice and butter. When mixture simmers again, remove it immediately from the heat. Pour the lemon filling over the cream cheese filling and let the pie cool. Chill pie in the refrigerator until completely cool.

For the Garnish: Beat together the whipping cream, powdered sugar, and vanilla. Pipe around edge of pie. Decorate with fresh raspberries, sliced lemon, sliced almonds, and raspberry jam. Refrigerate until ready to serve.

Lemon Cream Cheese Pie

SNICKERDOODLE PIE

Grace Thatcher, Delta, OH
2014 National Pie Championships
Amateur Division 3rd Place Cream Cheese

CRUST
1½ cups graham cracker crumbs
3 tablespoons sugar
½ teaspoon cinnamon
5 tablespoons butter

CREAM CHEESE FILLING
8 oz. cream cheese
8 tablespoons butter
⅓ cup confectioners' sugar
⅓ cup granulated sugar

2 teaspoons vanilla
¼ teaspoon cinnamon
2 large eggs

TOPPING
½ cup confectioners' sugar
¼ teaspoon cinnamon
2 tablespoons water, hot
¼ cup sliced almonds, toasted

For the Crust: Put crumbs, sugar, and cinnamon into a bowl and mix. Add melted butter and mix well with a large fork. Press into a shallow pie plate and bake at 350 for 10 minutes or until slightly browned.

For the Filling: Place room-temperature cream cheese into the work bowl of a food processor with the room-temperature butter and process until smooth. Add sugars, vanilla, and cinnamon. Process again, until smooth. Add eggs and pulse for three (1-second) pulses. Do not over-mix. Pour into a mixing bowl and finish mixing by hand. Pour into cooled crust and bake at 350 degrees for 22 minutes or until edges are slightly puffed and the center is set.

For the Topping: Put sugar, cinnamon, and water in a small saucepan. Bring to a rolling boil. Pour hot syrup over top of warm pie. Sprinkle with the almonds. This pie is good served warm or cooled.

Snickerdoodle Pie

SEA SALT CARAMEL BUTTERSCOTCH CRUNCH PIE

Patricia Lapiezo, LaMesa, CA
2015 National Pie Championships
Amateur Division 1st Place Cream Cheese

CRUST
½ cup Pepperidge Farms Dulce de
 Leche cookies, finely ground
butter, melted

FILLING
⅓ cup semisweet chocolate chips
⅔ cup butterscotch chips
2 (8-oz.) packages cream cheese,
 softened
½ cup powdered sugar
½ teaspoon vanilla

2½ cups heavy cream, whipped
½ cup salted caramel sauce
½ cup toffee bits
sea salt

TOPPING
1¼ cups heavy cream
2 tablespoons brown sugar
½ cup salted caramel
sea salt
toffee bits

For the Crust: Combine crumbs and enough butter to have cookies the texture of wet sand. Press into 9-inch pie pan. Bake at 350 degrees for 8 minutes. Remove from oven and cool while preparing filling.

For the Filling: Melt the chocolate chips and butterscotch chips together. Stir to combine. In a large bowl, beat the cream cheese with the powdered sugar until smooth. Blend in the melted chips until smooth. Divide cream cheese batter in half. Into one half, blend in melted chips and toffee bits. Fold in half of the whipped cream. To the other half, beat in ½ cup caramel and fold in remaining whipped cream. Alternately, drop spoonfuls of each filling into the prepared crust and cover the bottom of the pie; run a knife through to marble. Repeat until all the filling is used.

For the Topping: In a mixing bowl, beat the cream and brown sugar until stiff. Spread the caramel over top of pie to within 1 inch of sides. Decoratively pipe a whipped cream border around edge of pie and sprinkle with toffee bits. Just before serving, lightly sprinkle sea salt over top of caramel.

Sea Salt Caramel Butterscotch Crunch Pie

FRESH AND FRUITY CREAM CHEESE PIE

Carol Socier, Bay City, MI
2015 APC National Pie Championships
Amateur Division 2nd Place Cream Cheese

CRUST
1¼ cups all-purpose flour
½ teaspoon salt
½ cup shortening, cold
3–4 tablespoons water, cold

FILLING
8 oz. cream cheese
⅓ cup powdered sugar
⅓ cup heavy whipping cream
¾ cup granulated sugar
¼ cup cornstarch
1 cup pineapple juice
2 cups fresh raspberries, divided
1 cup fresh blackberries

For the Crust: Preheat oven to 425 degrees. In a bowl, combine flour and salt. Cut in shortening until mixture is crumbly. Add water 1 tablespoon at a time until dough forms a ball. Chill for 1 hour. Roll out on lightly floured surface to fit 8-inch pie pan. Bake 10 to 12 minutes or until golden brown. Cool before filling.

For the Filling: In a medium-sized bowl, beat cream cheese and powdered sugar until smooth. Slowly add whipping cream while beating until peaks form. Transfer to cooled pastry shell and refrigerate for a least 30 minutes.

In a small saucepan, combine sugar and cornstarch. Gradually whisk in pineapple juice until smooth. Bring to a boil. Cook and stir for 2 minutes or until thickened. Remove from heat. Mash ½ cup of raspberries. Stir into juice mixture. Cool to room temperature. Fold in remaining raspberries and blackberries. Spoon mixture over top of cream cheese layer. Garnish if desired with sweetened whipped cream and fresh berries. Serves 8.

Fresh and Fruity Cream Cheese Pie

COOKIES AND DREAM PIE

John Sunvold, Orlando, FL
2015 APC National Pie Championships
Amateur Division 3rd Place Cream Cheese

CRUST

26 Oreos sandwich cookies
5 tablespoons butter
½ cup white chocolate chips, melted

FILLING 1

13.5 oz. Oreos (or similar cookie)
6 oz. cream cheese
½ cup white chocolate chips, melted

FILLING 2

8 oz. cream cheese, softened
½ cup powdered sugar
8 oz. Cool Whip

GARNISH

8 oz. Cool Whip
Oreo cookie crumbs
white chocolate chip drizzle

For the Crust: Place whole cookies in food processor and pulse until cookies resemble wet sand. Melt butter and pour over cookie crumbs, and mix until butter is evenly distributed. Press crumbs evenly into pie pan. Bake crust at 375 degrees for 10 minutes. Let cool. Drizzle melted chocolate chips on crust. Chill.

For Filling 1: Place Oreos in food processor and pulverized until cookies are fine crumbs. Add cream cheese to Oreos and pulse until well blended. Spread this mixture on crust. Drizzle chocolate chips on Oreo layer. Chill.

For Filling 2: Mix 8 ounces softened cream cheese with ½ cup powdered sugar. Fold in 8 ounces of Cool Whip and decorate top of Oreo-cheese layer. Chill.

For the Garnish: Top with favorite whipped topping (if desired). Garnish with fudge topping, Oreo crumbs, white chocolate pieces or drizzle, chocolate, or nuts, as desired. Decorate as desired.

Cookies and Dream Pie

WE'RE ALL NUTS PIE

Raine Gottess, Pompano Beach, Fl
2014 APC National Pie Championships
Professional Division 1st Place Open

CRUST
1 package Keebler Pecan Sandie
   cookies
1 stick butter

FILLING 1
8 oz. Philadelphia cream cheese
2 tablespoons milk
1 teaspoon pure vanilla
1¾ cup powdered sugar

6 oz. Cool Whip
1 cup Nutella chocolate hazelnut
   spread

FILLING 2
8 oz. Philadelphia cream cheese
2 tablespoons milk
1 teaspoon pure vanilla
6 oz. Cool Whip
1¾ cups powdered sugar
1 cup almond butter spread

For the Crust: Food process to crumble cookies. Toss in bowl with melted butter. Press into 10-inch deep dish pie pan with back of spoon to shape. Freeze.

For Filling 1: Beat well-softened cream cheese with milk and vanilla. Add in powdered sugar, Cool Whip, and Nutella chocolate hazelnut spread. Spread over crust and freeze.

For Filling 2: Beat well-softened cream cheese with milk and vanilla. Add on Cool Whip and powdered sugar. Add in almond butter and spread evenly over Filling 1. Cover well and refrigerate to firm overnight. Decorate with Cool Whip and serve.

We're All Nuts Pie

BLUEBERRY HARVEST CHEESE PIE

Evette Rahman, Orlando, FL
2012 APC Crisco National Pie Championships
Amateur Division 2nd Place Cream Cheese

CRUST
2 cups coconut cookie crumbs, finely ground
¼ cup sugar
8 tablespoons unsalted butter, melted

FILLING 1
3 cups fresh blueberries, divided
½ cup sugar
½ tablespoon lemon juice
1½ tablespoons cornstarch
2 tablespoons water
1 tablespoon unsalted butter

FILLING 2
1 (8-oz.) Philadelphia cream cheese, softened
¾ cup sweetened condensed milk
¼ cup lemon juice
½ cup powdered sugar
1 (8 oz.) container of extra creamy frozen whipped topping, thawed

GARNISH
sweetened whipped cream
toasted almonds, mint sprigs, blueberries (optional)

For the Crust: Preheat oven to 350 degrees. Mix together cookie crumbs and sugar. Stir in butter and oil. Press in bottom and up sides of a deep dish pie plate. Bake for 8 minutes. Cool completely.

For Filling 1: In small saucepan over medium heat, place 1 cup of blueberries, sugar, lemon juice, cornstarch, and water. Cook, stirring frequently, until blueberries have burst and mixture is very thick. Remove from heat and stir in butter. Scrape into a medium-sized bowl. Cool 10 minutes. Stir in remaining blueberries. Refrigerate.

For Filling 2: In large bowl, beat cream cheese until fluffy. Add in condensed milk, lemon juice, and powdered sugar. Beat until well combined. Fold in whipped topping. Spread half of cheese filling in prepared pie crust. Top with half of the blueberry filling. Repeat with remaining fillings, leaving a border for whipped cream on top.

For the Garnish: Pipe sweetened whipped cream around border. Garnish with toasted almonds, mint sprigs, and blueberries, if desired. Refrigerate at least 4 hours before serving. Keep refrigerated.

Blueberry Harvest Cheese Pie

WHITE CHOCOLATE BLACKBERRY TOFFEE PIE

Phyllis Szymanek, Toledo, OH
2012 APC Crisco National Pie Championships
Amateur Division 3rd Place Cream Cheese

CRUST
1½ cups Pillsbury all-purpose flour
1 tablespoon sugar
½ teaspoon salt
½ cup Crisco, chilled
2 tablespoons butter, chilled
1 teaspoon vinegar
2–4 tablespoons water, cold
1 egg + 1 teaspoon water (egg wash)
¾ cup white chocolate chips

FILLING
3 cups fresh blackberries, reserving
    ½ cup for topping
1 cup white chocolate chips
8 oz. cream cheese, softened
2 teaspoons vanilla

1 cup powdered sugar
⅓ cup malted milk powder
8 oz. whipped topping
½ cup English toffee bits

TOPPING
2 tablespoons Smucker's Blackberry
    Jam
4 oz. cream cheese
¼ cup powdered sugar
2 teaspoons vanilla extract
½ cup white chocolate chips (melted)
¼ cup toffee bits
8 oz. whipped topping

For the Crust: In food processor, combine flour, salt, and sugar. Process on low to blend. Add Crisco and butter; pulse 6 to 8 times until mixture resembles coarse meal. Add vinegar to water, and add 1 tablespoon at a time to mixture until the mixture just begins to clump together. Shape dough into disk shape; cover in plastic wrap and chill 1 hour. Remove disk from refrigerator; roll out on floured surface into a 12-inch circle. Place in 9-inch deep pie dish. Fold dough under around edges and crimp. Brush bottom and sides with egg wash. Prick bottom and sides and bake at 425 degrees for 12 to 15 minutes or until golden brown. Remove from oven, and sprinkle white chocolate chips on bottom of crust to melt. Cool on wire rack.

For the Filling: Place 2½ cups of fresh blackberries in blender; cover and purée, then set aside. In a small microwave-safe bowl, melt chocolate chips for about 1 minute or until melted; cool slightly. Beat cream cheese until smooth. Add vanilla, powdered sugar, and malted milk powder until well blended. Fold in melted chocolate; beat in blackberries, then add whipped topping. Fold in ½ cup toffee bits. Pour mixture into pie crust and chill 4 hours or overnight.

For the Topping: Mix remaining ½ cup of blackberries with blackberry jam. Arrange in the center of pie. Beat cream cheese; add powdered sugar and vanilla until smooth. Add cooled melted chocolate; mix in whipped topping until well blended. Place in a pastry bag with a star tip. Pipe around edge of pie. Sprinkle with toffee bits. Decorate with white chocolate flower or mint leaves, if desired.

White Chocolate Blackberry Toffee Pie

CAMPFIRE FUN PIE

Raine Gottess, Pompano Beach, FL
2009 APC Crisco National Pie Championships
Professional Division 1st Place Cream

CRUST
1½ cup graham cracker crumbs
2½ tablespoons sugar
6 tablespoons butter, melted

FILLING 1
⅔ cup sugar
3 tablespoons flour
⅛ teaspoon salt
¾ cup milk
2 egg yolks, slightly beaten
½ tablespoon butter
½ teaspoon vanilla
1 oz. chocolate, or 2 tablespoons cocoa
   powder + 1 tablespoon shortening.

FILLING 2
6 oz. Philadelphia cream cheese
1 tablespoon milk
1 teaspoon vanilla
2⅛ cup powdered sugar
5 oz. Cool Whip
1 cup marshmallow cream
2 Hershey's bars, chopped

FILLING 3
6 oz. Philadelphia cream cheese
1 tablespoon milk
1 teaspoon vanilla
2⅛ cup powdered sugar
5 oz. Cool Whip
2½ tablespoons cocoa powder
1 tablespoon shortening
½ Hershey's Bar, shaved with a
   potato peeler

TOPPING
1 cup Cool Whip
½ cup hard shell topping
1 Hershey's bar, shaved

For the Crust: Preheat oven to 350 degrees. In a bowl, mix all ingredients with a fork. Press with the back of a large spoon into a 9-inch deep dish pie pan to form a crust. Bake for 7 minutes. Cool.

For Filling 1: In a saucepan, add the first three ingredients gradually, adding milk on medium heat to boil, and thicken about 2 minutes on a slow boil. Remove ½ cup of mixture and add egg yolks, return to saucepan. Stir about 2 more minutes and remove from heat. Add the butter, vanilla, and your choice of the chocolates. Blend well. Pour over crust and place in freezer.

For Filling 2: Using a mixer, beat well the first five ingredients. Add marshmallow cream. Carefully spread over chocolate cream layer. Sprinkle with 2 chopped Hershey's bars. Place in freezer.

For Filling 3: Mix together and carefully spread over previous layer.

For the Garnish: Edge with Cool Whip to decorate. Refrigerate about 6 hours. Slice to serve top with drizzled chocolate hard shell topping and cut up Hershey's bar pieces. Freeze a minute to harden shell and serve.

Campfire Fun Pie

ISLAND ESCAPE TROPICAL PIE

Tammi Carlock, Chickamunga, GA
2015 APC National Pie Championships
Professional Division Honorable Mention Open

CRUST
1½ cup graham cracker crumbs
1 tablespoon sugar
6 tablespoons butter, melted
½ cup pecans, chopped

FILLING
2 (8-oz.) packages cream cheese, softened
½ cup sugar
3 eggs
1 cup cream of coconut
¼ cup sour cream
1 (8-oz.) can crushed pineapple, drained
3 teaspoons coconut extract

TOPPING
1 (8-oz.) can crushed pineapple
1 tablespoon cornstarch
1 tablespoon water
¼ cup sugar
2 tablespoons lemon juice

GARNISH
1 cup heavy cream
¼ cup powdered sugar
½ cup toasted coconut

For the Crust: Preheat oven to 325 degrees. Mix ingredients together and press into a 10-inch pie plate. Set aside.

For the Filling: Beat together cream cheese and sugar until fluffy. Add eggs, one at a time. Add cream of coconut, sour cream, and pineapple, beating until well combined. Stir in extract. Pour into pie crust and bake for 40 to 45 minutes, or until set in the middle. Cool on wire rack.

For the Topping: In a small saucepan, combine cornstarch and water, stirring until smooth. Add pineapple, sugar, and lemon juice and cook over medium heat until very thick. Let cool.

For the Garnish: Whip together with electric mixer until stiff peaks form. Spread topping over pie and refrigerate several hours. Garnish with whipped cream and toasted coconut.

FRUIT & BERRY

BLACKBERRY KEY LIME PIE

Grace Thatcher, Delta, OH
2014 APC National Pie Championships
Amateur Division 2nd Place Fruit/Berry

CRUST
3 teaspoons sugar
1 tablespoon lime zest
1½ cups graham cracker crumbs
5 tablespoon butter

FILLING 1
1 tablespoon cornstarch
1 cup sugar
pinch salt
3 cups blackberries, divided
2 tablespoons blackberry Jell-O
¼ cup water

FILLING 2
1¼ tablespoons gelatin
¼ cup water
¼ cup sugar
1 tablespoon lime zest
8 oz. cream cheese
1 (14-oz.) can sweetened condensed milk
⅓ cup instant vanilla pudding mix
¾ cup lime juice

For the Crust: In a food processor, process the sugar with the lime zest for 1 minute. Add graham cracker crumbs and process just until mixed. Melt the butter and add to the processor and mix just until the mixture clumps together. Press into a deep dish pie pan and bake at 350 degrees for 10 minutes or until slightly browned. Set aside.

For Filling 1: Mix the cornstarch with the sugar and salt and put into a medium-sized saucepan. Mash 1 cup of blackberries and add to the pan and mix well. Bring to a boil over medium heat and cook for 2 minutes, stirring constantly. Remove from heat and add the Jell-O and mix well. Strain mixture to remove seeds. Add 2 cups of blackberries and pour into pie shell. Refrigerate until set.

For Filling 2: Put gelatin in water to soften. Put sugar and lime zest in a food processor and process for 1 minute. Add cream cheese and mix until smooth. Add sweetened condensed milk And the pudding mix and process until smooth. Microwave the gelatin and water mixture for 15 seconds and stir until dissolved. Add to the processor with the juice. When completely smooth, pour over top of the blackberry layer and smooth the top. Refrigerate at least 4 hours and garnish with whipped cream, fresh blackberries, and lime zest.

Blackberry Key Lime Pie

APPLE, PEAR & BERRIES OF MY FOREST PIE

Deb Knicos, Bangor, PA
2014 APC National Pie Championships
Amateur Division 3rd Place Fruit/Berry

PIE DOUGH:

2½ cups unbleached all-purpose
   flour
1 teaspoon table salt
2 tablespoons sugar
12 tablespoons (1½ sticks) unsalted
   butter, cold, cut into ¼-inch slices
½ cup vegetable shortening, cold
½ cup water, cold

FILLING:

3 medium apples (1 Braeburn, 1
   Royal Gala, 1 Macintosh) peeled,
   cored, and cut into ¼-inch cubes
1 Bosc pear, peeled, cored, and cut
   into ¼-inch cubes
¼ cup blackberries

½ cup blueberries, picked over for
   stems
½ cup strawberries, hulled and
   sliced
¼ cup wineberry jam
1 cup sugar
¼ teaspoon ground nutmeg
¼ teaspoon ground cinnamon
½ Madagascar vanilla bean, seeds
   scraped from pod
¼ teaspoon salt
2 tablespoon fresh lime juice
2 tablespoons butter
3 tablespoons half-and-half
2 tablespoons vanilla sugar

For the Crust: Preheat oven to 400 degrees. Process 1½ cups flour, salt, and sugar in food processor until combined, about two (1-second) pulses. Add butter and shortening and process until homogenous dough just starts to collect in uneven clumps, about 15 seconds (dough will resemble cottage cheese curds and there should be no uncoated flour). Scrape bowl with rubber spatula and redistribution dough evenly around processor blade. Add remaining cup flour and pulse until mixture is evenly distributed around bowl and mass of dough has been broken up, 4 to 6 quick pulses. Empty mixture into medium bowl. Sprinkle cold water over mixture. With rubber spatula, use folding motion to mix, pressing down on dough until dough is slightly tacky and sticks together. Divide dough into two even balls and flatten each into 4-inch disk. Cover each in plastic wrap and refrigerate at least 45 minutes or up to 2 days.

For the Filling: Combine the apple, pear, berries, and jam in a large bowl, stir to combine, pouring over the sugar, then add in the nutmeg, cinnamon, and vanilla beans, salt, lime juice. Stir, and set aside for 10 minutes. Take pie crust out of refrigerator, and roll out one disk to be placed in 9-inch pie pan, fill with apple mixture, and add dollops of butter all around. Roll out second pie disk, cut strips to create lattice top, flute edges to design edge of pie. Bake for 20 minutes. Then reduce heat to 350 degrees and bake an additional 35 minutes, take pie out of oven and brush with half-and-half and sprinkle with vanilla sugar. When putting pie back in oven, rotate 180 degrees, so the part that is facing the back of the oven now faces forward. Bake until steam vents bubble thickly for additional 20 minutes. Loosely tent top and crust of pie if it starts to get too brown. Transfer the pie to a wire rack and let cool before serving.

Apple, Pear & Berries of My Forest Pie

BOUNTIFUL BERRY DELIGHT PIE

David Harper, Lone Rock, WI
2015 APC National Pie Championships
Amateur Division 2nd Place Fruit/Berry

CRUST
1 cup flour
1 teaspoon salt
½ cup butter-flavored Crisco
5 tablespoons water, cold

BERRY JUICE
1 pint fresh/frozen strawberries/
    blueberries/blackberries/raspber-
    ries, a mix is best
2 cups water

BERRY GLAZE
2 cups prepared berry juice
1½ cup sugar
⅓ cup raspberry gelatin
3 heaping tablespoons cornstarch
2–3 tablespoons water
4–6 cups fresh strawberries, blueber-
    ries, blackberries, or raspberries
    (whatever is fresh and in season,
    but try to have three different kinds)

RASPBERRY FILLING
1 cup raspberry purée (2 cups of
    fresh raspberries yields about 1
    cup purée)
1 tablespoon fresh lemon juice
1 envelope plain gelatin
1½ cup heavy cream, whipped stiff

TOPPING
1 cup whipping cream
¼ cup powdered sugar
1½ teaspoons vanilla
fresh berries for garnish

For the Crust: Preheat oven to 375 degrees. Whisk the flour and the salt together in a large bowl. Add the Crisco and mix with your fingers until combined. Add the ice water and use a fork to combine. Turn pie dough out onto a floured surface and gather into a circular disk. Roll out the dough big enough to fit into a pie plate. Flute edges for decoration. Prick the bottom and sides of crust with a fork. Place into the refrigerator for 20 minutes. Bake crust until edges are golden brown and bottom is browned also, about 15 to 20 minutes. Cool on wire rack and set aside.

For the Juice: Combine berries and water in a small pan and cook for about 5 to 8 minutes. Strain the juice through a sieve and mash the berries with a spatula to get all the berry pulp. Discard the seeds.

For the Glaze: Combine the berry juice and sugar and bring to a boil. Boil until sugar dissolves, about 2 to 3 minutes. Add the raspberry gelatin and stir for about 30 seconds. Combine the cornstarch with the water and mix until dissolved. Add cornstarch mixture to the gelatin mixture, stir to combine, and then pour over fresh berries. Set aside to cool for about 30 minutes. Make raspberry filling.

For the Filling: Put raspberry purée in a small saucepan. Combine lemon juice and gelatin to-

Bountiful Berry Delight Pie

gether to soften in a small bowl, about 2 minutes. Heat raspberry purée until very hot but not boiling. Add the gelatin mixture to hot purée and stir until gelatin has dissolved. Remove from heat. Cool until room temperature, about 20 to 25 minutes. While mixture is cooling, whip the 1½ cups of heavy cream until stiff peaks. When raspberry mixture is room temperature, fold in the whipped cream until no white streaks remain. Place ¾ cup raspberry filling on pie crust and smooth out. Place about 2 cups berries on top of this. Cover the berries with the berry glaze. Spoon the raspberry filling again over the glaze layer and smooth the top. Place another 2 cups berries on top and cover with berry glaze. You may have a little of the glaze left over. Place in refrigerator and let cool overnight. Top with whipped cream and fresh berries.

PINKY'S STRAWBERRY-LICIOUS PIE

John Sunvold, Orlando, FL
2015 APC National Pie Championships
Amateur Division 1st Place Fruit/Berry

CRUST
1½ cup graham cracker crumbs
3 tablespoons sugar
6 tablespoons melted butter
1 jar Dolchi hard chocolate shell

FILLING 1
2 tablespoons butter
2 tablespoons corn syrup
2 tablespoons cream
⅓ cup chocolate chips (semisweet)
1 cup powdered sugar

FILLING 2
6 oz. cream cheese, softened
⅓ cup powdered sugar
6 oz. cool whip

TOPPING
1 cup sugar
2 cups strawberries, mashed (frozen work well)
1 cup water
2½ tablespoons cornstarch
1½ pints fresh strawberries

GARNISH
whipped cream

For the Crust: Mix graham cracker crumbs and sugar, add the melted butter, and press into a 9- to 10-inch pie plate. You may not use all of it if you use a shallow pan. Bake 8 to 12 minutes at 350 degrees.

Coat cooled crust with a light layer of Dolci hard chocolate shell. Chill.

For Filling 1: Mix butter, corn syrup, and cream, and heat over medium until boiling. Stir constantly. Add chocolate chips and stir until melted. Once fully combined, slowly add powdered sugar. Mix completely, then carefully spread the chocolate onto the bottom of the crust. It cools quickly, so you must spread immediately. Chill. When chilled, cover this layer with another light layer/drizzle of Dolci hard chocolate shell.

For Filling 2: Mix softened cream cheese with powdered sugar. Fold in Cool Whip and spread on top of the cooled chocolate layer. For extra crunch, apply a thin layer or two of Dolci hard chocolate shell between thin layers of cream cheese layer. Chill.

For the Topping: Place all ingredients in a pot, bring to a boil, and boil for 10 minutes. Stir frequently. Strain and collect the syrup in a bowl. Place cornstarch and 3 tablespoons of the cooled syrup in a bowl. Make a paste. Add drops of syrup until all of the starch is incorporated into the paste. Slowly add another ½ cup of the syrup and stir. Place all of the syrup and the starch into a pot, bring to a bowl, boil for 1 minute or until thick and clear. Remove from heat, let cool, then chill. Coat fresh strawberries in the chilled glaze and arrange on the pie as you like. Strawberries may be sliced, quartered, and/or kept whole.

For the Garnish: Top/decorate with favorite whipped topping. Top with nuts, strawberries, chocolate, syrup, or chocolate-covered strawberry pieces, if desired. Chill for at least 4 hours.

Pinky's Strawberry-Licious Pie

HULA SKIRT PINEAPPLE COLADA DREAM PIE

Naylet LaRochelle, Miami, FL
2015 APC National Pie Championships
Amateur Division 1st Place Fruit/Berry

CRUST

1¾ cups graham crackers, finely
  crushed
¼ cup sugar
7 tablespoons butter, melted
½ cup roasted macadamia nuts,
  chopped

FILLING 1

8 oz. cream cheese, softened
1 tablespoons sugar
1 (8.5-oz.) can cream of coconut
2 eggs
¼ teaspoon rum extract
¼ teaspoon coconut extract

FILLING 2

3½ cups pineapple, chopped
3 tablespoons light brown sugar
½ cup sugar
¼ cup cornstarch
1½ cup milk
¼ cup pineapple juice
¼ teaspoon salt
3 egg yolks
1 tablespoon butter
¼ teaspoon vanilla extract

TOPPING

sweetened whipped cream
½ cup roasted and salted macadamia
  nuts, chopped
½ cup coconut flakes, toasted

For the Crust: Preheat oven to 375 degrees. Lightly spray a 9-inch pie plate with cooking spray. In a large bowl, combine crushed cookie crumbs, sugar, and butter until well combined. Stir in nuts. Press mixture onto bottom and up the sides of pie plate. Bake 8 to 10 minutes. Let cool.

For Filling 1: Preheat oven to 350 degrees. In a large bowl, beat cream cheese and sugar until light and fluffy. Add cream of coconut a little bit at a time, beating between each addition. Add eggs and extracts; beat until well combined and smooth. Pour cream cheese onto pie crust. Bake 30 to 35 minutes or until set.

For Filling 2: Preheat oven to 425 degrees. In a large bowl, toss pineapple and light brown sugar. Spread pineapple onto a rimmed baking sheet lined with nonstick foil. Bake until caramelized and edges begin to brown. Mash lightly. In a medium saucepan, over medium heat, combine sugar, cornstarch, milk, pineapple juice, and salt. Cook 2 to 3 minutes, whisking frequently. Add egg yolks, one at a time, whisking constantly. Continue to cook, whisking, until mixture comes to a boil. Let boil 1 to 2 minutes, whisking constantly. Remove from heat. Add butter and vanilla extract. Set aside ½ cup roasted pineapple for topping; stir in remaining pineapple into custard. Spoon pineapple custard over coconut/cream cheese layer. Press a sheet of plastic wrap directly on the surface. Refrigerate 4 to 5 hours, or until completely set.

For the Topping: Top pie with whipped cream, nuts, coconut flakes, and reserved ½ cup chopped roasted pineapple.

Hula Skirt Pineapple Colada Dream Pie

PEACHES AND CREAM PIE

Evette Rahman, Orlando, FL
2015 APC National Pie Championships Professional Division
1st Place Fruit/Berry

CRUST
2 cup coconut cookie crumbs
2 tablespoons sugar
½ cup unsalted butter, melted

FILLING 1
3 cups peaches, peeled, finely
    chopped, and divided
½ cup sugar
2 tablespoons cornstarch
1 tablespoon water

FILLING 2
8 oz. cream cheese, softened
1 cup powdered sugar
1 tablespoon lemon juice
1 (8-oz.) container frozen whipped
    topping, thawed

GARNISH
sweetened whipped cream
fresh sliced peaches

For the Crust: Preheat oven to 350 degrees. Mix together crust ingredients and press into bottom and sides of deep dish pie plate. Bake for 8 minutes. Cool.

For Filling 1: In saucepan over medium heat, mix 1 cup of peaches, ½ cup sugar, cornstarch, and water. Cook until very thick, stirring constantly. Remove from heat and stir in remaining 2 cups of peaches. Cool in refrigerator.

For Filling 2: Beat together cream cheese, powdered sugar, and lemon juice until smooth. Fold in whipped topping. Spread half of cream filling into pie shell. Spread half of peach mixture on top. Spread the other half of the cream filling on top of peach mixture. Spread remaining peach mixture on top. Chill. Garnish pie with whipped cream and sliced peaches.

Peaches and Cream Pie

RASPBERRY BLUEBERRY CREAM CHEESE PIE

Devin Davis, Plant City, FL
2015 APC National Pie Championships
Professional Division Honorable Mention Fruit/Berry

CRUST
2 cups shortbread cookie crumbs
(about 20 shortbread cookies)
6 or 7 tablespoons* butter, melted
1 tablespoon Crisco shortening,
melted
2 tablespoons flour
1 tablespoon sugar

FILLING 1
1½ cups heavy cream
5 tablespoons powdered sugar
12 oz. cream cheese, softened
½ cup sugar

FILLING 2
12 oz. fresh or frozen blueberries
½ cup sugar
½ teaspoon lemon zest
¼ cup + 2 tablespoon water, divided
2 tablespoon cornstarch

FILLING 3
1 quart fresh raspberries, halved,
divided
½ cup sugar
¼ cup + 2 tablespoons water, divided
¼ teaspoon lemon zest
2 tablespoons cornstarch

*You may need more or less butter depending on the variety or brand of cookies you use. So add it gradually until moistened.

For the Crust: Preheat oven to 350 degrees. Mix all ingredients in a bowl until well combined, pour into 9-inch round pie plate and press up sides and bottom of pie plate till firm, and bake for 10 minutes. Let cool completely.

For Filling 1: Beat heavy cream to soft peaks, stir in powdered sugar, and set aside. In a separate bowl, beat the cream cheese and sugar until smooth and the sugar has dissolved; then fold in the whipped cream. Spread half of this mixture into cooled pie crust and refrigerate until ready to use.

For Filling 2: In a small pot, combine first three ingredients and ¼ cup of water and bring to a boil; cook for 5 minutes or until the blueberries are soft and begin to break down. Using a spoon or fork, mash the blueberries. Return the blueberries to a boil. Whisk together the cornstarch and remaining water in a small bowl and then whisk into the boil-ing blackberry sauce. Cook for 30 more seconds or until thick and let cool completely.

For Filling 3: In a small pot, combine half the raspberries, the sugar, ¼ cup of water, and lemon zest and bring to a boil. Cook for 5 minutes. In a small bowl, whisk together the cornstarch and remaining water and then whisk into the boiling strawberry mixture. Cook for 30 more seconds or until thick and let cool. Once cool, stir in the remaining raspberries and set aside to cool completely. To assemble the pie, spread half the cream cheese mixture into the bottom of the cooled crust and then spread over the blueberry filling and put in the refrigerator until the blueberry filling is set. Then spread over the remaining cream cheese filling and top with the strawberry filling. Refrigerate for 4 hours or over-night and garnish with whipped cream and fresh blueberries and raspberries, if desired.

Raspberry Blueberry Cream Cheese Pie

KAPPA PIE

Dionna Hurt, Longwood, FL
2014 APC National Pie Championships
Professional Division Honorable Menton Fruit/Berry

CRUST
3 cups Nilla Wafer cookies
½ cup butter, melted
2–3 tablespoons sugar

FILLING
2 (8-oz.) packages cream cheese, softened
½ cup sugar + 1 cup sugar
1 tablespoon vanilla extract
12 oz. frozen raspberries
2 pints fresh raspberries
½ cup water
1 envelope unflavored gelatin

For the Crust: Preheat oven to 350 degrees. In food processor, grind cookies into crumbs. Transfer crumbs to mixing bowl. Add melted butter and sugar, toss with fork. Pour into pie dish and press into bottom and up the sides. Bake for 15 minutes, let cool, and fill.

For the filling: In large bowl, whip cream cheese and ½ cup sugar till fluffy. Add vanilla. Set aside. In medium saucepan, place frozen raspberries, 1 cup sugar, ½ cup water, and bring to a simmer. Add unflavored gelatin, let simmer 2 more minutes. Remove from heat. In crust, sprinkle half of the raspberries, then top with cheese mixture. Take cooled raspberry mixture, add remaining raspberries, and stir to combine. Do not break berries. Pour over custard mixture. Chill for at least 2 hours or more.

Garnish with sweetened whipped cream and additional berries.

Kappa Pie

SENSATIONAL STRAWBERRY CHEESE PIE

Evette Rahman, Orlando, FL
2014 APC National Pie Championships
Professional Division Best of Show

CRUST
2 cups coconut cookie crumbs
2 tablespoons sugar
½ cup unsalted butter, melted

FILLING 1
3 cups fresh strawberries, divided
½ cup sugar
2 tablespoons cornstarch
1 tablespoon water

FILLING 2
8 oz. cream cheese, softened
1 cup powdered sugar
½ cup puréed strawberries
1 tablespoon lemon juice
8 oz. container of frozen whipped
    topping, thawed
few drops red food coloring
    (optional)

GARNISH
sweetened whipped cream
fresh strawberries

For the Crust: Preheat oven to 350 degrees. Mix together crust ingredients and press into bottom and sides of deep dish pie plate. Bake for 8 minutes. Cool.

For Filling 1: In saucepan over medium heat, mix 1 cup of strawberries, ½ cup sugar, cornstarch, and water. Cook until very thick, stirring constantly. Remove from heat and stir in remaining 2 cups of strawberries. Cool in refrigerator.

For Filling 2: Beat together cream cheese, powdered sugar, puréed strawberries, and lemon juice, until smooth. Fold in whipped topping and food coloring, if using. Spread half of cheese mixture into pie shell. Spread half of strawberry mixture on top. Repeat with remaining fillings.

For the Garnish: Garnish pie with whipped cream and strawberries.

Sensational Strawberry Pie

STRAWBERRY YIELDS FOREVER PIE

Beth Campbell, Belleville, WI
2015 APC National Pie Championships
Amateur Division 1st Place Duncan Hines Comstock/Wilderness Strawberry

CRUST
14 Oreo cookies
½ cup almonds, ground
4 tablespoons butter, melted

FILLING
½ pound marshmallows
¼ cup whole milk
1 (21-oz.) can Wilderness strawberry
    pie filling
1 teaspoon strawberry extract
½ pint heavy whipping cream,
    whipped until stiff peaks form
1 quart fresh strawberries

For the Crust: In a food processor, combine the cookies and ground almonds; cover and process until the cookies are finely chopped. Add butter; cover and pulse until the mixture resembles coarse crumbs.

Press onto the bottom and up the sides of ungreased 9-inch deep dish pie plate. Bake at 350 degrees for 8 to 10 minutes or until set. Cool on a wire rack.

For the Filling: Put the marshmallows and milk in a double boiler and melt over hot water. Combine 1 can of Wilderness strawberry pie filling and the strawberry extract into the melted marshmallow mixture until combined completely. When completely cooled, fold gently into the whipped cream.

Cut the strawberries in half and line the prebaked pie shell with the halved strawberries. Gently spread the whipped cream/strawberry pie filling mixture over top of the halved strawberries. Garnish with whipped cream, fresh strawberries, and crushed Oreo cookie crumbs. Refrigerate overnight.

Strawberry Yields Forever Pie

SAVANNAH PICNIC PEACH PIE

Naylet LaRochelle, Miami, FL
2015 APC National Pie Championships
Amateur Division 1st Place Comstock/Wilderness Peach

CRUST
1¾ cups honey graham crackers,
   finely crushed
¼ cup sugar
6 tablespoons butter, melted
½ cup roasted macadamia nuts,
   chopped

FILLING
1 (8-oz.) cream cheese
2 tablespoons sugar
1 (14-oz.) can sweetened condensed
   milk

3 egg yolks
1 whole egg
½ teaspoon vanilla bean paste
2 teaspoons lime zest
⅔ cup lime juice*
1 (17-oz.) can grated coconut in
   heavy syrup, drained, divided

TOPPING
1¼ cup heavy whipping cream
¼ cup powdered sugar
roasted macadamia nuts, chopped
lime slices

*Exact amount of lime juice may vary slightly depending on tartness of the
   lime. Taste to adjust.

For the Crust: Preheat oven to 375 degrees. Lightly spray a 9-inch pie plate with cooking spray. In a large bowl, combine ground cookie crumbs, sugar, and butter, until well combined. Stir in nuts. Press mixture onto bottom and up the sides of pie plate. Bake 8 to 10 minutes. Let cool.

For the Filling: In a large bowl, beat cream cheese and sugar until light and fluffy. Slowly add condensed milk; beat until combined. Add egg yolks, egg, vanilla, lime zest, and lime juice; beat until just combined. Stir in ⅓ cup of grated coconut (drained) and 3 tablespoons of heavy syrup. (Reserve remaining grated coconut for later use.) Pour into cooled crust. Bake 30 to 35 minutes or until pie is set. Refrigerate pie 4 to 5 hours or until well set.

Before topping pie with whipped cream, sprinkle remaining grated coconut (well drained) over top of pie to about 1 inch from the edge.

For the Topping: In a large bowl, beat heavy whipping cream until soft peaks form. Add powdered sugar; continue to beat until stiff peaks form. Pipe whipped topping over pie. Top with nuts; garnish with lime slices.

Savanah Picnic Peach Pie

WILDERNESS STRAWBERRY SCHAUM TORTE PIE

Beth Campbell, Belleville, WI
2014 APC National Pie Championships
Amateur Division 1st Place Duncan Hines Comstock/Wilderness Strawberry

CRUST
3 egg whites
¼ teaspoon cream of tartar
1 teaspoon vanilla extract
1 cup sugar

FILLING 1
2 teaspoons strawberry Jell-O
1 (21-oz.) can Wilderness Strawberry
  Pie Filling

FILLING 2
1 cup heavy whipping cream
½ cup powdered sugar
1 (8-oz.) cream cheese, softened
1 teaspoon almond extract
1 tablespoon lemon juice

FILLING 3
1 cup semisweet chocolate chips

TOPPING
1 quart fresh strawberries

For the Crust: In a mixing bowl, beat egg whites and cream of tartar on medium speed until soft peaks form. Add vanilla extract. Gradually beat in sugar, 1 tablesppon at a time, on high until stiff glossy peaks form and sugar is dissolved. Spread onto the bottom and up the sides of a greased 10-inch deep dish pie plate. Bake at 350 degrees for 25 to 30 minutes or until meringue is lightly browned. Cool on a wire rack.

For Filling 1: Stir the strawberry Jell-O into the strawberry pie filling and cook over medium heat until the Jell-O is all dissolved. Cool the Wilderness strawberry filling completely and spread over the cooled meringue crust. Chill in the refrigerator until completely set.

For Filling 2: Beat the heavy whipping cream until soft peaks form. Add the powdered sugar and beat until still peaks form. Add the softened cream cheese, almond extract, and lemon juice. Beat until the cream/cream cheese mixture is smooth and creamy. Take half the mixture and spread over the strawberry filling layer. Refrigerate the pie until set.

For Filling 3: Melt the chocolate chips in the microwave (watching carefully so they don't burn). Cool completely and fold into the remaining half of the cream/cream cheese filling mixture until it is thoroughly mixed. Carefully spread this over the first cream cheese mixture on the pie to form the second layer.

For the Topping: Wash the strawberries and cut them in half. Dry completely and place on top of the chocolate cream cheese layer. You can garnish the strawberries with white chocolate, semisweet chocolate, and sliced almonds, if desired.

SAVANNAH'S LADIES CLUB

John Sunvold, Winter Springs, FL
2014 APC National Pie Championships
Amateur Division 2nd Place Paramount Pictures Peach

CRUST
1¼–1½ cups speculoos cookie
   crumbs
3 tablespoons sugar
5–6 tablespoons butter, melted

FILLING 1
1 (8-oz.) cream cheese
½ cup powdered sugar
8 oz. Cool Whip

FILLING 2
8–12 peaches (fresh, frozen, or
   canned all work)
1⅓ cup brown sugar
½ teaspoon cinnamon
5 tablespoons cornstarch
1 cup water
3 tablespoons butter

For the Crust: Preheat oven to 350 degrees. Mix all ingredients together and press mixture into a deep pie plate. Bake for 8 to 10 minutes. Allow to cool to room temperature.

For Filling 1: Mix softened cream cheese and powdered sugar. Fold in thawed Cool Whip. Spread half of this into the crust and place in the refrigerator.

For Filling 2: Chop half of the peaches in ½–1-inch chunks. The other half of the peaches can be chunks, slices, or halves, depending how you want to decorate the top of your pie.

Mix the brown sugar, cinnamon, and starch into an oven-safe pot. Add the water, butter, and the half of the peaches that were cut into chunks. Top with the rest of the peaches. Place top on the pot and bake in 350-degree oven for 30 minutes, stirring the mixture carefully occasionally. Bake this mixture until the peaches are cooked and soft, yet not breaking apart. Take out of oven and let cool to room temperature. Then, place in the refrigerator. Take the remaining half of Filling 1 and divide in half. Fold half of the smaller peach pieces into it. Spread evenly on top of pie. Take the remaining Filling 1 and spread on top of pie. Arrange as much of the rest of the peaches on top in an attractive manner.

Top with your favorite whipped topping, plus nuts, caramel, or cookie pieces, if desired. Refrigerate 2 hours.

Savannah's Ladies Club Pie

COMSTOCK PEACH RASPBERRY CRUMB-TOPPED PIE

Carol Socier, Bay City, MI
2014 APC National Pie Championships
Amateur Division 1st Place Comstock Peach

CRUST
1½ cups all-purpose flour
¼ teaspoon baking powder
½ teaspoon salt
½ cup + 1 tablespoon shortening
4–5 tablespoon water, cold

FILLING
1 can Comstock Peach Pie Filling
2 tablespoon fresh lemon juice
1 cup red raspberries
½ cup granulated sugar

2 tablespoons quick-cook tapioca
½ teaspoon cinnamon
¼ teaspoon nutmeg

TOPPING
⅔ cup quick oats
¼ cup all-purpose flour
¼ cup slivered almonds
¼ cup packed brown sugar
½ teaspoon cinnamon
3 tablespoons butter

For the Crust: Mix together flour, baking powder, and salt. Cut in shortening until coarse crumbs form. Add cold water 1 tablespoon at a time, tossing with a fork until dough ball forms. Roll out pastry into 11-inch circle on lightly floured surface. Line 9-inch pie plate with pastry. Flute edges. Refrigerate for 15 minutes.

For the Filling: Place peach filling in large bowl. Add lemon juice, stirring well. Fold in raspberries and set aside. Combine sugar, tapioca, and spices in small bowl. Sprinkle over peach mixture. Toss to coat. Spoon evenly into prepared crust.

For the Topping: Combine oats, flour, almonds, brown sugar, and cinnamon in bowl. Cut in butter with a fork until mixture forms coarse crumbs. Sprinkle over filling.

Bake 15 minutes in 400-degree oven. Reduce oven temperature to 350 degrees. Continue baking for 30 minutes or until bubbly. Serve with whipped cream, if desired. Makes 8 tasty servings.

Comstock Peach Raspberry Crumb-Topped Pie

PEACH CRUMB PIE

Devin Davis, Plant City, FL
2014 APC National Pie Championships
Amateur Division 1st Place Peach

CRUST
1⅓ cup flour
½ teaspoon salt
2 tablespoons sugar
4 tablespoons butter, cold, cut into
    cubes
4 tablespoons butter-flavored Crisco,
    cold, cut into cubes
4–5 tablespoons water, cold

FILLING
8 peaches
juice of half a lemon
1⅓ cup sugar

½ cup cornstarch
3 tablespoons instant tapioca
¼ cup peach preserves
½ stick butter, melted
½ teaspoon cinnamon
1 teaspoon vanilla extract

TOPPING
½ cup pecans, chopped
½ cup oats
½ cup Bisquick mix
½ cup brown sugar
½ stick butter, softened

For the Crust: Preheat oven to 425 degrees. Combine flour, salt, and sugar in a small bowl. Add the butter and Crisco to the flour mixture. Toss it to coat each piece in flour. Using a pastry cutter, cut the butter and Crisco into the flour mixture until it is the size of green peas. Using a spoon, carefully stir in the water 1 tablespoon at a time until it is moistened and starts to come together. Form dough into a ball and wrap tightly in plastic wrap. Refrigerate for 30 minutes. Once chilled, roll out the dough on a floured surface to about $\frac{1}{8}$ inch in thickness. Fit the dough into a 9-inch pie plate and trim the excess off the edges. Then crimp the edges and mold into desired fashion. Prick the dough with a fork and set aside.

For the Filling: Peel, pit, and slice the peaches into $\frac{1}{4}$-inch slices and toss with lemon juice. Combine the sugar, cornstarch, and tapioca in a bowl and then toss with the peaches. Whisk together the preserves, butter, cinnamon, and vanilla and mix into the peaches and pour into the prepared crust.

For the Topping: In a small bowl, stir together the first four ingredients and then mix in the butter with your hands until it comes together into a loose dough. Then top the peaches and bake for 10 minutes. Reduce the temperature to 350 degrees and bake for 45 to 55 more minutes. Let cool and serve. If the topping and crust is browning too quickly, lay a piece of tin foil loosely over the pie until finished baking.

PEAR & BLACKBERRY CRUNCH PIE

John Lew, Orlando, FL
2013 APC Crisco National Pie Championships
Amateur Divison 1st Place Fruit/Berry

CRUST
1½ cups all-purpose flour
½ teaspoon salt
½ cup Crisco
5–6 tablespoons water, cold

FILLING
4 cups pear nectar
fresh grated ginger, cut into dime-
 sized coins
¾ cup sugar
¾ stick butter
7 large pears (rock hard fruit is the
 best)

1 teaspoon cinnamon
½ teaspoon nutmeg
zest of 1 lime
2 tablespoons flour
juice of 1 lime
5 tablespoons minute tapioca
6 oz. fresh blackberries

TOPPING
¾ cup flour
3 oz. sugar
3 oz. butter, softened
½ cup almonds, chopped
1 tablespoon vanilla extract

For the Crust: Preheat oven to 350 degrees. In a mixing bowl, combine flour and salt; cut in Crisco until crumbly. Add water 1 tablespoon at a time until dough forms into a ball. Roll out on floured surface to fit a 10-inch pie dish. Set aside.

For the Filling: Pare and dice the pears. Pour nectar into a pan and add ginger. On medium heat, bring to a slow boil. Reduce content until 1 cup is left and liquid is thickening. Add ¼ cup sugar and continue to heat until reduced to ½ cup. Remove from stove, remove ginger pieces and cool. In a pan, heat the butter. Add the diced pears, cinnamon, and nutmeg, and sauté until soft (about 15 minutes). Add ½ cup sugar and

lime zest and continue to cook for a few minutes. Remove from heat. Add flour and lime juice and stir. Remove from heat and allow to cool for 5 minutes. Add reduced nectar and tapioca and stir. Pour two-thirds of pears into prepared pie shell. Add two-thirds of blackberries. Add last one-third of pear and blackberries.

For the Topping: In a mixing bowl, combine flour and sugar; cut in butter until crumbly. Add almonds and toss. Add vanilla and mix. By hand, drop the crumbles on top of the pie. Top pie with crumble mixture. Bake at 350 degrees for 40 to 45 minutes or until bubbles appear.

NUT

CARIBBEAN COCONUT CASHEW PIE

Patricia Lapiezo, LaMesa, CA
2015 APC National Pie Championships
Amateur Division 1st Place Nut

CRUST
4 coconut granola bars, finely ground
10 coconut flavored cookies, finely ground
butter, melted

FILLING
32 Kraft coconut marshmallows
¾ cup vanilla bean or coconut ice cream, softened
1½ cups heavy whipping cream
8 oz. cream cheese, softened
½ cup toasted coconut
½ cup roasted cashews, finely chopped
⅓ cup cashew butter, heated in microwave until it can be drizzled

TOPPING
25 caramels
⅓ cup heavy cream
1 cup roasted and salted cashews, coarsely chopped
4 oz. Lindt chocolate coconut bar, finely chopped
2 tablespoons heavy cream

GARNISH
1 cup heavy whipping cream
2 tablespoon powdered sugar
½ teaspoon coconut extract
toasted coconut

For the Crust: Preheat oven to 350 degrees. Combine enough coconut cookie crumbs with the granola bar crumbs to equal 1½ cups. Add butter until the consistency of wet sand. Press into bottom and up sides of 9-inch pie pan. Bake for 8 minutes. Remove from oven and cool while preparing filling.

For the Filling: In a microwave-safe bowl, combine the marshmallows and softened ice cream. Heat until marshmallows are melted. Cool. Beat the cream cheese until softened. Beat in marshmallow filling. Beat the cream until stiff. Fold into marshmallow filling and fold in toasted coconut and cashews. Spread half in prepared crust and drizzle half of the cashew butter over filling. Run knife through to marble. Repeat.

For the Topping: In a saucepan, heat the cream with the caramels until melted. Stir in ¾ cup cashews and pour over top of pie. Sprinkle with remaining ¼ cup cashews. In microwave, heat the chocolate with the cream. Drizzle over caramel. Chill pie 3 hrs.

For the Garnish: In a large bowl, beat the cream, powdered sugar, and extract until stiff. Pipe decoratively around edge of pie. Sprinkle with toasted coconut just before serving.

Caribbean Coconut Cashew Pie

SWEET AND SALTY VERY NUTTY PIE

Carol Socier, Bay City, MI
2015 APC National Pie Championships
Amateur Division 2nd Place Nut

CRUST
1½ cups all-purpose flour
½ teaspoon salt
½ cup + 1 tablespoon shortening
¼ cup cold water

FILLING
3 large eggs
¾ cup Smucker's simple delight salted caramel topping
½ cup sugar

¼ cup light corn syrup
2 tablespoons butter, melted
1 teaspoon vanilla extract
⅛ teaspoon sea salt
1 (7-oz.) bag Milky Way unwrapped bites
1 (10-oz.) can honey roasted mixed nuts, chopped

For the Crust: In medium bowl, stir together flour and salt. Using a pastry blender, cut in shortening until crumbly. Add water 1 tablespoon at a time, tossing with a fork until dough ball forms. On lightly floured surface, roll to fit 9-inch pie pan. Crimp edges as desired. Set aside.

For the Filling: In a bowl, whisk the eggs, topping, sugar, corn syrup, melted butter, vanilla, and salt. Gently fold in Milky Way bites. Pour into prepared pastry shell. Top with chopped nuts. Cover edges with foil or pie protector. Bake in 400-degree oven for 10 minutes. Reduce oven temperature to 350 degrees and continue baking for 20 to 25 minutes or until filling is almost set. Cool on wire rack to room temperature, then refrigerate until ready to serve. Garnish as desired.

Sweet and Salty Very Nutty Pie

NUTTY HARVEST PIE

Ron Bronitsky, NM
2015 APC National Pie Championships
Amateur Division 3rd Place Nut

CRUST

2½ cups all-purpose unbleached
    flour
1 teaspoon salt
2 tablespoons sugar
12 tablespoons butter, cut into
    ¼-inch pieces
½ cup Crisco, chilled
½ cup water, cold

FILLING

1 cup golden raisins
2 tablespoons bourbon
8 tablespoons unsalted butter, halved
½ cup toasted pecans, cut into
    coarse pieces
½ cup toasted walnuts, cut into
    coarse pieces
½ cup toasted slivered almonds

¾ cup apple, cored and peeled,
    medium diced (jonagold, pink lady,
    or granny smith works best)
½ cup carrots, peeled and shredded
1 cup packed light brown sugar
½ teaspoon salt
¾ cup dark corn syrup
3 large eggs
1 tablespoon vanilla extract
2 tablespoons flour
½ teaspoon cinnamon
¼ teaspoon fresh ground nutmeg
¼ teaspoon ground cloves

For the Crust: Combine dry ingredients in food processor. Cut in the butter using 5 to 6 (1-second) pulses. Add shortening, and using 1-second pulses, blend until pea-sized bits form (about 6 pulses). Empty into large bowl and sprinkle water over ingredients while tossing with a spatula. Using spatula press until dough comes together. Using your hands, form the dough into one large ball (do not overwork the dough). Cut in half and form two 6-inch patties. Cover with plastic wrap and refrigerate at least two hours or overnight. They are now ready to be rolled out for the pies. Blind bake the crust: Preheat oven to 420 degrees. Roll out 1 pie crust into a 9-inch pan, crimp edges. Refrigerate at least 1 hour. Place aluminum foil on crust to cover all of the pie, especially the edges. Add pie weights of your choice. Bake for 20 minutes. Remove weights and foil. Continue to cook until crust turns light brown. Remove from oven and brush the bottom and sides with egg yolk wash (prepared by whisking 1 egg yolk with 1 teaspoon water). Return crust to oven and bake from 1 to 2 more minutes. Inside of pie shell should be shiny. Remove from oven and cool.

For the Filling: Mix the raisins with the bourbon and set aside a few minutes. Over medium heat melt 4 tablespoons of butter in a skillet. Add nuts, raisins, apple and carrots. Stir frequently until apple, and carrots are tender. Remove from heat and cool and set aside.

Nutty Harvest Pie

Place a large mixing bowl over double boiler (or pan of water brought to mild boil). Melt 4 tablespoons of butter in bowl. Add brown sugar and salt, stirring until completely mixed. Add corn syrup and mix thoroughly. Remove from heat. Add eggs, 1 at a time, mixing well after each egg. Add vanilla, then the flour, cinnamon, nutmeg, and cloves. Using a whisk to beat, return the bowl to the water bath. Whisk thoroughly and heat to 130 degrees, using cooking thermometer to gauge temperature. Remove from heat.

Stir in nuts, raisins, apple, and carrots. Pour into prebaked pie shell and bake at 275 degrees until filling barely jiggles when moved. This takes about 1 hour to 1 hour and 15 minutes (you will have to be the judge). Remove and allow to cool completely before serving.

MACADAMIA NUT COCONUT PIE

Devin Davis, Plant City, FL
2015 APC National Pie Championships
Professional Division 1ˢᵗ Place Nut

CRUST
1⅓ cup flour
½ teaspoon salt
2 tablespoons sugar
4 tablespoons butter, cold, cut into cubes
4 tablespoons butter-flavored Crisco, cold, cut into cubes
4–5 tablespoons water, cold

FILLING
½ cup butter
3 large eggs
¾ cup light corn syrup
¼ cup maple syrup
¾ cup sugar
1 teaspoon vanilla extract
¼ teaspoon salt
1¼ cup macadamia nuts, chopped
½ cup coconut flakes

For the Crust: Combine flour, salt, and sugar in a small bowl. Add the butter and Crisco to the flour mixture. Toss it to coat each piece in flour. Using a pastry cutter, cut the butter and Crisco into the flour mixture until it is the size of green peas. Using a spoon, carefully stir in the water 1 tablespoon at a time until it is moistened and starts to come together. Form dough into a ball and wrap tightly in plastic wrap. Refrigerate for 30 minutes. Once chilled, roll out the dough on a floured surface to about ⅛ inch thick. Fit the dough into a 9-inch pie plate and trim the excess off the edges. Then crimp the edges and mold into desired fashion. Prick the dough with a fork and set aside.

For the Filling: Preheat oven to 425 degrees. In a small saucepan, heat the butter over medium-low until it turns golden brown and set aside to cool. In a medium-sized bowl, whisk the eggs until smooth. Add the next five ingredients, cooled butter, and whisk until combined. Stir in the nuts and coconut and pour into the prepared pie crust. Bake for 10 minutes and then reduce heat to 325 degrees. Lay a piece of tin foil over the pie and bake for 30 minutes. After 30 minutes, remove the foil and bake for 15 more minutes. Remove from oven and let cool completely. Serve with whipped cream, if desired.

Macadamia Nut Coconut Pie

CHOCOLATE PECAN PIE

James Gallo, Atlanta, GA
2015 APC National Pie Championships
Professional Division Honorable Mention Nut

CRUST

2½ cups King Arthur Flour
½ teaspoon salt
½ cup unsalted butter, very cold, cut into small cubes
½ cup Crisco all-purpose shortening
½ cup water, cold
1 tablespoon vinegar

FILLING

1½ cups pecan pieces
3 oz. chopped semisweet chocolate
⅓ cup + 2 tablespoons all-purpose flour
1⅓ cups firmly packed light brown sugar
2 cups Karo light corn syrup
8 large eggs
2 (8-oz.) sticks butter, melted and hot

For the Crust: Combine flour and salt in a food processor. Pulse to mix.

Add butter and shortening, pulse until it the butter and shortening are small crumb size. Mix vinegar with water. Add the water, 1 or 2 tablespoons at a time. The dough is ready when it is pinched together and it stays together. Remove the dough from the machine and place on the table. Press it to for thinner layers of the butter and shortening. Shape into round disks and wrap with plastic wrap. Refrigerate for at least 3 hours and up to 2 days. Remove from refrigerator and let sit for about 10 minutes. This will help it soften slightly to make rolling easier. Line pie pans with the dough.

For the Filling: Place the pecans and chocolate in the pie shells. Mix the flour and brown sugar in a mixer with a paddle attachment. Add the corn syrup. Mix well. Scrape the bowl and add the eggs one at a time until each is well combined. Lastly, add the butter in a slow, steady stream. Mix until well combined. Strain through a mesh sieve. Pour the filling over the pecans and chocolate. Bake at 325 degrees for 60 minutes or until done.

NANNY McP'S PECAN PIE

Barbara Polk, Albuquerque, NM
2014 APC National Pie Championships
Amateur Division 3rd Place Nut

CRUST
1½ cups flour + ¼ cup for roll out
½ teaspoon salt
½ cup butter-flavored Crisco
¼ heaping cup pecans, finely
   chopped
¼ cup water, cold (or as needed)

FILLING
½ cup granulated sugar
2 tablespoons butter, melted
2 eggs, lightly beaten
2 tablespoons flour
½ teaspoon salt
1 teaspoon almond extract
1 cup dark Karo syrup
1 cup pecans, chopped
2 whole pecans for decoration

For the Crust: Combine flour, salt, and Crisco. Cut in Crisco with pastry cutter until crumbly. Slowly add cold water and ground nuts, fluffing with a fork until all is moist. Form into a ball, roll out on floured surface larger than 8-inch pie plate. Place in pie plate, trim edges next to rim with 1½-inch over hang, fold under, and flute edges.

For the Filling: Add all filling ingredients and mix until well blended. Pour into crust, place whole pecans in center for decoration, bake for 30 to 35 minutes at 400 degrees. Let cool before cutting.

NUT   255

CREAMY DELUXE CARAMEL PECAN PIE

Patricia Lapiezo, LaMesa, CA
2014 APC National Pie Championships
Amateur Division 1st Place Nut

CRUST
1¼ cups all-purpose flour
¼ cup powdered sugar
¼ cup + 2 tablespoons pecans, finely
  chopped
⅛ teaspoon salt
½ cup Crisco butter shortening
3 tablespoons water, cold

FILLING
2 (8-oz.) packages cream cheese
¼ teaspoon pecan praline flavoring
¼ cup granulated sugar

¼ cup light brown sugar
1¼ cups heavy whipping cream,
  stiffly beaten
½ cup caramel topping
¾ cup candied pecans, chopped

TOPPING
½ cup chocolate caramel topping
1 cup candied pecans, coarsely
  chopped
¼ cup caramel topping
sweetened whipped cream

For the Crust: Combine flour, powdered sugar, finely chopped pecans, and ⅛ teaspoon salt; cut in shortening until flour is blended to form pea-sized chunks. Sprinkle mixture with water, 1 tablespoon at a time. Toss lightly with fork until dough forms a ball. Form a disc. Roll and press crust into a 9-inch pie plate. Bake in a preheated 375-degree oven until lightly browned. Set aside to cool while preparing filling.

For the Filling: In a large bowl, beat the cream cheese until creamy. Beat in flavoring and sugars. Fold in whipped cream. Spread half into pre-pared crust. Combine the caramel topping and chopped candied pecans. Drizzle over filling and swirl with a knife. Spread the remaining filling over this, smoothing the top.

For the Topping: Heat the chocolate caramel just until spreadable. Spread over top of pie. Top with chopped pecans and then drizzle with caramel topping. Pipe a border of sweetened whipped cream around edge of pie. Refrigerate 2 hours or until set.

Creamy Deluxe Caramel Pecan Pie

CROWNED ROYAL PECAN

Kathryn Hanson, Orlando, FL
2014 APC National Pie Championships
Professional Division 1st Place Nut

CRUST

1¼ cups all-purpose flour
½ teaspoon salt
⅓ cup Crisco shortening, cold
3–5 tablespoons water, cold

FILLING

4 eggs
½ cup dark Karo corn syrup
½ cup light Karo corn syrup
⅓ cup butter
⅔ cup sugar
½ teaspoon vanilla extract
3 tablespoons Crown Royal
1½ cups pecan halves

For the Crust: In medium bowl, combine flour and salt. Using pastry blender, cut in the Crisco until particles are size of small peas. Sprinkle flour mixture with water, 1 tablespoon at a time, with a fork. Add water until dough is just moist enough to hold together.

For the Filling: In a large mixing bowl, lightly beat the eggs until they are slightly frothy. Stir in both of the corn syrups, butter, sugar, and vanilla. Mix well and add the Crown Royal and the pecan halves. Pour filling into a prepared unbaked pie shell, cover the edge of crust with foil or edge cover. Preheat the oven to 350 degrees. Bake the pie for 25 minutes and remove the foil or edge cover. Continue to bake for 20 to 25 minutes, or until a knife is inserted close to the center comes out clean. Cool the pie completely and refrigerate until ready to serve.

Crowned Royal Pecan Pie

REACHING HIGH CHOCOLATE PECAN PIE

Susan Boyle, DeBary, FL
2014 APC National Pie Championships
Professional Division Honorable Mention Nut

CRUST
1 cup Crisco shortening, cold
¼ teaspoon salt
2½ cups all-purpose flour
1 egg
1 tablespoon white distilled vinegar
¼ cup water, cold

FILLING
4 large eggs
¼ cup butter, melted
1 cup white corn syrup
⅓ cup sugar
1 teaspoon vanilla bean paste
1⅔ cups pecan halves (reserve 16 pecan halves for garnish)
1 cup semisweet chocolate chips (reserve 3 tablespoons of chips)

For the Crust: Preheat oven to 325 degrees. Mix together Crisco, salt, and flour, until it resembles corn meal. In another bowl, mix together egg, water, and vinegar; add to flour mixture all at once. Toss with fork until mixture forms a ball. Knead and pat into a disk and refrigerate until ready to use. Roll out pastry and place in prepared pie pan. Chill before filling.

For the Filling: In a large bowl, mix eggs, melted butter, corn syrup, sugar, vanilla bean paste, and hand whip with a whisk until frothy. Add pecans and chocolate chips and fold into mixture. Pour and spread evenly into prepared crust. Bake at 325 degrees for 60 to 70 minutes. Cool completely before cutting.

For the Garnish: Bake 16 half pecans for 2 to 5 minutes to just toast to light brown. Cool and melt the 3 tablespoons of reserved chocolate chips in microwave. When pecans are cool, dip half of pecan in melted chocolate, place on parchment to dry. Use to garnish top of pie.

Reaching High Chocolate Pecan Pie

HONEY BOO BOO PRALINE MUD PIE

Phyllis Szymanek, Toledo, OH
2013 APC Crisco National Pie Championships
Amateur Division 2nd Place Nut

CRUST
1½ cups Pillsbury all-purpose flour
½ teaspoon salt
1 tablespoon sugar
½ cups Crisco shortening, chilled
3 tablespoons butter, chilled
1 teaspoon vinegar
3–4 tablespoons water, cold
1 egg + 1 teaspoon water (egg wash)

FILLING
½ cup packed brown sugar
¼ cup Pillsbury all-purpose flour
¼ cup butter, melted
1 teaspoon vanilla
3 eggs, slightly beaten

1 (12-oz.) bag semisweet chocolate
   chips, melted
1 cup pecans, chopped

TOPPING
4 oz. cream cheese (not softened)
1 cup powdered sugar
1 teaspoon vanilla
3 teaspoon caramel topping
1½ cup whipped topping

GARNISH
2 tablespoons butter
2 tablespoons brown sugar
1 cup chopped pecans

For the Crust: In a mixing bowl, combine flour, salt, and sugar. Cut in shortening and butter until crumbly. Add vinegar to ice water. Add vinegar/ice water mixture 1 tablespoon at a time until dough forms into a ball. Shape dough into a disc shape, wrap in plastic, and chill for 1 hour. Roll out on floured surface to fit a 9-inch pie dish. Trim crust and flute edges.

For the Filling: In a large bowl, stir brown sugar, flour, butter, and vanilla; add eggs and mix until well blended. Stir in melted chocolate and pecans. Pour into pie shell and bake at 375 degrees for 25 to 30 minutes or until filling is set. Cool on wire rack.

For the Topping: Beat cream cheese, add sugar and vanilla. Beat until combined, add caramel. Fold in whipped topping. Spread a thin layer over pie. Pipe mixture around edge of pie.

For the Garnish: In a small skillet, melt butter and sugar over medium heat. Add pecans. Cook for about 3 minutes, remove from heat. Let dry. Place pralines in center of pie and around edge to garnish.

Honey Boo Boo Praline Mud Pie

MAPLE NUT GOODIE PIE

Judy Sunvold, Chicago IL
2013 APC National Pie Championships
Amateur Division 3rd Place Nut

CRUST
1½ cup maple cookies, crushed
¼–½ cup sugar (depending on
   sweetness of cookie)
4 tablespoons butter, melted

FILLING 1
1 cup chocolate chips, melted
8 oz. cream cheese
2 tablespoons cocoa
2 tablespoons sugar
2 tablespoons corn syrup
¾ cup chunky peanut butter

FILLING 2
½ cup caramel sauce
1 tablespoon maple extract
¾ cup salted peanuts, whole or
   slightly chopped

For the Crust: In a medium bowl, mix cookies, sugar, and butter. When fully incorporated, press into a greased 9- to 9½-inch pie plate and bake 6 to 8 minutes in a 350 degree oven or until golden in color. Cool. (Note: Depending on depth of pie pan, you could have a little extra.)

For Filling 1: In microwave-safe dish, melt chocolate chips. Add cream cheese to melted chips and blend. Add cocoa, sugar, and corn syrup. When fully incorporated, add peanut butter. Press mixture evenly into crust, coming up the sides slightly.

For Filling 2: Mix together all ingredients and spread over Filling 1.

For the Garnish: Top with your favorite whipped topping. Garnish and decorate as desired.

Maple Nut Goodie Pie

IT'S NOT CRAZY, IT'S NUTS! PIE

Susan Boyle, Debary, FL
2013 APC Crisco National Pie Championships
Professional Division Honorable Mention Nut

CRUST

1 cup cold Crisco, original or
    butter-flavored
¼ teaspoon salt
2½ cups all-purpose flour
1 egg
1 tablespoon white distilled vinegar
¼ cup water, cold

FILLING 1

3 eggs
¼ cup light brown sugar
¼ cup sugar
2 teaspoons pumpkin pie spice
½ cup pumpkin
¼ teaspoon salt
⅔ cup of half-and-half

FILLING 2

3 eggs
½ cup dark corn syrup
3 tablespoon light brown sugar
1 teaspoon molasses
½ teaspoon salt
1½ teaspoons vanilla bean paste
1 tablespoon flour
¾ cup pecans, chopped
¼ cups pecan halves

For the Crust: Mix together Crisco, salt, and flour, until it resembles coarse crumbs. Mix together in another bowl egg, vinegar, and water. Whisk and add all at once to flour mixture. Toss with fork until mixture forms a ball. Knead and pat into a disk, refrigerate until ready to use. Roll out pastry and crimp edges. Chill before filling.

For Filling 1: Mix together ingredients. Fill pie shell with Filling 1. Bake at 425 degrees for 12 minutes; reduce heat to 350 degrees and continue baking for 15 minutes.

For Filling 2: Whip eggs. Add corn syrup, brown sugar, molasses, salt, vanilla bean paste, and flour. Mix well and pour over first filling. Place nuts decoratively on top. Bake at 350 degrees for an additional 35 to 40 minutes.

It's Not Crazy, It's Nuts! Pie

CHOCOLATE CARAMEL PECAN PIE

Patricia Smith, Deltona, FL
2015 APC National Pie Championships
Amateur Division 3rd Place Innovation

CRUST
1 egg
¼ cup water, cold
1 tablespoon white vinegar
¼ cup coffee
2½ cups flour
¾ cup Crisco

FILLING 1
½ cup ice cream caramel
⅓ cup toasted pecans

¼ cup chocolate chips
¼ cup toffee bits

FILLING 2
1⅓ cup dark Karo
⅓ cup sugar
1 tablespoon vanilla bean paste
4 eggs
1½ cup toasted pecans
2 tablespoons clear
¼ cup Lindt milk chocolate, chopped

For the Crust: Whip egg in water, vinegar, and coffee. Add to flour, mix well. Add Crisco, knead and roll into ball, and chill before rolling out. Roll out, place in pan, and flute edges. Chill before filling.

For Filling 1: Mix together by hand and spoon into chilled crust. Set back in refrigerator until Filling 2 is ready.

For Filling 2: Mix well and pour into crust on top of first filling. Bake in preheated oven at 360 degrees for 50 minutes. Cool several hours before slicing

PEANUT BUTTER

PEANUT BUTTER PARFAIT PIE

Patricia Lapiezo, LaMesa, CA
2014 APC National Pie Championships
Amateur Division 1st Place Peanut Butter

CRUST
12 Nutter Butter cookies
4 peanut butter granola bars
⅓ cup butter, melted

FILLING
1 (8-oz.) package cream cheese,
  softened
⅓ cup light Karo syrup
1 cup peanut butter chips, melted
½ cup creamy peanut butter

1¼ cups heavy whipping cream,
  stiffly beaten
chocolate-covered peanut brittle,
  chopped
caramel topping
3 cups whipped cream sweetened
  with 2 tablespoons powdered
  sugar

For the Crust: In a food processor, process cookies and granola bars until finely ground. Stir in butter until blended. Press crumbs into bottom and sides of a 9-inch pie dish. Bake in a preheated 350-degree oven for 8 minutes. Remove and cool completely.

For the Filling: Beat the cream cheese and Karo together until well blended. Blend in melted chips and peanut butter. Fold in whipped cream. Spread one-half in prepared crust. Top with 1 cup whipped cream, chopped peanut brittle, and caramel drizzle. Repeat. Use remaining whipped cream to decoratively pipe a border on the pie.

Peanut Butter Parfait Pie

CHICK-O-STICK PIE

Judy Sunvold, Chicago, IL
2014 APC National Pie Championships
Amateur Division 2nd Place Peanut Butter

CRUST
1¼ cup crushed graham crackers
¼ cup sugar
¼ cup toasted coconut
5 tablespoons butter, melted

FILLING
1 (12-oz.) can evaporated milk
2 large egg yolks
1–1½ tablespoons cornstarch
    (optional)
2 cup Reese's peanut butter chips

TOPPING
1 cup peanuts, chopped, and/or 1 cup
    chunky peanut butter

For the Crust: Preheat oven to 350 degrees. Mix in a medium bowl crackers, sugar, coconut, and butter. When fully incorporated, press into pan and bake 6 to 8 minutes or until golden in color. Cool. (Note: Depending on depth of pie pan, you could have a little extra.)

For the Filling: Whisk together milk and egg in medium saucepan. (If using cornstarch, start by mixing a little milk and cornstarch, so that it doesn't have any lumps. You may have to add a little more milk to get it fully incorporated. When ready, add it to the rest of the milk and egg in saucepan.)

Heat over medium-low heat, stirring constantly until mixture is very hot and thickens; do not boil. Remove from heat and stir in chips and continue stirring until chips are melted. Pour into pie crust. Place plastic wrap on top of surface tightly, and chill for 3 hours or until set. Spread peanuts and/or peanut butter on cooled filling. Top with your favorite whipped topping. Garnish and decorate as desired.

Chick-o-Stick Pie

IT PUTS THE GLEAM IN RUTHIE'S EYE PIE

Janet Ropp, Edgewater, FL
2014 APC National Pie Championships
Amateur Division 3rd Place Peanut Butter

CRUST
2¼ cups chocolate graham cracker crumbs
10 tablespoons unsalted butter, melted
3 tablespoons sugar
2 tablespoons chocolate extract
2 tablespoons all-purpose flour
½ tablespoons vanilla extract
3 tablespoons powdered peanut butter

FILLING 1
¾ cup heavy whipping cream
1½ cup + 1 tablespoon confectioners' sugar, divided
5 tablespoons powdered peanut butter, divided
8 oz. mascarpone cheese, softened
4 oz. cream cheese, softened
¾ cup white chocolate peanut butter
2 oz. white chocolate, finely chopped

FILLING 2
¾ cup heavy whipping cream
1½ cup + 1 tablespoon confectioners' sugar, divided
5 tablespoons powdered peanut butter, divided
8 oz. mascarpone cheese, softened
4 oz. cream cheese, softened
¾ cup chocolate peanut butter
½ teaspoon chocolate extract
2 ounces semisweet chocolate, finely chopped

TOPPING
2 cups heavy whipping cream
6 tablespoons confectioners' sugar
6 tablespoons powdered peanut butter

For the Crust: Preheat oven to 350 degrees. Combine all the crust ingredients and press into 9½-inch glass pie plate. Bake at 350 degrees for 13 minutes. Remove from oven and cool completely on wire rack.

For Filling 1: In a cold bowl, heat whipping cream till soft peaks form. Add 1 tablespoon confectioners' sugar and 2 tablespoons powdered peanut butter; beat well. Refrigerate. Beat together mascarpone cheese and cream cheese till well blended. Add 1½ cup confectioners' sugar and 3 tablespoons powdered peanut butter and beat till combined. Add white chocolate peanut butter and chopped white chocolate and mix to blend. Beat in whipped cream mixture. Spoon into cooled pie crust. Refrigerate.

For Filling 2: In a cold bowl, beat whipping cream till soft peaks form. Add 1 tablespoon confectioners' sugar and 2 tablespoons powdered peanut butter; beat till combined. Refrigerate. Beat together mascarpone and cream cheese. Add 1½ cup confectioners' sugar and 3 tablespoons powdered peanut butter and mix well. Add chocolate peanut butter, chocolate extract, and chopped semisweet chocolate and beat till blended. Add whipped cream mixture and mix till combined. Spoon on top of white chocolate layer. Refrigerate.

For the Topping: In a cold bowl, beat whipping cream till soft peaks form. Add confectioners' sugar and powdered peanut butter and beat till well blended. Spoon onto pie. Garnish with white and semisweet chocolate, if desired. Refrigerate; serve cold.

It Puts the Gleam in Ruthie's Eye Pie

FIVE-LAYER PEANUT BUTTER SURPRISE PIE

Lisa Sparks, Atlanta, IN
2014 APC National Pie Championships
Professional Division 1st Place Peanut Butter

CRUST

9 Nutter Butter cookies, finely crushed
9 Oreo cookies, finely crushed
3 tablespoons sugar
⅓ cup butter/margarine
½ cup Hershey's chocolate syrup

FILLING 1

1½ cup sugar
½ cup milk
½ stick salted butter
7 oz. marshmallow cream
7 oz. crunchy peanut butter

FILLING 2

8 oz. cream cheese
1 cup powdered sugar
½ cup peanut butter (use crunchy for more texture)
1 cup heavy cream

FILLING 3

1½ cups Reese's peanut butter chips
18 marshmallows
½ cup milk
½ can sweetened milk
1 cup whipping cream

For the Crust: Combine all ingredients well. Press into pie plate and bake for 5 minutes in 350-degree oven. Place on rack to cool completely. Spread a thin layer of Hershey's chocolate syrup over bottom and sides of crust. Cool.

For Filling 1: Bring first three ingredients to a boil and boil for 5 minutes, stirring constantly. Remove from heat and stir in marshmallow cream and peanut butter. Cool.

For Filling 2: Blend all ingredients, except heavy cream, completely. Whip cream and fold into peanut butter mixture. Pour approximately half of first 1 over chocolate syrup. Reserve the rest for garnish. Pour over Filling 1.

For Filling 3: Place all ingredients in double boiler, except whipping cream, and melt over medium heat until marshmallows are melted. Cool completely. Whip cream and fold into peanut butter mixture. Pour over Filling 2.

Garnish with whipped heavy cream, chocolate sauce, and bits of fudge.

Five-Layer Peanut Butter Surprise Pie

POSITIVELY PERFECT PEANUT BUTTER PIE

Dionna Hurt, Longwood, FL
2014 APC National Pie Championships
Professional Division Honorable Mention Peanut Butter

CRUST
12 peanut butter sandwich creme
    cookies
¼ cup granulated sugar
6 tablespoons butter, melted

FILLING
8 oz. cream cheese
small jar marshmallow fluff
1 cup peanut butter
2 cups whipped cream
½ cup chocolate hazelnut spread
¼ cup honey roasted peanuts,
    chopped

For the Crust: Process the peanut butter sandwich creme cookies in a food processor until fine crumbs are formed. Add in sugar and melted butter and process until blended. The mixture will resemble wet sand. Press mixture into a 9-inch pie plate that has been sprayed with nonstick cooking spray

For the Filling: Blend cream cheese, marshmallow cream, and peanut butter with an electric mixer until smooth. Add in the whipped cream and mix with the mixer until blended. Place half of filling in the crust. Spread chocolate spread over filling and sprinkle with chopped honey roasted peanuts. Spread the remaining filling over chocolate spread and nuts. Garnish with additional chopped nuts and whipped cream.

Positively Perfect Peanut Butter Pie

PEANUT BUTTER EXTRAVAGANZA PIE

Christopher Taylor, Atlanta, GA
2015 APC National Pie Championships
Amateur Division 1st Place Peanut Butter

CRUST

1½ cup all-purpose flour
1¼ teaspoon sugar
½ teaspoon salt
⅛ teaspoon baking powder
8 tablespoons unsalted butter, cold,
    in 8 pieces
4 tablespoons vegetable shortening, cold
1 teaspoon cider vinegar
¼ cup water, cold

PEANUT BUTTER CREAM TRUFFLES

½ cup creamy peanut butter
1 cup powdered sugar, sifted
2 tablespoons butter, melted

CHOCOLATE PEANUT BUTTER GANACHE

5 oz. bittersweet chocolate, coarsely
    chopped
¼ cup creamy peanut butter
½ cup heavy cream
½ teaspoon vanilla extract

FILLING

6 oz. cream cheese, softened
3 tablespoons light brown sugar
¼ teaspoon salt
¾ teaspoon vanilla extract
¾ cup creamy peanut butter
1 cup heavy cream
8 fun-size Reese's Peanut Butter
    Cups, chopped

PEANUT BUTTER MOUSSE
6 oz. cream cheese, softened
¾ cup powdered sugar
pinch salt
¾ cup creamy peanut butter
¾ cup + 2 tablespoons heavy cream,
    divided

TOPPING
⅓ cup honey roasted peanuts,
    coarsely chopped
1½ oz. dark chocolate, melted
1 cup heavy cream
2 tablespoons piping gel
2 tablespoons powdered sugar

For the Crust: Preheat oven to 425 degrees. Mix flour, sugar, salt, and baking powder in the bowl of a food processor. Pulse in the butter until the pieces are the size of large beans. Pulse in the shortening until mixture resembles coarse, wet sand and there are no pieces larger than peas. Add the vinegar to the water. Pulse in the water mixture until incorporated but before a dough ball forms. Remove the dough from the processor and pat into a 4-inch disc on a sheet of plastic wrap. Wrap tightly and refrigerate for at least 3 hours.

Roll the pie dough out to a circle large enough to fill a 9½-inch deep dish pie pan. Line the pan with the rolled crust and crimp the edges as desired. Freeze for 30 minutes. Line the dough with parchment paper and pie weights. Bake for 18 minutes. After 18 minutes of baking, remove the weights and parchment. Continue baking until the crust is golden brown, 5 to 10 minutes more. Allow the crust to cool completely.

For the Truffles: Stir together the peanut butter and powdered sugar until smooth. Stir in melted butter. Scoop into 1½ teaspoon portions. Roll into balls and refrigerate.

For the Ganache: Place chopped chocolate and peanut butter in a medium bowl. Bring the heavy cream to a simmer. Pour the cream over the chocolate and stir to combine.

When chocolate is completely melted and mixture is smooth, stir in the vanilla extract. Reserve ¼ cup and set aside. Spread 3 tablespoons into the bottom of the prepared crust.

Evenly distribute the peanut butter truffles across the bottom of the pie.

Pour the remaining ganache (but NOT the reserved ganache) over the truffles, trying to cover the tops of each truffle ball. Refrigerate while preparing the filling.

For the Filling: In a large bowl, beat the cream cheese until smooth. Beat in the brown sugar, salt, vanilla extract, and peanut butter.
In a separate bowl, beat the heavy cream to stiff peaks. Fold the whipped cream into the peanut butter mixture. Spread mixture evenly in the pie pan.

Pour the remaining ¼ cup reserved ganache over top of the smoothed filling. Sprinkle the chopped peanut butter cups evenly over the top. Refrigerate while preparing the Peanut Butter Mousse.

For the Mousse: In a large bowl, beat the cream cheese until smooth. Beat in the powdered sugar, salt, peanut butter, and 3 tablespoons of heavy cream on low speed until combined. Increase speed to medium-high and whip until fluffy, about 1 minute.

Whip the remaining heavy cream to stiff peaks. Fold into the peanut butter mixture. Spread in an even layer over the chopped peanut butter cups.

For the Topping: Sprinkle the chopped peanuts evenly over the top of the pie. Drizzle the melted chocolate over the top of the pie. Whip the cream to soft peaks. Beat in the piping gel and powdered sugar. Continue to beat to stiff peaks. Pipe decoratively over the top of the pie, as desired.

Peanut Butter Extravaganza Pie

PEANUT BUTTER SATIN PIE

Evette Rahman, Orlando, FL
2015 APC National Pie Championships
Professional Division 1st Place Peanut Butter and Best of Show

CRUST
1½ cups peanut butter cookies,
   ground
2 tablespoons sugar
6 tablespoons unsalted butter, melted

FILLING
8 oz. cream cheese, softened
1 cup powdered sugar
½ cup creamy peanut butter
2 teaspoon vanilla extract
⅛ teaspoon salt
1 (8-oz.) container frozen whipped
   topping, thawed

TOPPING
sweetened whipped cream
peanut butter cups, chopped

For the Crust: Preheat oven to 350 degrees. Mix crust ingredients together.

Peanut Butter Satin Pie

Press in a deep dish pie plate and bake 8 minutes. Cool completely.

For the Filling: Beat together filling ingredients together until smooth. Spread in pie crust.

For the Topping: Garnish with whipped cream and chopped peanut butter cups.

PIPER'S FIVE-STAR PEANUT BUTTER PIE

John Sunvold, Orlando, FL
2015 APC National Pie Championships
Amateur Division 2nd Place Peanut Butter

CRUST
26 Oreos sandwich cookies
5 tablespoons butter
30 caramels
¼ cup milk
½ cup cocktail peanuts, chopped

FILLING 1
1 cup creamy or crunchy peanut butter
8 oz. cream cheese
1¼ cups powdered sugar

1 teaspoon vanilla extract
10 oz. Cool Whip

FILLING 2
3 oz. bittersweet or unsweetened
   chocolate
1⅛ cup fine sugar
¾ cup butter
1 teaspoon vanilla
3 pasteurized eggs

For the Crust: Preheat oven to 375 degrees. Place whole cookies in food processor and pulse until cookies resemble wet sand. Melt butter and pour over cookie crumbs and mix until butter is evenly distributed. Press crumbs evenly into pie pan. Bake crust for 10 minutes. Let cool. Melt caramels with milk. Add chopped cocktail peanuts. Spread into the bottom of the pie crust and cool.

For Filling 1: Beat peanut butter, cream cheese, sugar, and vanilla until smooth. Fold in the Cool Whip. Spread on crust.

For Filling 2: Melt chocolate and set aside to cool. Place sugar in food processor and make the sugar powdery. In a mixer, cream the butter and sugar. Add the cooled chocolate and vanilla, and beat with a mixer for 2 minutes. Add an egg and beat for 5 minutes. Scrape the bowl. Add another egg and beat for 5 minutes. Scrape the bowl. Add the last egg and beat for 5 minutes. Scrape the bowl and beat for 1 more minute. Spread on the pie, cover, and place in the refrigerator for two hours. Top with favorite whipped topping and/or some peanut butter mix. Garnish with caramel topping, Oreo crumbs, chocolate, chocolate/peanut or peanut butter candies, and/or nuts, as desired.

Piper's Five-Star Peanut Butter Pie

PROCEED WITH CAUTION PEANUT BUTTER PIE

Naylet LaRochelle, Miami, FL
2015 APC National Pie Championships
Amateur Division 3rd Place Peanut Butter

CRUST
2¼ cups peanut butter sandwich
    cookies, finely crushed
5 tablespoons butter, melted

FILLING
1⅛ cups milk chocolate chips
½ cup heavy cream whipped,
    whipped
½ cup salted caramel sundae topping
1¼ cup chopped mini chocolate-
    peanut butter candies (e.g., mini
    Reese's)
1 (8-oz.) cream cheese

1¾ cup powdered sugar
1 cup creamy peanut butter
2 tablespoons cream or milk
1 teaspoon vanilla extract
½ cup heavy whipping cream,
    whipped

TOPPING:
sweetened whipped cream
salted caramel sauce
honey roasted peanuts, chopped
peanut butter chocolate candy,
    chopped

For the Crust: Preheat oven to 350 degrees. Lightly spray a 9-inch pie plate with cooking spray. In a large bowl, combine ground cookie crumbs and butter until well combined. Press mixture onto bottom and up the sides of pie plate. Bake 8 to 10 minutes or until lightly toasted. Let cool.

For the Filling: In a microwavable bowl, add chocolate. Microwave until smooth. Let cool slightly. Fold in ½ cup cream, whipped. Spread onto bottom of crumb crust. Refrigerate about 1 hour or until set. Carefully spread caramel over top of chocolate layer. Top with chocolate-peanut butter candy. Return to refrigerator. In a large bowl, beat cream cheese until light and fluffy. Add powdered sugar; beat until combined. Add peanut butter, cream, and vanilla; beat until combined. Fold in ½ cup whipped cream. Carefully spread peanut butter mixture over top of chocolate-peanut butter candies. Refrigerate until completely set, about 3 to 4 hours.

For the Topping: Spread whipped cream over top of pie. Drizzle salted caramel sauce over whipped cream; swirl gently with a knife. Sprinkle with peanuts and candy.

Proceed with Caution Peanut Butter Pie

SAVANNAH DAYDREAMIN' PIE

Janet Ropp, Edgewater, FL
2012 APC Crisco National Pie Championships
Amateur Division 1st Place Peanut Butter

CRUST
¾ cup graham cracker crumbs
1½ cups gingersnap cookie crumbs
2 teaspoon cinnamon
1 tablespoon all-purpose flour
pinch salt
¼ teaspoon mace
½ cup butter, melted

FILLING
½ cup quick-cooking grits (not instant grits)
2 cups half-and-half
1 cup heavy cream
2½ cups + 3 tablespoons confectioners' sugar, divided

4 (3-oz.) packages cream cheese, softened
2 tablespoons butter, softened
6 tablespoons powdered peanut butter (PB2)
1½ cups crunchy peanut butter
pinch salt
½ teaspoon vanilla

TOPPING
3 cups heavy cream
9 tablespoons confectioners' sugar
6 tablespoons powdered peanut butter (PB2)

For the Crust: In a bowl, combine all dry ingredients. Add butter and blend well using a fork. Press crumb mixture into 9½-inch glass pie plate. Bake 12 minutes at 350 degrees. Place on wire rack to cool. Cool completely before filling.

For the Filling: Cook grits in half-and-half according to package directions. Measure out 1½ cup cooked grits to cool, then set aside. In a chilled bowl, beat whipping cream until soft peaks start to form. Add 3 tablespoons confectioners' sugar and beat until well blended. Set aside. In a medium mixing bowl, beat together cream cheese and butter until well blended. Add confectioners' sugar and powdered peanut butter and beat until smooth. Add grits and peanut butter, mixing well. Stir in whipped cream and mix until smooth. Add salt and vanilla. Mix well. Pour into prepared crust. Chill while preparing topping.

For the Topping: In a chilled bowl, beat cream until soft peaks form. Add sugar and continue to beat until well blended. Add powdered peanut butter and beat until well blended. Spread on top of chilled pie. Garnish with drizzle of caramel topping or peanut butter topping (made with powdered peanut butter and water).

PEANUT BUTTER CUP PIE

Rick Johnson, Belleville, IL
2012 APC Crisco National Pie Championships
Amateur Division 2nd Place Peanut Butter

CRUST
16 oz. semisweet chocolate
1½ cups cream
8 tablespoons butter + more for coating pan

FILLING
¾ cup cream
1 cup cream cheese
2 cups creamy peanut butter
¾ cup sugar
1½ teaspoons vanilla
3 tablespoons cream

For the Crust: Coat tart pan with butter and freeze. Microwave chocolate and cream until melted, then add butter, and stir until creamy. Pour approximately half the chocolate mixture into pan and coat the bottom and the sides, then freeze while preparing the filling. Reserve the remaining chocolate mixture to pour on top of filling.

For the Filling: Whip ¾ cup cream and set aside. Combine the rest of the ingredients and blend until creamy. Fold in the reserved whipped cream and fill pie shell. Refrigerate for at least several hours, then reheat leftover chocolate mixture and pour over top of pie. Freeze for 1 hour, then refrigerate. If desired, cut out portion of the pie to resemble bite mark.

Peanut Butter Cup Pie

PUMPKIN

PUMPKIN AND MAPLE CROWN PIE

Andy Hilton, Davenport, FL
2015 APC National Pie Championships
Professional Division 1st Place Pumpkin

CRUST
1¼ cups all-purpose flour
¼ cup butter
¼ cup shortening
½ tablespoon sugar
¼ teaspoon baking powder
4–5 tablespoons water, cold

FILLING 1
1¼ cup heavy whipping cream
4½ oz. white chocolate chips
1½ (8-oz.) packages cream cheese
½ cup sugar
⅛ cup maple syrup

FILLING 2
⅓ cup granulated sugar
½ teaspoon ground cinnamon
¼ teaspoon salt
¼ teaspoon ground ginger
⅛ teaspoon ground cloves
1 large egg
7.5 oz. canned pumpkin
7 oz. canned sweetened condensed
  milk

For the Crust: Preheat the oven to 350 degrees. Whisk together the dry ingredients in a bowl. Place cold butter and cold shortening on top of the flour mixture. Cut in with a pastry blender until the butter and shortening are the size of small peas. Sprinkle with 4 tablespoons of cold water and fluff with a fork, sprinkle with 4 or 5 more tablespoons of water and fluff until the dough comes together. Form a ball with the dough, wrap in plastic, and place in the refrigerator for 30 minutes.

For Filling 1: Using a heavy sauce pan, bring ¼ cup heavy cream to a simmer, remove from heat. Add the white chocolate and gently stir until smooth and creamy. Beat cream cheese and sugar with a stand mixer until smooth. Scrape the walls and beater, beat again for 1 minute. Mix in chocolate mixture, mix for 1 minute, add maple syrup and mix for 1 minute. Whip 1 cup heavy cream to stiff peaks, fold in cream cheese mixture to the whipped cream. Fill crust halfway full with maple cream. Gently cover with plastic and freeze overnight.

For Filling 2: Mix sugar, cinnamon, salt, ginger, and cloves in small bowl and set aside. Beat egg in large bowl. Stir in pumpkin and sugar and spice mixture. Gradually stir in the sweetened condensed milk. Pour into pie shell over the frozen cream. Bake in preheated oven for 40 to 50 minutes or until knife inserted near center comes out clean. Cool on wire rack for 2 hours. Top with sweetened whipped cream (optional); keep refrigerated until ready to serve.

Pumpkin and Maple Crown Pie

IT'S BETTER THAN THE GREAT PUMPKIN PIE

Kathryn Hanson, Orlando, FL
2015 APC National Pie Championships
Professional Division Honorable Mention Pumpkin

CRUST

1⅓ cups ginger snaps and shortbread cookies, finely crushed
2 tablespoons sugar
½ teaspoon vanilla
⅓ cup unsalted butter, melted

FILLING 1

⅓ cup pumpkin purée
½ cup cream cheese
½ cup powdered sugar
½ teaspoon saigon cinnamon
¼ teaspoon vanilla extract
pinch ground cloves
pinch ground nutmeg
pinch ginger

FILLING 2

⅔ cup pumpkin purée
½ teaspoon Saigon cinnamon
¼ teaspoon vanilla extract
pinch ground cloves
pinch ground nutmeg
pinch ginger
1 cup better cream

TOPPING

1¾ cup heavy whipping cream
¼ cup confectioners' sugar
½ teaspoon vanilla extract

For the Crust: Mix all of the ingredients in a bowl until blended; pour into a 9-inch pie dish sprayed with Crisco cooking spray. Press into the bottom and sides; bake in a 350-degree oven for 8 to 12 minutes or until lightly browned. Let cool.

For Filling 1: Using a mixer, cream together the pumpkin purée, cream cheese, and powdered sugar. Mix in the vanilla and spices. Pour into cooled crust.

For Filling 2: Combine the pumpkin purée, cinnamon, vanilla extract, cloves, nutmeg, and ginger. Set aside. Whip the Better Cream until stiff picks form. Gently fold the pumpkin mixture into the Better Cream. Pour onto Filling 1.

For the Topping: Whip the heavy cream and slowly add the powdered sugar and vanilla extract. Whip until stiff peaks form. Pipe the Pumpkin Chiffon filling over the cream filling. Finish by piping the whipped Chantilly Cream over the pie and garnish with pumpkin pie spice blend.

It's Better Than the Great Pumpkin Pie

PUMPKIN PARFAIT PIE

Patricia Lapiezo, LaMesa, CA
2015 APC National Pie Championships
Amateur Division 1st Place Pumpkin

CRUST
3 cups flour
1 teaspoon salt
1 cup + 2 tablespoon Crisco shortening
1 large egg
⅓ cup water, cold
1 tablespoon vinegar

PUMPKIN BREAD
2 cups cubed pumpkin bread (from a mix)

FILLING 1
1 (3.5-oz) package instant vanilla pudding
½ teaspoon cinnamon
½ teaspoon pumpkin pie spice
1 cup canned pumpkin
1 cup heavy whipping cream

FILLING 2
2 tablespoons powdered sugar
3 oz. cream cheese
½ cup white chocolate chips
1 cup heavy whipping cream, stiffly beaten
⅔ cup toffee bars, chopped
⅔ cup candied or toasted pecans, chopped
⅔ cup caramel sauce

CINNAMON MAPLE WHIPPED CREAM
1½ cups heavy whipping cream
2 tablespoons powdered sugar
¼ teaspoon cinnamon
½ teaspoon maple flavoring

For the Crust: Preheat oven to 425 degrees. In a large bowl combine the flour and salt. Cut in shortening. In a separate bowl, beat the egg and add water and vinegar. Gradually add to flour mixture until dough comes together. Divide in half and flatten into disks. Refrigerate at least 1 hour. Roll out to fit a 9½-inch pie dish. Flute edge and prick bottom and sides. Bake 20 minutes, or until light brown. Cool completely before filling.

For Pumpkin Bread: Prepare pumpkin bread from mix. Cool completely. Cube 2 cups of pumpkin bread.

For Filling 1: In a large mixing bowl, stir together the pudding and spices. Add pumpkin and whipping cream and beat on medium speed 1 to 2 minutes until combined. Spread half of mixture into prepared crust. Top with 1 cup cubed pumpkin bread.

For Filling 2: In a medium bowl, beat the powdered sugar and cream cheese together until blended. Blend in melted white chocolate and then fold in whipped cream. Spread half of mixture over the pumpkin bread. Top with ⅓ cup each chopped toffee, candied pecans, and caramel. Repeat the layers. Refrigerate until set (about 2 hours).

For the Topping: Beat the cream, powdered sugar, maple flavoring, and cinnamon, on high speed until stiff. Pipe around edge of pie.

Pumpkin Parfait Pie

BLOOMING PUMPKIN PIE

Terri Beaver, Hebron, KY
2015 APC National Pie Championships
Amateur Division 3rd Place Pumpkin

CRUST
1½ cups flour
2 tablespoons sugar
6 tablespoons shortening
2 tablespoons cold butter
2 tablespoons coconut oil
⅓ cup water, cold
½ teaspoon salt
½ teaspoon apple cider vinegar
1 egg, beaten, mixed with 1 table-
    spoon cream

FILLING
¾ cup sugar
½ teaspoon salt
2 teaspoons pumpkin pie spice
¼ teaspoon cardamom
2 large eggs, room temperature

1 (15-oz.) can pumpkin puree
1 (12-oz.) can evaporated milk

TOPPING
2 oz. cream cheese, softened to
    room temperature
1 tablespoon saved egg mixture
1 tablespoon sugar
¼ teaspoon vanilla
1 tablespoon cream
bottled chocolate sundae syrup

GARNISH
1 cup heavy whipping cream
2 tablespoon sugar
1 teaspoon vanilla
¼ teaspoon pumpkin pie spice

For the Crust: Preheat oven to 375 degrees. In a large bowl, mix together flour and sugar. Cut in shortening, butter, and coconut oil with a pastry cutter or two knives until the size of peas. Stir together water, salt, and vinegar. Add water in small amounts to flour mixture, stirring as you go until mixture holds together when a small amount is squeezed in your hand. You may not use all the water. Shape into a disc and wrap with plastic wrap and chill for at least 1 hour. When chilled, roll out on a floured surface to about 12 inches. Transfer to a 9-inch pie plate. Cut the edges so they come out slightly over the edge of the pie plate and flute the edges. Roll out the scraps and cut into leaf shapes. With a pastry brush, brush the backs of the leaves with the egg mixture and place around the edges. Chill pie shell while making filling. Save the rest of the egg mixture for the topping.

For the Filling: Mix sugar, salt, and spices in a small bowl. Beat eggs in a large bowl. Stir in pumpkin and sugar with spice mixture. Gradually stir in evaporated milk. Pour into pie shell.

For the Topping: In a bowl, beat first four ingredients until smooth. Garnish with cheesecake mixture by carefully putting a small amount in the middle to create a solid white circle about the size of a silver dollar. Using the bottle of chocolate sundae syrup, squeeze a line of syrup around the outside edge of the white circle. About ½ inch from the white circle, make another circle with the syrup so it looks a little like a bull's-eye. Take a wooden kabob skewer and draw a line from the outside of the circle to the center 6 to 8 times, wiping stick after each swipe. Then draw a line between these going from the outside to the center of the circle.

Bake in the lower center of the oven 40 to 50 minutes until set. Cool completely.

For the Garnish: Whip all ingredients. Pipe whipped cream onto pie. Serve cold.

PUMPKIN PIE DELIGHT

Jone Schumacher, Chapin, IL
2014 Illinois State Fair, APC Pumpkin Pie Contest
1st Place

CRUST

2½ cups all-purpose flour
1½ tablespoons dark brown sugar
1 teaspoon salt
¼ teaspoon cinnamon
⅛ teaspoon nutmeg
½ cup solid vegetable shortening, chilled
½ cup salted butter, cut into thin slices
1 egg yolk
6 tablespoons (or more) ice water
1 teaspoon vanilla extract
2 teaspoons apple cider vinegar
Florida Demerara Sugar Crystals
colored sanding sugars (optional)
butter-flavored cooking spray

FILLING

2 extra large eggs, separated
1 cup dark brown sugar
2 tablespoons all-purpose flour
¼ teaspoon salt
1 teaspoon cinnamon
¼ teaspoon nutmeg
¼ teaspoon ginger
1 (8-oz.) can pumpkin (or 1 cup)
1 cup scalded whole milk
2 tablespoons salted butter

GARNISH

whipped cream

For the Crust: Preheat oven to 400 degrees. Blend flour, sugar, and crust spices. Add shortening and butter and cut with pastry blender or food processor until the mixture resembles coarse meal. In a separate bowl, combine the egg yolk, water, vanilla, and vinegar, and stir until mixed. Gradually add the egg yolk mixture to the flour mixture and stir with fork until moist clumps form, adding additional water by the teaspoon if dough is dry. Gather dough into 2 balls, one slightly larger than the other. Wrap in plastic and chill 30 minutes.

Spray inside of pie plate with cooking spray. Roll larger dough to fit deep 9- or 10-inch pie dish. Place crust into pan, flute edge. Cut out shapes of leaves and pumpkins with other dough ball. Combine egg white with 1 teaspoon water and whip with fork, brush crust. Brush cut-outs and sprinkle the Demerara sugar on the leaves and colored sugar on the pumpkins. Press leaves onto the crust edge and place pumpkin shapes on a pan prepared with parchment paper and sprayed with butter-flavored cooking spray. Cut out foil to fit around edge of pie plate; spray one side of foil with cooking spray and lay lightly over crust edge. Set in refrigerator while preparing filling.

For the Filling: In a small mixing bowl, beat egg whites with an electric mixer until fluffy to somewhat stiff. Combine the sugar, flour, salt, and spices and add to pumpkin and egg yolk in a large mixing bowl of an electric mixer. Beat on medium speed until blended. In a separate microwaveable bowl, add milk and butter, heat in microwave for 2 to 2½ minutes. Add to pumpkin mixture. Fold in beaten egg whites. Pour mixture into the pie shell.

Place in the preheated oven on the lower ⅓ rack and bake for 10 minutes, then reduce temperature to 340 degrees for 45 to 50 minutes. Test with a toothpick for doneness. Remove from oven to cool to slightly warm and then chill in refrigerator until serving. Bake the pumpkin trims in 375-degree oven for 10 to 14 minutes until golden brown. Place on pie for decoration.

For the Garnish: Garnish with whipped cream, if desired.

PUMKINSCOTCH PIE

Emily Pearce, Sheboygan Falls, WI
2014 APC National Pie Championships
Amateur Division 3rd Place Pumpkin

CRUST
1⅓ cup flour
½ teaspoon salt
½ cup Crisco vegetable shortening
3–6 tablespoons water, cold
3 tablespoons pecans, finely crushed

FILLING 1
1 (3.4-oz.) package butterscotch
   pudding
1½ cup milk
1 (8-oz.) package cream cheese
2 tablespoons powdered sugar
¾ cup stabilized whipped cream
½ cup crème fraîche
¼ cup pecans, coarsely chopped
3 tablespoons caramel sauce

FILLING 2
1 (8-oz.) package cream cheese
1 cup pumpkin
¼ cup powdered sugar
1 teaspoon pumpkin pie spice
1¼ cup stabilized whipped cream
½ cup crème fraîche
⅓ cup pecans, coarsely chopped
2 teaspoons nutmeg

STABILIZED WHIPPED CREAM
3 teaspoons (1 packet) powdered
   unflavored gelatin
3 tablespoons water
3 cups heavy cream
¼ cup + 2 tablespoons sugar, or
   more to taste
1 tablespoon vanilla extract

CRÈME FRAÎCHE
1 cup heavy cream
1 tablespoon cultured buttermilk

For the Crust: Preheat oven to 400 degrees. Blend together flour and salt. Cut in chilled shortening with pastry blender, until resembles coarse crumbs. Sprinkle 3 tablespoons water over flour mixture: mix gently with fork. Add more water by the tablespoon, mix until dough holds together. Flatten dough into ½-inch-thick round disk, wrap in plastic wrap; refrigerate at least 30 minutes. Place dough on lightly floured surface. With floured rolling pin, sprinkle pecans over center then roll dough outward from center into a circle 2 inches wider than pie plate. Ease crust into pie plate and trim evenly around plate. Place a sheet of aluminum foil over crust and form up the sides, put in pie weights or unbaked beans. Bake for 10 to 15 minutes or until light golden brown. Set on rack to cool.

For Filling 1: Mix pudding and milk together, set aside. Soften cream cheese, put in mixer, and mix in powdered sugar. Add pudding, then fold in whipped cream. Pour in cooled crust. Spread crème fraîche over butterscotch layer. Sprinkle pecans over crème fraîche. Drizzle with caramel and chill.

For Filling 2: Soften cream cheese, put in mixer, mix in pumpkin, powdered sugar, pumpkin pie spice, then fold in whipped cream. Spoon over caramel pecan layer. Set aside to cool. Whip crème fraîche and spread over pumpkin layer. Sprinkle pecans and nutmeg over crème fraîche layer.

For the Stabilized Whipped Cream: Put the gelatin and water in a small bowl and let sit for about 10 minutes, or until it swells, or blooms, and absorbs the water. Stir the mixture with a rubber

Pumpkinscotch Pie

spatula (a rubber spatula allows you to pull the gelatin away from the sides of the bowl) until it is smooth. Don't heat it any more then is needed to dissolve the gelatin.

Combine the remaining cream with the sugar and vanilla and beat to medium peaks. Turn the mixer to low speed and pour in gelatin mixture in a steady stream, avoiding the whisk and sides of the bowl. If you're making the stabilized whipped cream by hand, stir the gelatin mixture into the cream with a whisk. Continue beating the cream just long enough to incorporate the gelatin. Set aside till needed.

For the Crème Fraîche: Combine the cream and buttermilk in saucepan and heat only to tepid (not more than 85 degrees on an instant reading thermometer). Pour into a clean glass jar. Partially cover and let stand at room temperature (between 65 and 75 degrees) for 8 to 24 hours, or until thickened. Stir and refrigerate at least 24 hours before using. The cream will keep about 2 weeks in the refrigerator.

PUMPKIN BUTTER PECAN PIE

Jeanne Ely, Mulberry, FL
2014 APC National Pie Championships
Amateur Division 2nd Place Pumpkin

CRUST
1 package butter pecan cookies
6 tablespoons butter, melted

FILLING 1
1 (4½-cup serving) package vanilla
 instant pudding
1 cup milk
1 tablespoon butter pecan flavoring
½ cup pecans, crushed and roasted
 in ¼ cup butter

FILLING 2
1 cup milk
1 (4½-cup serving) package vanilla
 instant pudding
½ cup sugar
1 can pumpkin purée
2 teaspoons pumpkin pie spice
1½ cup heavy whipping cream

GARNISH
¾ cup heavy whipping cream
¼ cup confectioners' sugar
¼ teaspoon vanilla bean paste

For the Crust: Crush butter pecan cookies and blend in butter. Press into 9-inch deep dish pie plate. Freeze 10 minutes or until set.

For Filling 1: Combine pudding mix, milk, butter pecan flavoring, and crushed pecans. Spoon into pie shell and cool until set.

For Filling 2: Beat on medium speed with the electric mixer the milk, pudding mix, pumpkin purée, sugar, and pumpkin pie spice until smooth and creamy. Whip the whipping cream on high speed until stiff peaks form. Fold the whipping cream into the pumpkin mixture and spoon on top of the butter pecan layer. Refrigerate until set, about 2 hours.

For the Garnish: Whip all ingredients together until stiff. Decorate as desired.

Pumpkin Butter Pecan Pie

I'LL HAVE ONE OF EACH . . . PUMPKIN APPLE PIE

Rick Johnson, Carbondale, IL
2015 APC National Pie Championships
Amateur Division 2nd Place Pumpkin

CRUST
3 cups all-purpose flour
1¼ cups butter
½ teaspoon salt
⅓ cup lard
½ cup cream cheese
½ teaspoon almond extract

FILLING 1
6 tablets vitamin C
3 cup water
5 cups Golden Delicious apples
¼ cup sugar
½ gallon apple cider
2 teaspoon cinnamon

½ teaspoon nutmeg
¼ teaspoon ground cloves
¼ teaspoon salt
2 tablespoons butter
2 tablespoons Clear Jel

FILLING 2
2 eggs
1 (15-oz.) can pumpkin
1½ cups heavy cream
½ cup sugar
⅓ cup light brown sugar
1 tablespoon pumpkin pie spice
½ teaspoon salt

TOPPING
1 cup flour
1 cup walnuts, chopped and divided
½ cup sugar
6 tablespoons butter
pinch salt

GARNISH
12 tablespoons powdered sugar
8 tablespoons piping gel

2 teaspoons vanilla
6 tablespoons reduced apple cider
  (from above)
1 quart heavy whipping cream
caramel sauce
walnuts, chopped

For the Crust: Add all ingredients to a food processor and process until it forms a ball. Refrigerate overnight then roll out into 1 large crust. Blind bake at 425 degrees for 15 minutes in the largest pie plate you can find (flute up edges to hold more filling.)

For Filling 1: Crush vitamin C tablets and dissolve in water. Cut apples and dip in solution then add to plastic bag with sugar and refrigerate overnight. Pour apple cider in large saucepan and simmer on medium high until reduced to a thick syrup. Combine apple mixture with 2 tablespoons butter in a large saucepan and sauté until apples are soft and fully cooked. Stir in approximately half of the cider syrup, spices, and Clear Jel. Pour into baked crust.

For Filling 2: Combine all ingredients for pumpkin filling and mix well. Pour pumpkin

mixture over apple filling right up to the edge of the crust. Bake at 350 degrees for approximately 45 minutes.

For Topping: Combine topping ingredients in food processor and process until coarsely chopped. Spread over top of pie and continue until internal temperature is 170 degrees (carry over will eventually get it to 175). Cover with aluminum foil if top is getting too brown.

For Garnish: Combine powdered sugar, piping gel, vanilla, and cider syrup in mixing bowl and mix until combined. Add whipping cream a little at a time until well combined, then whip on high until stiff peaks have formed and top pie. Drizzle with caramel sauce and chopped walnuts.

PRALINE PUMPKIN PIE WITH CARAMEL SAUCE

Jone Schumacher, Chapin, IL
2015 Illinois State Fair
Pumpkin Pie Contest Winner

CRUST
2½ cups unbleached all-purpose
   flour
2 tablespoons dark brown sugar
1 teaspoon salt
¼ teaspoon cinnamon
⅛ teaspoon nutmeg
1½ stick butter, cold and thinly sliced
½ cup cold shortening, cut into small
   pieces
¼ cup vodka, cold
¼ cup water, cold
½ teaspoon vanilla
¼ teaspoon caramel flavoring
1 egg + 1 teaspoon water
Florida Demerara Sugar crystals
   (optional)

OPTIONAL TRIM FOR CRUST
6–8 pecan halves
additional pastry leaves

FILLING
3 large or extra large eggs, separated
1 cup whole milk
3 tablespoons all-purpose flour
½ teaspoon salt
1 cup dark brown sugar
1½ teaspoons cinnamon
¼ teaspoon nutmeg
¼ teaspoon ginger
1 (8-oz.) can pumpkin puree
3 tablespoons salted butter, melted

TOPPING
⅓ cup dark brown sugar
1 tablespoon butter
½ teaspoon cinnamon
⅓ cup pecans, chopped

CARMEL SAUCE
2 tablespoons salted butter
2 tablespoons heavy cream
¼ cup brown sugar

For the Crust: Blend flour, sugar, and crust spices. Add butter and shortening and cut with pastry blender or food processor until mixture resembles coarse meal. Combine the vodka, water, and flavorings, and gradually add liquid to flour mixture. Stir with fork until moist clumps form. (All the liquid may not have been used.) Gather dough into 2 balls, one larger than the other. Flatten each into a disk. Wrap in plastic and chill for at least 30 minutes. Roll larger dough to fit a deep 9- or 10-inch deep dish pie plate. Place crust into pan and flute edge or cut out shapes or leaves. Beat egg with water and brush crust edge or cut-outs with egg and sprinkle with Demerara sugar. Brush edge of crust with water before applying optional leaves. Press leaves around edge. Cut an open circle of heavy foil and spray inside surface with cooking spray; place over edge of crust. Chill crust in refrigerator while preparing filling.

For the Filling: In a small mixing bowl of electric mixer, beat egg whites until fluffy to somewhat stiff. Scald the milk. Combine the flour, salt, brown sugar, and spices. Add to the pumpkin and egg yolks in the large mixing bowl of electric mixer. Blend in the melted butter. Beat on medium speed until well blended. Add the warm milk to the mixture. Fold in the beaten egg whites. Pour mixture into the prepared pie shell. Place in a 400-degree oven on lower ⅓ rack and bake for 10 minutes; reduce oven temperature to 350 degrees and bake for an additional 40 minutes.

Praline Pumpkin Pie with Caramel Sauce

For the Topping: Combine topping ingredients. Remove pie from oven and quickly sprinkle on the topping over the pumpkin filling. Remove the foil of the crust edge and return pie to oven for 10 minutes or until knife inserted comes out clean. Combine the caramel ingredients in a small sauce pan. On medium heat, bring to a boil and stir constantly and cook for 2 minutes. Drizzle caramel over warm pie. Place in refrigerator after cooled until served.

Optional Trim: Prepare several extra pastry crust leaves as in crust edge. Use a little caramel sauce and brush over the pecan halves. Bake leaves and pecans on small tray in a 400-degree oven for 4 to 6 minutes until golden brown. Place on pie top.

OPEN

RASPBERRY WHITE CHOCOLATE BOMB

By David Harper, Richland Center, WI
2013 APC National Pie Championships
Amateur Division 2nd Place Innovation

CRUST
1 cup flour
1 teaspoon salt
½ cup butter-flavored Crisco
5 tablespoons water, cold

FILLING 1
4 oz. cream cheese
½ cup powdered sugar
1 cup heavy cream
4 oz. white chocolate, melted and cooled
1 teaspoon vanilla extract

FILLING 2
1 cup raspberry purée (2 cups of fresh raspberries yields about 1 cup purée)
2 tablespoons fresh lemon juice
1 envelope plain gelatin
2 cups heavy cream
2 cups fresh raspberries

GARNISH
1½ cup whipping cream
¼ cup powdered sugar
1½ teaspoons vanilla
4 oz. white chocolate curls/shavings

For the Crust: Preheat oven to 400 degrees. Place baking stone in oven to preheat. Whisk the flour and the salt together in a large bowl. Add the Crisco and mix with your fingers until combined. Add the water and use a fork to combine. Turn pie dough out onto a floured surface and gather into a circular disk. Roll out the dough big enough to fit into a pie plate. Flute edges for decoration. Place into the refrigerator for 20 minutes. After 20 minutes, place a piece of parchment paper in the pie shell and fill with pie weights or pennies. Bake crust until edges are golden brown and bottom is browned also, about 15 to 20 minutes. Remove crust from oven and take out the parchment and pie weights. If bottom crust is not browned enough, place back in oven without parchment and pie weights and bake until bottom is browned, about 5 min. Cool on wire rack and set aside.

For Filling 1: In the bowl of a stand mixer, combine the cream cheese, powdered sugar, heavy cream, melted and cooled white chocolate, and vanilla and mix until combined and fluffy. Cover the bottom of the pie crust with the white chocolate cream cheese mixture.

For Filling 2: Put raspberry purée in a small saucepan. Combine lemon juice and gelatin together to soften in a small bowl, about 2 minutes. Heat raspberry purée until very hot but not boiling. Add the gelatin mixture to hot purée and stir until gelatin has dissolved. Remove from heat. Cool until room temperature, about 20 to

Raspberry White Chocolate Bomb

25 minutes. While mixture is cooling, whip the 2 cups of heavy cream until stiff peaks. When raspberry mixture is room temperature, fold in the whipped cream until no white streaks remain. Spoon one-third of the raspberry mixture on top of the white chocolate layer. Place one cup of the fresh raspberries on the filling, pushing them into filling so that only half the raspberry is seen. Spoon another one-third raspberry filling on top of the raspberries, covering them completely. Place another cup of fresh raspberries on the filling, gently pushing them down into the filling. Spoon the last of the filling on top of the raspberries, covering them completely. Chill until set, about 4 hours or overnight.

For the Garnish: Combine all ingredients for whipped cream and beat until stiff. Cover the top of the pie with whipped cream and garnish with the white chocolate shavings/curls. Refrigerate until ready to eat.

CARROT CAKEY PIE

Patricia Lapiezo, LaMesa, CA
2015 APC National Pie Championships
Amateur Division 1st Place Innovation

CRUST

3 cups flour
1 teaspoon salt
1 cup + 2 tablespoon Crisco shortening
¾ cup pecans, finely chopped
1 large egg
⅓ cup water, cold
1 tablespoon vinegar

CARROT CAKE

1 cup flour
1 teaspoon baking powder
½ teaspoon baking soda
½ teaspoon salt
1 teaspoon cinnamon
1½ teaspoon unsweetened cocoa
   powder
2 large eggs
½ teaspoon vanilla
½ cup granulated sugar
½ cup dark brown sugar
½ cup + 2 tablespoons corn oil
½ pound carrots, shredded
½ cup raisins

FILLING

¼ cup heavy cream
6 oz. white chocolate
12 oz. cream cheese, softened
½ cup powdered sugar
¼ teaspoon cream cheese flavoring
1½ cups heavy whipping cream,
   stiffly beaten

TOPPING

1 (20-oz.) can crushed pineapple,
   drained, reserving juice
½ cup sugar
3 tablespoons cornstarch
½ teaspoon vanilla extract
1 tablespoon butter
¾ cup pecans, finely chopped

For the Crust: In a large bowl, combine the flour and salt. Cut in shortening. Stir in chopped pecans. In a separate bowl beat the egg and add water and vinegar. Gradually add to flour mixture until dough comes together. Divide in half and flatten into disks. Refrigerate at least 1 hour. Roll out to fit a 9½-inch pie dish. Flute edge and prick bottom and sides. Bake in a 425-degree oven 20 minutes, or until light brown. Cool completely before filling.

For the Cake: Preheat oven to 350 degrees. Spray two 8-inch round cake pans with nonstick spray and line bottoms with parchment paper. Sift together the flour, baking powder, baking soda, salt, cinnamon and cocoa; set aside. In a large bowl, beat the eggs. Add vanilla, sugars, and oil and beat well. Gradually add dry ingredients on low speed just until incorporated. Stir in carrots and raisins. Pour batter evenly between the two pans. Bake until a toothpick inserted in center comes out clean. Cool completely and remove from pans.

For the Filling: Heat the ¼ cup heavy cream and the white chocolate until just melted. In a large mixing bowl, beat the cream cheese and powdered sugar until creamy and well blended. Blend in melted chocolate mixture. Blend in flavoring. Fold in whipped cream. Place one cake round in bottom of pie crust. Spread half of filling over cake. Top with second cake layer. Spread with remaining filling. Prepare pineapple topping.

For the Topping: Stir together the pineapple and sugar in a medium saucepan over low heat until the sugar is dissolved. Combine the pineapple juice and cornstarch and stir into the pineapple. Bring the mixture to a boil, stirring constantly until thickened. Remove from heat and stir in the vanilla and butter. Cool slightly and spread over top of pie to within 1 inch of crust. Sprinkle finely chopped toasted pecans around edge of pie (between crust and filling). Chill pie 2 hours.

Carrot Cakey Pie

ROCKIN' POPPIN' ROOT BEER FLOAT PIE

Christopher Taylor, Atlanta, GA
2014 APC National Pie Championships
Amateur Division 1st Place Innovation

CRUST
1½ cups all-purpose flour
1¼ teaspoons maple sugar
½ teaspoon salt
⅛ teaspoon baking powder
1 stick unsalted butter, cold
¼ cup Crisco vegetable shortening, cold
1 teaspoon cider vinegar
¼ cup water, cold
2 oz. white chocolate, melted

FILLING 1
1½ teaspoon unflavored gelatin
½ cup whole milk, divided
¼ cup granulated sugar
¼ teaspoon salt
½ cup Ghirardelli white chocolate chips
½ cup SodaStream root beer soda mix

1 teaspoon McCormick root beer extract
1 cup heavy cream
5 packs (0.33 oz. each) Chocolate Pop Rocks

ROOT BEER WHIPPED CREAM
1 cup whipping cream
2 tablespoons powdered sugar
2 tablespoons piping gel
¼ teaspoon McCormick root beer extract

VANILLA WHIPPED CREAM
1 cup whipping cream
2 tablespoons powdered sugar
2 tablespoons piping gel
¾ teaspoon vanilla paste

GARNISH
10 French Vanilla Pirouette cookies
10 maraschino cherries, well drained

For the Crust: Mix flour, sugar, salt, and baking powder in the bowl of a food processor. Add butter pieces and pulse until butter is the size of beans. Add the shortening and pulse together until the mixture resembles coarse, wet sand and butter pieces are no larger than peas. Add the vinegar to the water. Add 3 tablespoons of the water mixture to the flour mixture and briefly pulse until the water is incorporated. Add the remaining water if the mixture looks dry. Remove the dough from the processor and pat into a 4-inch disc on a sheet of plastic wrap. Wrap tightly and refrigerate for at least 3 hours. Roll out the pie dough out to a circle large enough to fill a 9½-inch deep dish pie pan. Line the pan with the rolled crust and crimp the edges as desired. Freeze for 30 minutes. Meanwhile, preheat oven to 425 degrees. Line the dough with parchment paper and pie weights. Bake for 20 minutes. After 20 minutes of baking, remove the weights and parchment. Reduce the oven temperature to 375 degrees and continue baking until the crust is lightly golden brown, 5 to 10 minutes more. Allow the crust to cool completely. Brush bottom and sides with a thin layer of melted chocolate and refrigerate to set before filling.

For the Filling: In a small bowl, sprinkle the gelatin over 2 tablespoons of the milk. Set aside. Combine the remaining milk, sugar, salt, and white chocolate chips. Cook over medium heat until the chips are melted. Add the reserved gelatin mixture and continue to cook until the gelatin is dissolved, about 1 minute. Stir in the root beer soda mix and extract. Transfer to bowl. Allow mixture to cool at room temperature for 20 minutes.

Whip the cream until stiff peaks form. Gently fold the whipped cream into the root beer mixture. Refrigerate for 1 hour. Sprinkle the Pop Rocks evenly over the top of the pie. Refrigerate until set, at least 2 more hours, before topping with the Root Beer Whipped Cream.

For the Root Beer Whipped Cream: Combine whipping cream and sugar in large bowl. Whip until soft peaks form. Add piping gel and extract. Continue to whip until stiff peaks form. Spread the mixture evenly over the Pop Rocks layer. Refrigerate while preparing the Vanilla Whipped Cream.

For the Vanilla Whipped Cream: Combine whipping cream and sugar in large bowl. Whip until soft peaks form. Add piping gel and vanilla paste. Continue to whip until stiff peaks form. Decorate the top of the pie, as desired. Garnish before serving.

For the Garnish: Trim the cookies to 3-inch lengths. Evenly space cookies and cherries across the top of the pie, allowing one cookie and cherry for each slice. Makes 10 servings.

PIÑA COLADA PIE

Angela Cacciola, Windemere, FL
2015 APC National Pie Championships
Amateur Division 3rd Place Open

CRUST
6 tablespoons butter
1¾ cup Nilla wafer crumbs
2 tablespoons flour
2 tablespoons brown sugar
½ teaspoon cinnamon
pinch salt
1–2 teaspoons water

FILLING 1
1 (5.1-oz.) box of instant vanilla
   pudding mix
1 (15-oz.) can cream of coconut
¼ cup coconut milk
12 oz. cream cheese, softened
2 cups Cool Whip

FILLING 2
2 cups crushed pineapple, drained
⅔ cup frozen piña colada concentrate, thawed
½ cup sugar
3 tablespoons cornstarch
2 tablespoons rum extract
1 teaspoon coconut extract
pinch salt

GARNISH
2 teaspoons unflavored gelatin
2 tablespoons water, cold
2 cups heavy whipping cream
4 tablespoons white sugar
½ teaspoon vanilla extract
¼ teaspoon rum extract

For the Crust: Preheat oven to 350 degrees. Lightly grease pie pan. Microwave butter on low until melted. Pulse wafers and flour in food processor until the consistency of fine crumbs. Add brown sugar, cinnamon, salt, butter, and water. Mix well. Press into 8-inch pie tin or plate (bottom and sides) and bake for 12 to 14 minutes until edges are golden brown. Set aside to cool.

For Filling 1: Mix pudding mix, cream of coconut, and coconut milk together until well combined. Beat the cream cheese until light and fluffy using an electric mixer. Slowly add the pudding mixture to the cream cheese and beat until incorporated. Fold in the Cool Whip, mixing until smooth. Fill pie until it is two-thirds full and refrigerate.

For Filling 2: Combine pineapple and piña colada concentrate in a medium saucepan. Mix sugar and cornstarch together in a small bowl. Stir the sugar mixture into the pineapple mixture. Stir in the rum and coconut extracts and salt. Cook mixture over medium heat until thickened. Allow mixture to cool. Pour mixture over coconut cream filling and refrigerate pie for at least 3 hours.

For the Garnish: Combine gelatin and cold water in a microwave-safe container. Allow to sit for one minute, microwave on high for 15 seconds and allow to cool (not long enough to set). Begin whipping cream in mixer, add gelatin, sugar, vanilla, and rum extract. Whip until soft peaks are formed. Pipe onto pie.

Piña Colada Pie

HOPSCOTCH BUTTERSCOTCH PIE

Beth Campbell, Belleville, WI
2015 APC National Pie Championships
Amateur Division 2nd Place Open

CRUST
1 cup flour
2 tablespoons powdered sugar
1 stick (½ cup) butter
1 cup pecans, finely chopped

FILLING
2 tablespoons butter
1¼ cup firmly packed brown sugar
4½ teaspoons cornstarch
2 cups milk

3 egg yolks
½ teaspoon vanilla
¼ teaspoon salt
2 tablespoons water

TOPPING
½ cup heavy cream, whipped
2 large Butterfinger candy bars
chocolate curls

For the Crust: Preheat oven to 350 degrees. Cut butter, flour, and powdered sugar with pastry blender or fork to make coarse crumbs. Stir in pecans and pat into a 9-inch pie plate. Bake for about 12 to 15 minutes or until light golden brown. Do not overcook. Cool completely.

For the Filling: Melt butter in a pan over medium heat. Stir in brown sugar and cook together, stirring constantly for about 3 minutes. Remove from heat. In a small bowl, whisk cornstarch and ½ cup of the milk until smooth, then whisk in egg yolks. Whisk the remaining milk into the brown sugar mixture, then whisk in the cornstarch mixture. Return the pan to the stove on medium heat. Bring to a boil, whisking often. Reduce heat to low, simmer, whisking constantly until the filling thickens for about 1 minute. Remove from heat and add vanilla. Spoon the filling into the baked crust. Cool completely in the refrigerator.

For the Topping: Top the completely cooled pie with the whipped cream. Chop up Butterfinger bars and garnish with them and chocolate curls, as desired.

Hopscotch Butterscotch Pie

CARROTLICIOUS PIE

Juliana Evans, Orlando, FL
2015 National Pie Championships
Professional Division 1ˢᵗ Place Open

CRUST
1½ cups graham crackers, crushed
2 tablespoons brown sugar
1 tablespoon cinnamon
¼ cup salted butter, melted

FILLING
2 cups carrots, shredded
1 tablespoon buttermilk
½ cup packed brown sugar
¼ cup granulated sugar
2 eggs

¼ teaspoon salt
1 tablespoon cinnamon
¼ teaspoon nutmeg
¾ cup heavy cream

TOPPING
8 oz. cream cheese, softened
4 marshmallows
¾ cup powdered sugar
1 tablespoon clear imitation vanilla
   extract
1½ cups heavy cream

For the Crust: Preheat oven 350 degrees. In a food processor, combine all the crust ingredients. Pulse until well combined. Press into a 9-inch pie dish.

For the Filling: Place the 2 cups of shredded carrots in a pot with enough water to cover completely. Boil for 10 minutes until cooked. Drain well. Purée cooked carrots in a food processor. When carrots are almost smooth, add in 1 tablespoon of buttermilk to help them along. Still using a food processor, add in both sugars. Mix well. Next, add in eggs, then vanilla, salt, cinnamon, and nutmeg. Finish by streaming in the heavy cream. When carrot filling is well mixed, pour into graham crust. Bake 350 degrees for 45 to 50 minutes or until center is set. If edges of graham start to darken, cover edges with tin foil to prevent burning. Remove and allow to cool completely. You may place in the freezer to hurry the process.

For the Topping: In a stand mixer with the whisk attachment, beat cream cheese until smooth. Microwave marshmallows for 12 to 15 seconds until they puff up. Add and beat into cream cheese to help stabilize the whipped cream. Add in powdered sugar. Then mix in vanilla and heavy cream. Beat on high until thick, careful not to overmix. On top of carrot-filled cooled pie, pile on the cream cheese whipped cream. Sprinkle some cinnamon on top of topping for decor. Chop up some store-bought pralines and add for crunch.

DENNIS'S SOUTHERN HOSPITALITY PIE

John Sunvold, Orlando, FL
2014 APC National Pie Championships
Amateur Division 2nd Place Open

CRUST
1½ cup Nilla Wafer crumbs
2 tablespoons sugar
5 tablespoons butter, melted

FILLING 1
4 oz. cream cheese
½ teaspoon vanilla
$^3/_8$ cup powdered sugar
½ cup whipping cream

FILLING 2
$^5/_8$ cup sugar
¼ teaspoon salt
¼ cup cornstarch
1½ cup cream
1 cup milk
5 egg yolks
1 tablespoon vanilla extract
2 tablespoons butter
¼ teaspoon banana extract (optional)
2–3 bananas
1 cup Nilla Wafer pieces

For the Crust: Mix crumbs and sugar, add the melted butter, and press into a 9- to 10-inch pie plate. Bake for 8 to 12 minutes at 350 degrees.

For Filling 1: Beat cream cheese, vanilla, and powdered sugar until smooth. Whip cream and fold into the cream cheese. Spread onto cooled chocolate later and chill in refrigerator.

For Filling 2: Mix sugar, salt, and starch in a pot. In a bowl, whisk cream, milk, and egg yolks slightly. To the pot, slowly add the egg yolk/cream/milk mixture. Heat over medium heat, whisking frequently, until thick and bubbling (but not rapidly boiling). Once the cream is bubbling, continue to cook and whisk for 30 more seconds. Finally, add the vanilla, butter, and banana extract, and mix until the cream is smooth. Set aside. Cut 2 to 3 large bananas, and cover the cream layer with bananas and half of warm pudding. Cover with layer of Nilla wafer pieces (as many as you prefer), and cover with the remaining pudding. Place a plastic sheet over the cream to prevent a skin from forming on the cream filling. Place in refrigerator until completely chilled. Top with your favorite whipped topping. Garnish wafer crumbs or pieces, as/if desired. Chill 4 hours before serving.

Dennis's Southern Hospitality Pie

COCONUT CASHEW APRICOT PIE

Andrea Spring, Bradenton, FL
2013 APC Crisco National Pie Championships
Professional Division 1st Place Innovation

CRUST
4 oz. Crisco shortening
⅛ cup powdered sugar
1¼ cups all-purpose flour
½ egg (beat whole egg but only
 use half)
1½ teaspoon water, cold
¼ teaspoon salt
¼ cup salted cashews, chopped
¼ cup dried apricots, diced small

FILLING
⅔ cup granulated sugar
⅓ cup flour
1⅓ cup milk
⅓ cup heavy cream

4 egg yolks
1½ cups shredded coconut
¼ cup white chocolate chips
½ teaspoon salt

TOPPING
½ cup butter-flavored Crisco
½ cup coconut
¾ cup all-purpose flour
2 tablespoons brown sugar
2 tablespoons salted cashews,
 chopped
2 tablespoons dried apricots, diced
 small

For the Crust: Preheat oven to 400 degrees. Cut Crisco into powdered sugar and flour. Add egg, water, and salt. Form into disc and chill for at least 4 hours. Roll out dough and place in 10-inch pie plate. Press cashews and apricots into bottom of pie dough. Blind bake for 8 minutes and lower temperature to 325 degrees. Bake 20 to 30 minutes or until brown.

For the Filling: Mix sugar and flour. Add milk and cream. Cook, stirring until mixture becomes thick. Beat in egg yolks quickly and cook for another minute. Remove from heat and mix in coconut, chocolate chips, and salt. Cool slightly and pour into pie shell. Chill well.

For the Topping: Mix topping ingredients in frying pan over medium heat, stirring often. Cook until flour is cooked and medium brown in color. Pour onto greased aluminum foil and chill. Break into small pieces and garnish top of pie.

Coconut Cashew Apricot Pie

PERFECT ISLAND HARMONY PIE

Susan Boyle, Debary, FL
2013 APC Crisco National Pie Championships
Professional Division 1st Place Innovation

CRUST
21 coconut or shortbread cookies
¼ cup butter, melted
⅓ cup sugar
¼ cup macadamia nuts, finely chopped

FILLING 1
½ cup crushed pineapple, drain and reserve syrup
¼ cup sugar
½ cup reserved syrup
1 tablespoon Clear Jel

FILLING 2
½ cup cream cheese
1½ cups marshmallows, melted
1 teaspoon vanilla bean paste

¼ teaspoon salt
½ cup cream of coconut
1¼ cups drained crushed pineapple, reserving juice
1 cup heavy whipping cream
½ cup reserved pineapple juice
1 teaspoon rum flavoring (optional)

GARNISH
2 teaspoons meringue power
2 tablespoons water
1¼ cups superfine sugar
40 edible flower blossoms or petals (pansies, edible orchids, rose petals)

For the Crust: In a food processor, pulse cookies until finely chopped. Add melted butter, sugar, and nuts; pulse until mixed. With a small glass, press firmly on bottom and sides and bake at 350 degrees for 8 minutes cool before filling.

For Filling 1: Cook on medium-low all four ingredients until mixture is clear and thick. Set aside to cool. Add first filling to crust. Refrigerate.

For Filling 2: Mix cream cheese, marshmallows, vanilla bean paste, salt, cream of coconut, rum extract, and pineapple juice; blend until smooth. Add whipping cream and whip until thick and creamy, then remove and add crushed pineapple, folding into mixture. Spoon second filling on top of first filling. Refrigerate.

For the Garnish: Mix meringue and water together and brush all sides of flowers to coat. Sprinkle with sugar. Let dry on wax paper lined baking sheet for 1 to 2 days; use as garnish on pie.

Perfect Island Harmony Pie

NOT MY GRANNY'S EGG CUSTARD PIE

Amy Freeze, Avon Park, FL
2012 APC Crisco National Pie Championships
Amateur Division 3rd Place Custard

CRUST
1⅓ cups all-purpose flour, chilled
½ teaspoon salt
½ cup Crisco shortening, chilled
4–6 tablespoons water, cold
1 egg
1 tablespoon water

FILLING
4 large eggs
1 (15-oz.) can Eagle Brand condensed milk
1 cup whole milk
1 teaspoon vanilla extract
½ cup light brown sugar
½ cup pecans, chopped

For the Crust: In a medium bowl, combine flour and salt. Cut in shortening. Gradually add water until dough forms. Roll out and line pie plate. Create an egg wash of egg and 1 tablespoon water. Brush over crust edges. Refrigerate crust while preparing custard.

For the Filling: In a medium bowl, beat eggs until light. Add condensed milk and beat well. Add milk and vanilla, and beat well. Pour custard into prepared crust. Bake at 325 degrees for 30 minutes. Sprinkle the top of the pie with brown sugar and pecans. Increase the heat to 350 degrees, and bake an additional 10 minutes or until custard is done. (To test custard doneness, insert a wet butter knife into the center of the pie. If it comes out clean, it's done. If it comes out with custard on it, continue cooking, but re-check for doneness every 5 minutes.)

Not My Granny's Egg Custard Pie

RASPBERRY ALMOND BLISS PIE

Patricia Lapeizo, LaMesa, CA
2012 APC Crisco National Pie Championships
Amateur Division 1st Place Custard

CRUST
3 cups all-purpose flour
1 teaspoon salt
1¼ cups Crisco butter-flavored
    shortening
5 tablespoons water, cold
1 tablespoon vinegar
1 egg, lightly beaten

FILLING 1
10 oz. box frozen raspberries in
    syrup, thawed
1 tablespoon cornstarch
1 tablespoon granulated sugar
1 cup fresh raspberries

FILLING 2
5 large egg yolks
¼ cup cornstarch
3 cups heavy cream, divided
2 cups granulated sugar
1 vanilla bean, split and scraped
¼ teaspoon amaretto flavoring

TOPPING
2 cups heavy whipping cream
2 tablespoons powdered sugar
candied or toasted almonds for gar-
    nish (optional)

For the Crust: Combine flour and salt in large bowl. Cut in shortening. In a small bowl, combine water, vinegar, and egg. Stir into flour mixture until dough comes together. Shape dough into two disks. Cover in plastic wrap and refrigerate at least 1 hour. Roll 1 disk out onto floured surface to fit a 9-inch pie dish. Prick bottom and sides with fork. Bake at 400 degrees blind for 15 minutes. Remove pie weights and bake another 10 minutes, or until light golden brown. Remove from oven and cool while preparing filling.

For Filling 1: In a blender or food processor, purée the thawed raspberries. Strain and discard seeds. In a small saucepan, stir together the cornstarch and sugar. Gradually add the raspberry purée. Over medium heat, constantly stir until the mixture thickens and just begins to boil. Cool 5 minutes. Spread over bottom of prepared pie crust. Top with fresh raspberries and chill while preparing filling.

For Filling 2: In a mixing bowl, combine the egg yolks, cornstarch, and 1 cup of the heavy cream. Whisk to blend. Set aside. Combine the remaining 2 cups cream, sugar, and vanilla bean in a large saucepan over medium heat. Whisk to dissolve sugar and bring to a gentle boil, about 10 minutes. Slowly add the egg yolk mixture, whisking constantly until it thickens, about 5 minutes. Stir in flavoring. *This mixture must break and look curdled or it will not set up properly.* Pour into a glass bowl and press plastic wrap over the surface. Let cool completely at room temperature. When cooled, remove the vanilla bean and pour into the bowl of an electric mixer with a wire whip. Beat at medium speed to combine mixture. Whip until you have a thick and creamy custard. Pour over raspberry layer. Cover with plastic wrap until set.

For the Topping: Beat the cream and powdered sugar together until stiff. Decoratively pipe over top of pie. Sprinkle edges with candied or toasted almonds, if desired.

Raspberry Almond Bliss Pie

WHITE CHOCOLATE RAISIN NUT PIE

Francine Bryson, Pickens, S.C.
2012 APC National Pie Championships
Amateur Division 1st Place Raisin

CRUST
1¼ cups all-purpose flour
¼ teaspoon salt
½ cup shortening, chilled
3 tablespoons ice water

FILLING
1½ cups apple juice
2 cups raisins
2 (8-oz.) packages indulgence white
  chocolate cream cheese

⅔ cup sugar
¼ teaspoon salt
2 eggs
⅔ cup heavy cream
1 teaspoon vanilla extract
1 cup toasted pecans, chopped

TOPPING
1 cup heavy cream
⅔ cups powdered sugar
1¼ teaspoons vanilla extract

For the Crust: Whisk the flour and salt together in a medium-sized bowl. With a pastry blender, cut in the cold shortening until the mixture resembles coarse crumbs. Drizzle 2 to 3 tablespoons water over flour. Toss mixture with a fork to moisten, adding more water a few drops at a time until the dough comes together

Gently gather dough particles together into a ball. Cover in plastic wrap, and chill for at least 30 minutes before rolling.

Roll out dough, and put in a pie plate. Set aside

For the Filling: In pan over medium-high, heat apple juice and raisins till rehydrated or plump, approximately 15 minutes. Drain apple juice off raisins and discard juice and let raisins cool. In mixer, beat cream cheese till smooth then add sugar, salt, eggs, cream, and vanilla. Stir in raisins and nuts and pour into prepared crust. Bake at 350 degrees for 35 to 40 minutes. Center should be soft. Chill in fridge for 2 hours.

For the Topping: Whip cream with sugar and vanilla till stiff peaks. Spread on chilled pie.

White Chocolate Raisin Nut Pie

RAISIN REGALIA PIE

Bev Johnson, Crookston, MN
2012 APC Crisco National Pie Championships
Amateur Division 3rd Place Raisin

CRUST
1½ cups graham cracker crumbs
⅓ cup chopped pecans
2 tablespoons light brown sugar
¼ teaspoon salt
4 tablespoons unsalted butter, melted
1 tablespoon unsweetened
 applesauce

FILLING
1 cup raisins
3 cups water
⅔ cup sugar
3 tablespoons lemon juice

1 package + 2 teaspoons unflavored
 gelatin
¼ cup water
2 cups heavy whipping cream

TOPPING
1 cup heavy whipping cream
3 tablespoons powdered sugar
1 teaspoon vanilla
3 teaspoons piping gel

For the Crust: Combine graham crumbs, pecans, brown sugar, and salt; mix in melted butter and applesauce. Press mixture into a 9-inch deep dish pie plate. Refrigerate for 10 minutes; bake in 350 degree oven for 8 minutes. Cool.

For the Filling: Cook raisins in 3 cups water for 12 minutes. Drain cooked raisins; save the liquid. Place raisins in food processor and pulse 5 to 6 times. Return raisins and 1 cup of the reserved liquid to a medium saucepan. Add the sugar and lemon juice; cook for 2 minutes. Dissolve gelatin in ¼ cup water. Add gelatin to hot raisin mixture, stirring. Cool until set. Whip the heavy whipping cream, fold the thickened raisin mixture into the whipped cream. Fill the cooled pie shell. Refrigerate until the pie is set.

For the Topping: Whip the heavy cream in a mixing bowl. Beat until stiff; add powdered sugar, vanilla, and piping gel. Place in piping bag and decorate the edge of the pie.

Raisin Regalia Pie

COFFEE TOFFEE CRUNCH A BUNCH PIE

Susan Boyle, DeBary, FL
2012 APC Crisco National Pie Championships
Professional Division 1st Place Open & Best of Show

CRUST
1½ cups graham cracker crumbs
½ cup sugar
½ cup unsalted butter, melted
1 bar melted toffee crunch milk
   chocolate bar

FILLING
1 large box vanilla pudding mix
2 cups heavy whipping cream
½ cup half-and-half

½ cup strong coffee
1 teaspoon caramel flavoring
5 crushed English toffee bars
½ cup caramel ice cream topping

GARNISH
2 cups heavy whipping cream
¼ cup sugar
crushed or whole toffee bits

For the Crust: Combine crumbs and sugar. Slowly add butter and mix well. Press into bottom and sides of pie plate. Preheat oven to 400 degrees. Bake for 8 to 10 minutes. Let cool. Once cool, brush melted toffee crunch milk chocolate bar on bottom and sides of crust before filling.

For the Filling: Whip pudding mix, heavy whipping cream, half-and-half, coffee, and caramel flavoring until creamy but firm. Fold in the crushed toffee bars. Refrigerate for about 15 minutes. Spoon ½ cup caramel topping on bottom of pie crust brushed with melted chocolate. Spoon filling on top of caramel layer. Return to refrigerator for 6 to 8 hours.

For the Garnish: Whip cream and sugar until stiff. Decorate pie as desired with whipped cream and toffee bits.

Coffee Toffee Crunch A Bunch Pie

BLACK BOTTOM SOUS VIDE SPICED BANANA CREAM PIE

David Eaheart, Kansas City, MO
2015 APC National Pie Championships
Professional Division Honorable Mention Innovation

CRUST
1½ cups graham cracker crumbs
¼ cup powdered milk
2 tablespoons sugar
½ teaspoon salt
4 tablespoons butter, melted
¼ cup heavy cream

SOUS VIDE SPICED BANANAS
16 tablespoons unsalted butter
6 tablespoons spiced rum
½ cup sugar
1½ cups golden raisins
2 teaspoon ground mace
¼ teaspoon cardamom
1 teaspoon ground ginger
4 cinnamon sticks
6 ripe bananas

BLACK BOTTOM CHOCOLATE FILLING
105 grams milk
60 grams heavy cream
2 grams vanilla
54 grams sugar
9 grams cornstarch
25 grams egg yolks
1 grams salt
25 grams butter
45 grams bittersweet chocolate

CARAMELIZED SOUS VIDE BANANAS
2 tablespoons butter
5 sous vide spiced bananas, sliced
2 tablespoons sous vide poaching liquid

BANANA PASTRY CREAM
520 grams milk
5 grams vanilla
130 grams sugar
42 grams cornstarch
156 grams egg yolks
2 grams salt
104 grams butter
1 sous vide spiced banana, blended
  smooth
1 tablespoon spiced rum

SOUS VIDE SWISS MERINGUE
500 grams sugar
330 grams egg whites
10 grams lemon juice

GARNISH
chocolate, for shaving
banana chips

For the Crust: Preheat oven to 350 degrees. Mix crumbs, powdered milk, sugar, and salt. Mix the butter and heavy cream. In greased 10-inch pie pan, mold crumb mixture. Bake for 8 to 10 minutes. Remove from oven and cool completely.

For the Sous Vide Spiced Bananas: In a saucepan, heat to simmer butter, rum, sugar, raisins, mace, cardamom, ginger and cinnamon sticks. Remove from heat. Let steep for about 15 minutes. Strain and cool rum sauce in ice bath. Once cool, stir to bring together liquid and butter. Peel bananas and place in vacuum bag with cooled rum sauce. Vacuum seal. Heat sous vide machine or immersion circulator to 140 degrees. Place vacuum packages in sous vide water bath and cook for 20 minutes. Remove vacuum bags and place bags in water bath to chill. Hold until ready for pie assembly.

For the Chocolate Filling: Bring milk, cream, vanilla, and half of the sugar to a boil. Combine remaining sugar, cornstarch, egg yolks, and salt. to make a paste. Temper starch mixture with half of hot milk. Return remaining to pot. Pass tempered mixture through chinois back into pan. With whisk, bring entire mixture to a boil. Cook 1 minute. Stir in butter and chocolate, pour in pie shell, and cover with plastic wrap. Chill.

For the Caramelized Sous Vide Bananas: Melt butter in a skillet. Add sliced bananas and brown sugar. Cook until golden and syrupy, about 2 to 4 minutes. Remove. Let cool. Layer on top of chilled chocolate filling.

For the Banana Pastry Cream: Bring milk, cream, vanilla, and half of the sugar to a boil. Combine remaining sugar, cornstarch, egg yolks, and salt to make a paste. Temper starch mixture with half of hot milk. Return remaining to pot.

Pass tempered mixture through chinois back into pan. With whisk, bring entire mixture to a boil. Cook 1 minute. Stir in butter and banana and pour on top of bananas. Cover with plastic wrap and chill.

For the Sous Vide Meringue: Whisk sugar and egg whites just until thoroughly incorporated. Place in vacuum bag and seal. Place sealed bag in a 165-degree water bath for 25 minutes. Pour sous vide cooked egg mixture into a whipping siphon. Add 4 nitrous oxide chargers. Test meringue for stiffness as you add chargers. Pipe on chilled pie with charger. Torch to brown meringue. Optional: Garnish with shaved chocolate and/or dried banana chips.

Black Bottom Sous Vide Spiced Banana Cream Pie

SPECIAL DIETARY

We have added some special categories that might help with some dietary restrictions, such as gluten free or no sugar added. This chapter includes some of those recipes.

FOUR APPLE PIE WITH GLUTEN-FREE GRATED PECAN PASTRY CRUST

Mike Soszynski, Easthampton, NJ
2014 APC National Pie Championships
Amateur Division 3rd Place Special Dietary

CRUST
3 cups gluten-free Namaste flour
1 tablespoon sugar
1¼ teaspoon salt
1 cup unsalted butter
½ cup water, cold

FILLING
4 Granny Smith apples
1 Fuji apple
1 Gala apple
2 Honey Crisp or Pink Lady apples
   (or other good baking apple)
2 tablespoons Namaste gluten-free
   flour

1 tablespoon cornstarch
2 teaspoons candied ginger, minced
1 teaspoon cinnamon
a few sprinkles ground ginger
½ cup white sugar
⅝ cup brown sugar

TOPPING
1 cup pecans
½ teaspoon cinnamon
sugar for sprinkling (large crystals
   preferably)

For the Crust: Preheat oven to 400 degrees. Combine dry ingredients in bowl of standing mixer. Cut up butter into teaspoon-sized pieces. Turn on mixer (low) and drop pieces of butter in bit by bit until it is a crumbly mixture. Drizzle the water in. As soon as the dough starts to form large clumps, stop the mixer. Pack the dough together. Rip it in half and form one half into a flat disk and the other into a cylinder/brick shape. Refrigerate for at least 1 hour. Dust your pie pan with a little Namaste flour. Roll out the disk-shaped dough using two pieces of parchment or two silicon mats dusted with a little bit of Namaste gluten-free flour. Flip rolled-out dough into the pan and form it nicely into place.

For the Filling: Peel and core the apples. Cut them thinly (about an eighth of an inch) and put them in a bowl. Add the dry ingredients to the bowl and stir/fold to combine. Dump the apple mixture into the pie pan with the dough pressed into it.

For the Topping: Pulse the pecans in a food processor until they are a semi-coarse meal (like a streusel topping consistency). Grate the dough brick, using the big holes of a box grater, into a bowl. Toss the pecans and dough shreds together. Top the apples with the grated pastry mixture. Sprinkle sugar and cinnamon on top. Put the pie in the oven and lower the temperature to 375 degrees. Bake for 30 minutes. Turn the pie 180 degrees and check its progress: place aluminum on the top it if its browning too fast. Bake for 25 to 35 more minutes at 350 degrees. The pie is done when a stick goes in and out without much resistance. Take out the pie and cool completely before cutting/serving.

Four Apple Pie with Gluten-Free Pecan Pastry Crust

CAFÉ MEXICANA PIE

Patricia Lapiezo, LaMesa, CA
2014 APC National Pie Championships
Amateur Division 2nd Place Special Dietary

CRUST
3 cups all-purpose flour
1 teaspoon salt
1¼ cups Crisco shortening
5 tablespoons water, cold
1 tablespoon vinegar
1 egg, lightly beaten

FILLING
1 (8-oz.) package cream cheese, softened
1 (8-oz.) package Hershey's sugar-free semisweet chocolate chips

½ cup heavy cream
1½ teaspoon instant espresso powder
½ teaspoon cinnamon
Splenda, to taste (⅓ to ½ cup)
1 carton Sugar-Free Cool Whip

GARNISH
⅓ cup heavy cream
½ cup Hershey's sugar-free chocolate chips
Sugar-Free Cool Whip
cinnamon

For the Crust: Combine flour and salt in large bowl. Cut in shortening. In a small bowl, combine water, vinegar, and egg. Stir into flour mixture until dough comes together. Shape dough into two disks. Wrap in plastic wrap and refrigerate at least 1 hour. Roll 1 disk out onto floured surface to fit a 9½-inch pie dish. Preheat oven to 425 degrees. Prick bottom and sides of crust. Line crust with aluminum foil and fill with pie weights. Bake for 15 minutes. Remove weights and bake an additional 10 minutes or until crust is browned. Set aside to cool.

For the Filling: In a large mixing bowl, beat the cream cheese until creamy. Heat the chocolate chips, ⅓ cup heavy cream, and espresso powder over low heat, stirring until chocolate is melted. Cool. Blend into cream cheese. Beat in cinnamon. Fold in Cool Whip. Spread in crust, smoothing top.

For the Garnish: Heat the cream in the microwave and pour over chocolate chips; stir until melted. Pour over top of pie to within ½ inch of edge. Decorate edge of pie with Sugar-Free Cool Whip. Dust top of pie with cinnamon.

Café Mexicana Pie

CHERRIES FROM HEAVEN

Jeanne Ely, Mulberry FL
2014 APC National Pie Championships
Amateur Division 1st Place Special Dietary

CRUST
4 egg whites
½ teaspoon cream of tartar
¼ teaspoon salt
1 teaspoon vanilla bean paste
1 cup white sugar

FILLING
1 (8-oz.) package cream cheese, softened
⅓ cup powdered sugar
⅛ teaspoon salt
1 teaspoon vanilla bean paste
1 cup heavy whipping cream

TOPPING
2 (24.7-oz.) jars dark Morello cherries, drained
1 (12-oz.) jar Smuckers red tart cherry preserves
⅓ cup tart cherry juice
2 tablespoons cornstarch

GARNISH
¾ cup heavy whipping cream
¼ cup confectioners' sugar
¼ teaspoon vanilla bean paste

For the Crust: In a large bowl, beat egg whites, cream of tartar, and salt, until soft peaks form. Add vanilla and slowly beat in sugar until very stiff and glossy. Spread the mixture into a 9-inch pie plate to form a shell. Bake at 300 degrees for 50 minutes. Turn off the oven and leave the meringue in the oven for 1 more hour. Cool.

For the Filling: Beat cream cheese, sugar, salt, and vanilla on medium speed until smooth. Add the heavy whipping cream and beat on high until thick and smooth. Pour into cooled crust and chill until set.

For the Topping: Combine cherries, preserves, cherry juice, and cornstarch in a medium sauce pan. Cook till thickened stirring constantly. Cool completely and add to top of the cream cheese filling.

For the Garnish: Whip all ingredients together until stiff. Spoon into star-tipped pastry bag. Swirl into rosettes around the edge just inside the crust. Keep cold in the refrigerator until ready to serve.

Cherries from Heaven

WHITE AND YELLOW PEACH PIE WITH PECAN STREUSEL TOPPING

Susan Asato, Aliso Viejo, CA
2014 APC National Pie Championships
Amateur Division 3rd Place Paramount Pictures Peach

CRUST
8 tablespoons vegan butter (1 stick, Earth Balance recommend)
3 tablespoons vegan shortening (Earth Balance recommend)
1²⁄₃ cups all-purpose flour
2 tablespoons organic sugar
¼ teaspoon salt
3–6 tablespoons water, cold

FILLING
3 cups white peaches, peeled and cut into ¼-³⁄₈-inch slices (3–5 peaches)
3 cups yellow peaches, peeled and cut into ¼"-³⁄₈-inch slices (3–5 peaches)
1 cup organic sugar, divided
1 tablespoon lemon juice, freshly squeezed

2 tablespoons light brown sugar
6 tablespoons tapioca starch
2 tablespoons cornstarch
2 teaspoons orange zest, micro-planed
1 tablespoon orange juice, freshly squeezed
1 teaspoon vanilla extract
½ teaspoon cinnamon
½ teaspoon salt

TOPPING
3 tablespoons vegan butter,
½ cup pecans, coarsely chopped
¼ cup rolled oats
⅓ cup light brown sugar (non-bone char processed)
⅓ cup all-purpose flour
¼ teaspoon cinnamon
pinch nutmeg

GLAZE
½ cup organic powdered sugar
2–3 tablespoons lime juice, freshly squeezed

For the Crust: Cut the vegan butter and short-ening into ½-inch pieces and chill in freezer at least 10 minutes. Pulse in food processor with flour, sugar, and salt about 10 times or until crumbly. Add 3 to 6 tablespoons water (amount will vary depending on kitchen temperature and humidity) and pulse about another 5 times or un-til mixture holds its shape when a small amount is squeezed in fist. Form into a 5-inch disc then place in an airtight container and refrigerate for at least 1 hour. Preheat oven to 350 degrees. Roll out dough about ⅛-inch thick and press into a 9-inch deep dish pie plate. Dock bottom with fork, line with parchment paper, and fill with pie weights. Bake for 14 to 16 minutes or until very lightly browned. Allow to cool for at least 30 minutes.

For the Filling: Gently mix together sliced peaches with ½ cup of the sugar and 1 table-spoon lemon juice and place in a large colander over a bowl. Let sit for 1 hour, allowing liquid to drain out of the peaches. Place drained peaches in a separate large bowl with the remaining ½ cup of sugar, light brown sugar, tapioca starch, cornstarch, orange zest, orange juice, vanilla ex-tract, cinnamon, and salt. Toss gently. Pour filling into pie plate with cooled crust.

White and Yellow Peach Pie with Pecan Streusel Topping

For the Topping: Mix together all streusel topping ingredients well using a fork, then spoon evenly over the peach filling. Place pie on a cookie sheet and bake at 375 degrees for 55 to 65 minutes, or until filling starts bubbling around the edges. If the crust starts to get too dark, cover the entire pie loosely with aluminum foil. Allow to cool for at least 4 hours before adding glaze and slicing.

For the Glaze: Whisk together powdered sugar and 2 tablespoons lime juice. Gradually add additional lime juice, several drops at a time as needed, until desired consistency is reached. Drizzle onto cooled pie.

GLUTEN-FREE CHOCOLATE CREAMY PEANUT BUTTER PIE

Kathleen Costello, Tallmadge, OH
2015 APC National Pie Championships
Amateur Division 1st Place Gluten Free

CRUST
1 (6-oz.) package gluten-free double chocolate chip cookies (Glutino brand)
1 (6-oz.) package gluten-free double chocolate brownie (LiveGfree brand)
3 tablespoons sugar
5 tablespoons unsalted butter, melted

FILLING
2 (8-oz.) packages cream cheese, softened
1½ cups creamy peanut butter
1 (7-oz.) jar marshmallow crème
⅓ cup Bosco gluten-free fudge brownie syrup
1¾ cups powdered sugar
2 cups heavy whipping cream

GARNISH
1 tablespoon leftover cookie crumbs
1 tablespoon Bosco Syrup
2 tablespoons dry roasted peanuts, finely chopped

For the Crust: Mix cookies and brownies together in food processor, grinding into crumbs. In a small bowl, blend together the 1⅓ cups of the combined crumbs and sugar. Add melted butter and continue to mix until ingredients are incorporated. Mixture will be moist. (Save remaining crumb mixture for next time or use as a garnish on top of pie.) Prepare a 9-inch pie dish by lightly spraying it with Coconut Oil Cooking Spray. Press cookie mixture into the pie dish; spread the crumbs out evenly in the bottoms and sides. Place the prepared pressed crust into the refrigerator for 30 minutes to set before filling. Note: The ingredients are enough for two pie shells.

For the Filling: In a large bowl with an electric mixer, add cream cheese, peanut butter, and marshmallow creme, and mix until blended. Add powder sugar, chocolate syrup, and ½ cup whipping cream; continue mixing ingredients until incorporated and creamy. In a chilled mixing bowl, add remaining 1½ cups whipping cream, and mix with an electric mixer until cream is stiff. Add stiff cream to chocolate peanut butter mixture and mix all ingredients together until incorporated. Spoon filling into prepared pie crust.

For the Garnish: Sprinkle finely crushed mixed cookie crumbs on top of pie. With a fork, drizzle Bosco's Syrup over cookie crumbs. Next sprinkle the finely chopped dry roasted peanuts on top of pie. Chill for 8 hours or more before serving. Refrigerate leftovers.

Gluten-Free Chocolate Creamy Peanut Butter Pie

NEW-FASHIONED BANANA CREAM PIE

John Sunvold, Orlando, FL
2015 APC National Pie Championships
Amateur Division 2nd Place Special Dietary

CRUST

1⅛ cups gluten-free graham cracker
    crumbs (or substitute crumbs
    from vanilla gluten-free cookie)
⅛ cups nuts, chopped
3 tablespoons sugar
3–6 tablespoons butter, melted
½ cup Dolci Hard Chocolate Shell

FILLING 1

2 tablespoons butter
2 tablespoons corn syrup
2 tablespoons heavy cream
⅓ cup chocolate chips (semisweet)
1 cup powdered sugar
½ cup Dolci Hard Chocolate Shell

FILLING 2

6 oz. cream cheese, softened
⅓ cup powdered sugar
6 oz. Cool Whip

FILLING 3

⅔ cup sugar
¼ teaspoon salt
¼ cup cornstarch
5 egg yolks
1½ cup heavy cream
1 cup milk
1 tablespoon vanilla extract
2 tablespoons butter
2–4 bananas

For the Crust: Preheat oven to 350 degrees. Mix graham cracker crumbs, nuts, and sugar, and add enough melted butter to make crumbs wet but not soggy (each brand reacts differently). Start with half of the butter and add it slowly until it is wet. Press into a 9- to 10-inch pie plate. You may not use all of it if you use a shallow pan. Bake for 8 to 12 minutes. Cool. Coat cooled crust with a light layer of Dolci Hard Chocolate Shell. Chill.

For Filling 1: Mix butter, corn syrup, and cream, and heat over medium until boiling. Stir constantly. Add chocolate chips and stir until melted. Once fully combined, slowly add powdered sugar. Mix completely, then carefully spread the filling onto the bottom of the crust over the hard shell (may include a thin layer around the sides of the crust to hold the crust together). It cools quickly, so you must spread immediately. Chill. When chilled, cover this layer with another light layer/drizzle of Dolci Hard Chocolate Shell.

For Filling 2: Mix softened cream cheese with powdered sugar. Fold in Cool Whip and spread on top of Filling 1. For extra crunch, apply a thin layer or two of Dolci Hard Chocolate Shell.

For Filling 3: Mix sugar, salt, and starch in a pot. In a bowl, whisk egg yolks, cream, and milk

New-Fashioned Banana Cream Pie

slightly. To the pot, slowly add the egg yolk/cream/milk mixture. Heat over medium heat, whisking frequently, until thick and bubbling (but not rapidly boiling). Once the cream is bubbling, continue to cook and whisk for 30 more seconds. Finally, add the vanilla and butter and mix until the cream is smooth. Set aside. Cut 2 to 4 bananas, and cover the cream cheese later with bananas and the warm Filling 3. Place a plastic sheet over the cream to prevent a skin from forming on the cream filling. Place in refrigerator until completely chilled.

For the Garnish: Top with favorite whipped cream topping. Garnish with chocolate, white chocolate, and nuts, as/if desired. May also cover with chocolate-covered banana pieces. Chill 4 hours before servings.

Index

Conversion Charts

METRIC AND IMPERIAL CONVERSIONS

(These conversions are rounded for convenience)

Ingredient	Cups/Tablespoons/Teaspoons	Ounces	Grams/Milliliters
Butter	1 cup=16 tablespoons= 2 sticks	8 ounces	230 grams
Cream cheese	1 tablespoon	0.5 ounce	14.5 grams
Cheese, shredded	1 cup	4 ounces	110 grams
Cornstarch	1 tablespoon	0.3 ounce	8 grams
Flour, all-purpose	1 cup/1 tablespoon	4.5 ounces/0.3 ounce	125 grams/8 grams
Flour, whole wheat	1 cup	4 ounces	120 grams
Fruit, dried	1 cup	4 ounces	120 grams
Fruits or veggies, chopped	1 cup	5 to 7 ounces	145 to 200 grams
Fruits or veggies, puréed	1 cup	8.5 ounces	245 grams
Honey, maple syrup, or corn syrup	1 tablespoon	.75 ounce	20 grams
Liquids: cream, milk, water, or juice	1 cup	8 fluid ounces	240 milliliters
Oats	1 cup	5.5 ounces	150 grams
Salt	1 teaspoon	0.2 ounce	6 grams
Spices: cinnamon, cloves, ginger, or nutmeg (ground)	1 teaspoon	0.2 ounce	5 milliliters
Sugar, brown, firmly packed	1 cup	7 ounces	200 grams
Sugar, white	1 cup/1 tablespoon	7 ounces/0.5 ounce	200 grams/12.5 grams
Vanilla extract	1 teaspoon	0.2 ounce	4 grams

OVEN TEMPERATURES

Fahrenheit	Celsius	Gas Mark
225°	110°	¼
250°	120°	½
275°	140°	1
300°	150°	2
325°	160°	3
350°	180°	4
375°	190°	5
400°	200°	6
425°	220°	7
450°	230°	8